INTERNATIONAL STRATEGIC MANAGEMENT AND GOVERNMENT POLICY

International Strategic Management and Government Policy

Peter J. Buckley

Foreword by John H. Dunning

First published in Great Britain 1998 by
MACMILLAN PRESS LTD
Houndmills, Basingstoke, Hampshire RG21 6XS and London
Companies and representatives throughout the world

A catalogue record for this book is available from the British Library.

ISBN 0–333–71086–X

First published in the United States of America 1998 by
ST. MARTIN'S PRESS, INC.,
Scholarly and Reference Division,
175 Fifth Avenue, New York, N.Y. 10010

ISBN 0–312–21440–5

Library of Congress Cataloging-in-Publication Data
International strategic management and government policy / by Peter J.
Buckley.
p.   cm.
Includes bibliographical references and index.
ISBN 0–312–21440–5 (cloth)
1. International business enterprises—Management.
2. Investments, Foreign—Government policy.   I. Buckley, Peter J.,
1949–   .
HD62.4.I5659 1998
658'.049—DC21   98–11551
                                                                      CIP

© Peter J. Buckley 1998
Foreword © John H. Dunning 1998

This book is printed on paper suitable for recycling and made from fully managed and
sustained forest sources.

10   9   8   7   6   5   4   3   2   1
07   06   05   04   03   02   01   00   99   98

Printed and bound in Great Britain by
Antony Rowe Ltd, Chippenham, Wiltshire

Contents

Foreword

This volume contains a rich panoply of scholarly essays written by Peter Buckley and his colleagues, mainly from Leeds and Bradford Universities. They embrace a variety of contemporary issues, all of which deal with the interface between government policy and the activities of multinational enterprises. The monograph is valuable in that it covers a broad canvass of countries and types of firms. More especially the reader is given some fresh and unusual insights into the comparative strategies of firms, and of the policies of national governments of countries at different stages of development and with widely different investment and other regimes. As might be expected, the authors show there is no one optimal course of action which either firms or governments should adopt towards the acquisition, creation, transfer and utilisation of wealth creating assets; nor of the economic benefits of alternative organisational forms in achieving their goals. Scholars working on the theory of foreign direct investment and international business activity do well to heed some of the findings of these essays, all of which reveal the importance of *context* in evaluating the causes and consequences of such investment and activity.

This monograph is to be commended in another respect, in that it blends together the interests, perceptions and analytical techniques of both economists and business scholars; and it does so without comprising the intellectual integrity of either discipline. I believe it represents a trend in interdisciplinary collaboration which will become increasingly common in the years ahead.

If I have one quibble about the thrust and contents of this volume it is that I do not think the authors pay sufficient attention to the impact of globalisation and alliance capitalism on the interface between firms, markets and governments. As I have written elsewhere, I believe this is leading to a greater synergy of interests between multinational enterprises and national governments, and is fundamentally changing the bargaining relationship between the two parties. At the same time, I accept that globalisation is a two-edged sword, and is generating new concerns and fears among various constituents in the world economy. It is these concerns and fears – and particularly those to do with the cross-border distribution of work and welfare, and the actual or perceived erosion of national sovereignty – which may cause at least some national governments to reconsider the liberal stance they have been adopting.

There is a good deal of new and interesting empirical material in this volume, all of which further clothes some of our ideas about the determinants and present course of economic integration, foreign direct investment and cross-border alliance formation; and of the strategies of MNE managers and the policies of national governments. I warmly commend these studies to a wide-ranging audience.

Rutgers and Reading Universities   JOHN H. DUNNING

Acknowledgements

I would like to thank my co-authors for all their efforts, help and understanding – and for permission to reprint our joint work here. The authors and publishers are grateful to the following for permission to reproduce copyright materials: Chapter 2 first appeared in Gavin Boyd and Alan M. Rugman (eds), *Euro-Pacific Investment and Trade* (Edward Elgar, Cheltenham, 1997); Chapter 3 in *Transnational Corporations*, vol. 5, no. 2, August 1996; Chapter 4 in *Journal of Management Studies*, vol. 33, no. 3, May 1996; Chapter 5 in *Small Business Economics*, vol. 9, no. 1, February 1997, by kind permission from Kluwer Academic Publishers; Chapter 6 in *Journal of Asian Business*, vol. 10, no. 3, August 1994; Chapter 7 in Henri-Claude de Bettignies (ed.), *Changing Markets in Asia* (Paris, INSEAD, 1998); Chapter 8 in *Management International Review*, vol. 35, no. 1.1, 1995; Chapter 9 in *Business Economics*, vol. XXXI, no. 1, January 1996; Chapters 10, 11 and 12 in *British Journal of Canadian Studies*, respectively vol. 9, no. 2, 1994; vol. 10, no. 1, 1995; and vol. 11, no. 2, 1996; Chapter 13 in *International Business Review*, vol. 3, no. 1, 1994 (with kind permission from Elsevier Science Ltd, The Boulevard, Langford Lane, Kidlington OX5 1GB, UK); and Chapter 14 in *Applied Economics Letters*, vol. 4, no. 1, January 1997.

I would like to thank my current and former secretaries, Sheila Fordham, Sylvia Ashdown and Chris Barkby, for their help and word-processing skills.

PETER J. BUCKLEY

Notes on the Other Contributors

Jane Frecknall-Hughes is Lecturer in Accounting, Leeds University Business School, UK.

Nick Freeman is Head of Indochina Research, ING Baring, International Pte. Ltd, based in Bangkok, Thailand.

Keith Glaister is Senior Lecturer in Strategic Management, at Leeds University Business School, UK.

Hafiz Mirza is Professor of International Business, Bradford University Management Centre, UK.

Christopher Pass is Reader in Comparative Industrial Economics, University of Bradford Management Centre, UK.

Kate Prescott is Lecturer in International Business Management at the University of Bradford Management Centre, UK.

Gordon Smith is Senior Lecturer in Business Strategy at Teesside Business School, UK.

John Sparkes is Professor of Business Economics at University of Bradford Management Centre, UK.

1 Introduction

This book treats the two key elements of its title as interdependent. There is not one section on 'international business strategy' and another on 'government policy' as the two cannot sensibly be treated in isolation. Part I of the book examines this interaction directly and concentrates on the strategy of multinational firms with particular attention to foreign direct investment (FDI) and international alliances, but with appropriate attention to government policy responses. Part II examines these issues as they play out in two key economies of Asia: Japan and Vietnam. This region has been an important focus of my research since the early 1980s and its fascination continues with the rise of a third wave of 'dragons' or 'tigers' after Japan: the four little tigers of Hong Kong, Taiwan, Korea and Singapore; after them, Malaysia, Thailand, Indonesia; and then, perhaps, China and Vietnam. European investment in Japan has been a weak link within the flows of FDI between the Triad (North America, Europe and Japan) but it provides a continuing focus of interest. Part III examines the role of trade blocs in the world economy and the ramifications of the growth of supra-national groupings. The three pieces on Canada–UK bilateral economic relations illustrate the impact of NAFTA and the EU on cross-Atlantic flows. The final two chapters return to the strategy of the multinational enterprise (MNE) and focus on a cross-national comparison of the structure of their foreign market servicing strategies and on the vital question of transfer pricing. Fittingly, the last piece is concerned with the transfer pricing policy in Japanese-owned MNEs, because this combines government policy, company strategy, international links and an Asian flavour!

INTERNATIONAL STRATEGIC MANAGEMENT AND GOVERNMENT POLICY

Part I consists of five pieces, all published in 1996 or 1997, which have a unity of approach and intent. They illustrate aspects of MNE strategy in an increasingly interdependent world economy and they illustrate the importance of strategic FDI by multinationals and its alternatives – alliances and external technology transfer.

Chapter 2 examines and assesses the role of foreign direct investment (FDI) as a strategic weapon in competition in the increasingly integrated world market. It presents a simple model of globalisation – conceived simply as the pace of integration of national markets of various kinds – and draws out the implications of the differential pace of integration of markets for capital, goods and services, and labour. FDI is seen as the crucial means by which integration occurs and its impact on trade and technology transfer is explained. A section in this chapter examines international alliances as complementary to FDI.

Chapter 3 extends this analysis to all forms of foreign market servicing strategy – whose generic elements are analysed as exporting, licensing and FDI. This chapter examines explicitly the possibility of effective government action in a world dominated by rent-seeking multinational firms which have the ability to switch between different modes of carrying out foreign business. It also takes on board the problem that governments have perforce to deal with both inward and outward investment, trade and technology flows, and shows that asymmetries in policies can lead to difficulties and distortions if all cells in the inward/outward matrix are not carefully monitored. Where firms have choices both in location of production and in mode of operation, government policies require reappraisal.

Chapter 4 examines the strategic motives for the formation of international alliances between companies. It tests hypotheses using a sample of UK firms with international alliances. Its key finding is that alliances are largely used as competitive weapons in a role analogous to FDI. The choice between FDI and alliances appears to be crucial.

The role of smaller firms in the international arena has been a long-term focus of interest for my work. Chapter 5 examines the key issues involved in the transfer of technology by small and medium-sized enterprises (SMEs). It is found that SMEs can play a significant niche role even in the most 'globalised' industries. Managerial processes, here, as elsewhere, play a crucial role in determining the role of success of these firms.

FOREIGN INVESTMENT IN VIETNAM AND JAPAN

In Part II, Chapter 6 examines the first six years of Vietnam's programme of economic reform (*doi moi*) with special attention to the role of joint ventures. Like many market opening processes, foreign involvement in Vietnam was at first seen in euphoric terms, followed by some inevitable disillusionment and sober reappraisal. Two extensive case studies are included in this piece (co-authored with Nick Freeman of ING Barings) to illustrate the practical challenges of this particular emerging market. The inevitable comparisons with China are also drawn. The following chapter (7) examines the role of country funds in the particular context of Vietnam. Country funds enable investment in relatively risky high growth economies by a packaging exercise, where a fund manager selects and re-selects a fluid portfolio of shares from the listed companies in the country. Country funds are then listed or privately placed.

Chapter 8 examines European direct investment in Japan – the weakest link in the triad of FDI flows introduced in Chapter 2. This chapter presents some results of a long (over 10-year) period of tracking key European investors in Japan. The paper explores the interesting phenomenon of 'double entry' (or re-entry) into Japan by firms whose first FDI entry (via joint venture) led to a dead end in terms of development, and a parallel second entry (usually wholly owned) had to be engineered. Chapter 9 builds on this perspective by comparing European FDI in Japan with American FDI. This comparison suggests that inhibitors to inward investment are declining but that inherent factors in the Japanese business environment, including the continuing difficulty of acquisition of Japanese companies, remain challenges to potential and existing investors. These problems are compounded by difficulties emanating from the parent companies, in many cases.

TRADE BLOCS, FOREIGN MARKET SERVICING STRATEGIES AND INTERNATIONAL TRANSFER PRICING

In Part III, three chapters explore the outcome of projects generously supported by the Canadian High Commission in London which examine Canada–UK bilateral economic relations in the context of integration on both sides of the Atlantic. Chapter 10 focuses on the Single European Market Act which consolidated market integration in the EU and the development of NAFTA. It examines the strategies of firms in a two-by-two matrix of Canadian and UK firms in the Single European Market and NAFTA. Chapter 11 concentrates on the attitude and policies of Canadian firms in respect of the Single European Market and it pays particular attention to the evolution of Canadian firms' foreign market servicing strategies as European Market integration has progressed. The final piece on Canada and Europe examines alliances between Canadian and European firms. It catalogues such alliances and seeks to establish the type, objectives and joint responsibilities of the alliance partners. Canadian firms exhibit a certain degree of reluctance to use this mode of operation in Europe and the reasons for this are explored.

Chapter 13 takes a broad international comparison of the structure of the foreign market servicing strategy of firms, aggregated at the national level. Analyses of the total foreign sales of firms (exports, foreign licensed sales,

sales from foreign located affiliates) have been shown to shed light on variations in strategy across groups of firms (by industry or nationality of ownership, for instance). Despite severe data limitations, significant differences in foreign market servicing strategies do emerge across both industries and nationalities (and, as far as can be ascertained by target market, too).

The final chapter (14) examines the international transfer pricing policy of Japanese multinational firms. The pricing structures of Japanese firms often seem to be designed for a different purpose from the 'Western' norm. The implications of these differences are explored in this chapter.

Part I

International Strategic Management and Government Policy

2 Strategic Foreign Direct Investment*

INTRODUCTION

This chapter examines foreign direct investment by multinational firms in the modern world economy, which is characterised by increasing integration across national markets. This process – often termed 'globalisation' – has radically altered firms' approaches to direct foreign investment. The following section introduces a simple model of the world economy which traces the effects of different degrees of integration across various types of markets and examines the consequences for direct foreign investment, paying particular attention to cross-investment in the 'Triad' of North America, Europe and Japan. The next section examines strategic foreign direct investment and its crucial relationships with trade and GDP. This section introduces some key data on the role of foreign direct investment in world economic activity in both the long run and short run. It demonstrates the crucial role of foreign direct investment in achieving the firm's strategic objectives, be they market access, control of key inputs or cost reduction. Then relationships among the Triad are examined in detail. International strategic alliances are introduced and analysed in a separate section and the conclusion brings various elements together.

A SIMPLE MODEL OF THE INTERNATIONAL ECONOMY

Figure 2.1 shows a highly simplified picture of the world economy. It attempts to show different degrees of integration across various types of market. The suggestion is that financial markets are substantially integrated so that the world financial market can, for many purposes, be regarded as a single market. The market for goods and services is differentiated on a regional basis with 'single markets' either existing or emerging (European Union (EU), North American Free Trade Area (NAFTA) and so on). Such markets are increasingly uniform in regulation, standards, codes of practice (for

---

*Originally published in G. Boyd and A.M. Rugman (eds), *Euro–Pacific Investment and Trade* (Edward Elgar, Cheltenham, 1996).

example, anti-trust) and business behaviour and so they offer the possibility of economies of scale across the market, but are substantially differentiated by these factors (and possibly by a common external tariff) from other regional markets. Labour markets, however, remain primarily national. Governments wish to regulate their own labour market and to differentiate it (protect it) from neighbouring labour markets. Many of the current difficulties in governmental regulatory policy arise from the difficulty of attempting to pursue independent labour market policies in the presence of regional goods and services markets and an international market for capital.

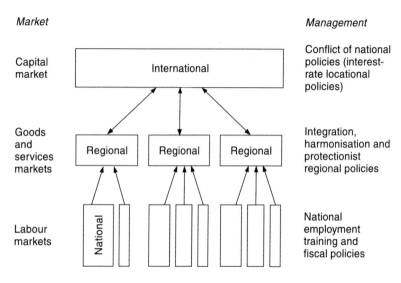

Figure 2.1   Internationalisation of firms – conflict of markets

In contrast, multinational enterprises are perfectly placed to exploit the differences in international integration of markets. The presence of an international capital market enables capital costs to be driven to a minimum. The existence of regional goods and services markets enables firms to exploit economies of scale across several economies. Differential labour markets enable costs to be reduced by locating the labour-intensive stages of production in cheap labour economies. Horizontal integration is served by regional goods and services markets, vertical integration by differentiated labour markets and the spatial distribution of supplies of key raw materials. Strategic trade and foreign direct investment can be seen to take place within this overall framework.

STRATEGIC TRADE, STRATEGIC FOREIGN DIRECT INVESTMENT AND GDP

Does the notion of 'strategic' when appended to trade or foreign direct investment make a difference? It adds the dimension of competition – rivalry – to that of the firm simply responding to external market signals. As Graham (1992) has pointed out, many models of multinational firms assume the firm to be a monopolist. Formal modelling becomes more difficult when 'strategies' are included, because an interaction term with other firms is being added to the firm's decision set. It is not now simply aiming for the least-cost operation, it has goals defined in opposition to its rivals (market share for example, national or global). This suggests an analysis in which strategic goals are proximate goals, shorter-run goals or means towards an end which may be long-run survival or profit maximisation. The competitive game is played under constraints. These constraints are the external environment, demand and technology conditions. Part of the modelling of strategy aims to make technology conditions endogenous by examining the creation of technology via R&D expenditure and combining this with assumptions on increasing returns to scale in the firm's various activities. These refinements can take place within the orthodox (non-strategic) environment. The twist is the market-share rivalristic game, such as the entry pre-emption case analysed by Horstmann and Markusen (1987). (See also Brander and Spencer, 1985; Krugman, 1990.)

From the point of view of the individual firm, trade can be strategic. Exports can be a weapon to gain access to a foreign market. When this is cast as a two-person game with national champions contending for a share of the prize (the international market) then subsidies can alter the payoffs and under certain restrictive assumptions can lead to gains in national welfare (payoffs to individual firms of national ownership) in the post-subsidy game.

As Casson (1990) points out, strategic trade policies suffer from the same difficulty as adversarial business strategies – they can be imitated and the results of the imitation can be disastrous. Classic strategic trade policy under which government subsidises 'national champions' (Brander and Spencer, 1985; Krugman, 1987b) can result in foreign governments matching the subsidies. This can result in escalation of threat and counter-threat as each government guarantees the credibility of its national champion's threat to spoil the rival's market. Only when slow response or poor liquidity of the foreign rival causes it to exit the industry is a permanent gain likely to be achieved. The analogy with protectionism ('beggar-my-neighbour') policies is strong. While a subsidised or protected firm may sometimes gain, domestic consumers and taxpayers will normally lose. The first part of this sentence explains rent-seeking lobbying for government intervention to protect or subsidise putative 'national champions'.

This leaves aside the political feasibility of the 'tax generally and subsidise specifically' policy combination. In the USA this must (at the least) be constrained by the budget deficit and in the European Union it is constrained by the lack of a centralised body (Holmes, 1995). In addition, observation suggests that the ability of governments to pick winners (national champions) is severely limited. Institutional failure is greater than market failure.

From a macro view, trade, based on comparative advantage, is a non-zero-sum game. It is from this viewpoint that Krugman views the notion of national competitiveness as a meaningless concept (Krugman, 1994).

Krugman (1987a) reviews the arguments based on externalities and strategic trade consideration for interventionist policies, but he concludes that the optimal policy is so sensitive to the technological and behavioural parameters that the results of intervention are uncertain even in areas where externality and monopoly arguments abound (like semiconductors). Information available to the government will be biased – not least by lying on the part of rent-seekers: 'We have a sadder but wiser argument for free trade in a world whose politics are as imperfect as its markets.'

Strategic trade theorists have played a valuable role in introducing elements of imperfect competition, such as product differentiation, into trade models and focusing attention on to increasing returns to scale. There has, perhaps, been too little attention paid to *firm*-level economies of scale rather than *plant*-level economies. It is often firm-level economies of scale – gaining the maximum return from a specific sunk cost in R&D – which leads to internationalisation rather than external transaction. The same logic, when combined with the firm's search for the most efficient operation by minimising its overall costs of production by optimally locating its sub-units, often dictates foreign direct investment.

Trade, however, is not redundant. The expansion of multinational firms by subdividing activities and locating them where overall costs are minimized creates a network of intra-firm trade. This intra-firm trade can take place at prices which diverge from market or 'arm's-length' prices in order to afford the corporation the ability to reduce its overall tax bill. Such transfer pricing policies add an additional, purely international (inter-tax jurisdiction) reason for firms to invest abroad.

This is not to say that foreign direct investment (FDI) will be always and everywhere the preferred means of doing business abroad. Figure 2.2 shows a simple model for the determination of the optimal form of doing business in a given foreign market (Buckley and Casson, 1981). It attributes fixed costs of entry and variables costs of exposure to each mode of doing business abroad: exporting, licensing and FDI. In the example given, the firm should switch from exporting to foreign direct investment only at point q, where the lower variable costs of foreign direct investment outweigh its higher fixed costs of entry. If q is large, then the point will never be reached where the firm should choose *FDI*. If *FDI* has unusually high set-up costs – large fixed capital requirements, for instance in a petrochemical complex – only in the largest markets will such a strategy be feasible.

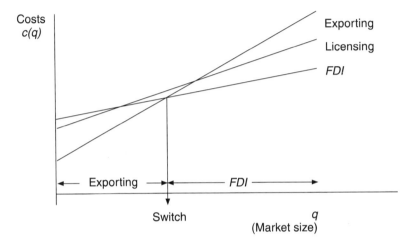

Figure 2.2   The timing of a foreign direct investment

Note: In this example, licensing is never the preferred alternative.

Source: Reproduced from Buckley and Casson (1981), p. 80.

Table 2.1 shows the role of foreign direct investment in selected years as a share of world output (stocks and flows), as a share of world capital formulation and an estimate of the world sales of foreign affiliates as a share of world exports. The importance of the sales of foreign affiliates as a percentage of world exports shows a rising long-term trend to the point at which the sales of foreign affiliates exceed the volume of world exports. This is particularly notable given the decline in tariffs (Table 2.2).

Intra-firm international trade is also a factor of growing importance variously estimated as between 30 and 40 per cent of world trade (Table 2.3). This arises in large part because of the increase in foreign sourcing of intermediate inputs as shown in Table 2.4.

Strategic foreign direct investment is a notion which arises from the competitive behaviour of firms. Foreign direct investment is carried out for a variety of motives, most notably:

(1) market access;
(2) resource control and foreign sourcing of key intermediate inputs;
(3) cost reduction (efficiency seeking).

Table 2.1   The role of foreign direct investment in world economic activity, 1913,
1960, 1975, 1980 and 1991 (percentage)

Item	1913	1960	1975	1980	1985	1991
World FDI stock as a share of world output	9.0[a]	4.4	4.5	4.8	6.4	8.5
World FDI inflows as a share of world output	–	0.3	0.3	0.5	0.5	0.7
World FDI inflows as a share of world gross fixed capital formation	–	1.1	1.4	2.0	1.8	3.5
World sales of foreign affiliates as a share of world exports	–	84[b]	97[c]	99[d]	9 9[d]	122

Notes:
[a] Estimate.
[b] 1967 based on United States.
[c] Based on United States and Japanese figures.
[d] 1982 based on German, Japanese and United States data

Source: UNCTAD. Division on Transnational Corporations and Investment, based on UNCTAD-DTCI, FDI data base, UN-DESIPA data base, Dunning (1993) and Bairoch (1994). Taken from *World Investment Report 1994, UNCTAD, Division on Transnational Corporations and Investment*, p. 130.

Table 2.2   Average tariff rates on manufactured products in selected developed countries, 1913, 1950 and 1990 (weighted average; percentage of value)

Country	1913	1950	1990
France	21	18	5.9
Germany	20	26	5.9
Italy	18	25	5.9
Japan	30	–	5.3
Netherlands	4	11	5.9
Sweden	20	9	4.4
United Kingdom	–	23	5.9
United States	44	14	4.8

Source: Bairoch (1993) table 3.3, taken from *World Investment Report 1994*, p. 123.

Table 2.3　United States and Japan: intra-firm trade, 1977, 1982 and 1989
(percentage of total exports or imports)

| Year | United States | | Japan[a] | |
	Exports	Imports	Exports	Imports
1977	36	40	24[b]	32
1982	33	37	31[c]	18
1989	34	41	33	29

Notes:
[a] Refers to Japanese TNCs only.
[b] Refers to 1980.
[c] Refers to 1983.

Source:　*World Investment Report 1993*, p. 143.

Table 2.4　Ratio of imported to domestic sourcing of intermediate inputs,
selected countries (percentage)

Country	Early 1970s	Mid- and late 1970s	Mid-1980s
Canada	34	37	50
France	21	25	38
Germany	–	21	34
Japan	5	6	7
United Kingdom	16	32	37
United States	7	8	13

Source:　*World Investment Report 1993*, p. 145.

Each of these motives contains the notion of 'stealing a march' on rivals either by securing (foreign) market share, excluding rivals from key inputs or raw materials and undercutting prices by least-cost location.

Foreign direct investment centrally incorporates the notion of control. This is the defining characteristic which distinguishes direct foreign investment from portfolio foreign investment. Control is easy to recognise but difficult to define. Control may be exercised not only through equity shares but also through control of technology, management and even information flows. The issue of foreign control raises a large number of questions related to conflicting national jurisdictions. It further complicates the targeting of policy. For whom should policy be designed? (All firms resident in the national economic space, including foreign-owned ones or all firms of 'our' nationality wherever they are located?)

Foreign direct investment represents a package of resources. Not only capital but also management skills, technology, labour services and access to markets are often elements of the package. These dimensions of the FDI give it a centrality in international economic relations which does not apply to trade flows. FDI represents a conduit through which flow information and resources.

The relationship between flows of trade and flows of foreign direct investment is a complex one. In some instances FDI will replace exporting by the parent corporation of a multinational firm. This so-called 'defensive investment' may be put in place to protect a market share initially established by exporting. 'Tariff-jumping' FDI would also be in this category. A local presence through FDI enables the firm to respond more rapidly to demand in a particular foreign market, but also serve as a 'listening post' in order to spot trends more quickly and to enable adjustment to the local business culture. Thus even when intended to be export replacing, FDI will often increase exporting capability and may serve to 'piggy-back' other products on to the original export line. FDI will be expected to enhance exports of semi-finished goods if it is aimed at a final foreign market (assembly, fabrication or finishing).

As pointed out above, it is not necessarily the case that the markets will be a key motive for FDI. Securing access to resources and cost reduction are alternative motivations. The latter motive may result in a more differentiated pattern of trade as the firm moves towards globally integrated production. Casson *et al.* (1986) attempted to capture some of the complexities of this pattern by classifying the structure and content of world trade by six types of industry: new product industry, mature product industry, rationalised product industry, resource-based industry, trading services and non-tradable services.

Thus foreign direct investment is a strategic weapon which can serve a variety of motives. In high-technology multinationals, FDI represents the most important conduit for the international transfer of technology. In these instances FDI is intended to diffuse technology spatially, at the same time protecting its proprietary nature (ownership). In contrast to licensing, FDI represents the internal transfer of information and knowledge, risking diffusion less by reducing exposure to the market.

Foreign direct investment is the major method of penetrating markets in the non-tradables sector (largely services) which actually make up a majority of world economic activity!

TRIAD RELATIONS IN THE INTERNATIONAL ECONOMY

North America, Europe and Japan (the Triad) represent the centres of the world's emerging regional trade blocs – NAFTA, the EU and the putative

Asia-Pacific Economic Cooperation (APEC) zone. Much of the analysis of flows of trade and FDI takes place on an implicit or explicit framework of this tripolar world. This must be held in mind as an abstraction or at best an approximation to trade and investment relations in the international economy. The decisions which are being aggregated are those of individual firms. The outcomes of these decisions are aggregated by national groups. Flows of trade are defined by spatial factors, flows of investment by ownership. There is a real sense that aggregating flows risk adding apples to pears. This is only useful when one wishes to know the weight of fruit. All such analyses should

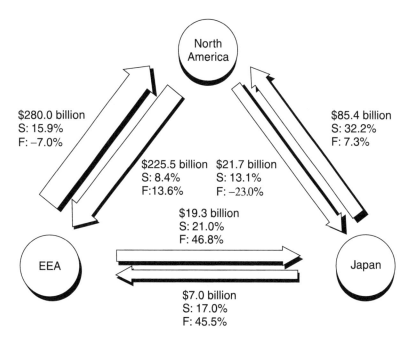

Figure 2.3 Intra-Triad foreign direct investment, 1990 (billions of dollars)

Note: Dollar figures show estimated values of stock of FDI based on data on inward and outward investment from North America and the European Economic Area (EEA), excluding Iceland and Liechtenstein. Intra-North American investment and intra-EEA investment have been netted out. Percentages show average annual growth rates for stocks (1980–90) and flows (1985–91). North America includes Canada and the United States. The European Economic Area includes the European Community (EC) and the European Free Trade Association, excluding Iceland and Liechtenstein.

Source: UNCTAD, Programme on Transnational Corporations, foreign-direct-investment database.

carry a health warning. Given these problems, analyses of flows across the Triad can be very revealing.

Figure 2.3 shows the imbalance of foreign direct investment stocks across the Triad. The weakest link is the European FDI in Japan which represented only $7.0 billion. North American FDI in Japan, too, accounted for only $21.7 billion as against $85.4 billion of Japanese direct investment in North America. Figure 2.4 shows clusters of countries attached to the main poles of the Triad. Developing countries have consistently declined as hosts to foreign direct investment, in terms of their share of world FDI (which is directed to a small number of less-developed countries (LDCs)). One Triad pole is the dominant investor in the countries listed. A pattern emerges of European dominance in Central and Eastern Europe and Africa, North American dominance in Latin America and Japanese dominance in non-Indian Sub-continent Asia (Figure 2.4).

In terms of firms' strategic positioning, it might be suggested that global firms need to maintain a (strategic) position in each of these three key markets in order not to let rivals have a 'free run' in any one market which would allow them to accumulate resources to enable the firm to mount a subsidised concerted attack on its rivals. This is a variant of the 'exchange of threat' model, usually expounded on a bilateral basis (Flowers, 1976; Graham, 1978, 1990).

TRADE AND INVESTMENT BETWEEN TRIAD POLES

Table 2.5 shows the shares of different national ownerships of the world foreign direct investment stocks. In terms of Triad investment only, the figures in Table 2.6 show inward stocks.

Table 2.5   Share in world outward stock of foreign direct investment, by selected countries, 1914, 1960, 1978 and 1992 (percentage of world total)

Country	1914	1960	1978	1992
France	12.2	6.1	3.8	8.3
Germany	10.5	1.2	7.3	9.2
Japan	0.1	0.7	6.8	13.0
United Kingdom	45.5	16.2	12.9	11.4
United States	18.5	49.2	41.4	25.3

Source: Dunning, 1993, annex table 4. Taken from *World Investment Report 1993*, p. 131.

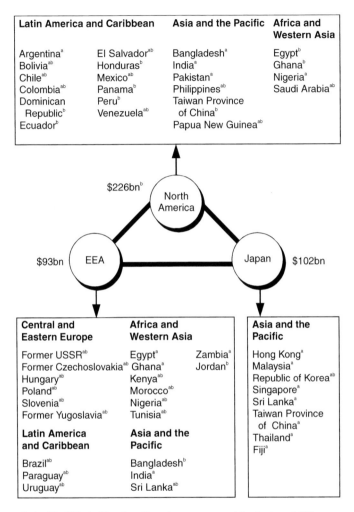

Figure 2.4 The Triad of foreign direct investment and its clusters, 1991

Notes:
[a] In terms of average inward FDI flows, 1987–91.
[b] In terms of inward FDI stock for 1991.

Source: UNCTAD, Division on Transnational Corporations and Investment.

The weak link is clearly inward investment to Japan. This issue brings us back to the idea of the 'centrality' of foreign direct investment (Buckley, 1994). FDI has a crucial role in cementing international economic relations.

FDI is more than just a strategic weapon in a multinational firm's armoury or a choice among several possible foreign market-servicing strategies (Buckley and Casson, 1976; Buckley and Prescott, 1989; Buckley and Smith, 1994). It is a manifestation of a serious competitive commitment in the increasingly interdependent international economy. In many markets, it is not possible to gain a sizeable market share without an investment presence. Increasingly, arm's-length exports to major markets are futile. Selling through agents or distributors does not allow control of the operation or effective flow-back of information to the principal (Buckley, Pass and Prescott, 1990). In markets such as Japan, the complexity of the distribution system demands a presence and the necessity for investment increases the cost of entering the market (Buckley, Mirza and Sparkes, 1987).

Table 2.6   Intra-Triad flows: inward stocks, 1990 (billions of dollars)

North America	365.4
EEA	244.6
Japan	28.7

Source: Figure 2.3 – Intra Regional Flow (e.g. US–Canada) netted out.

The institutional form of foreign direct investment is also important. Multinational firms have to make crucial choices on ownership strategy (wholly-owned subsidiary, majority- or minority-owned joint ventures) and in entry mode (takeover versus greenfield venture). The difficulties of takeover in certain countries such as Japan increase the costs and problems of market penetration by outsiders, particularly in a competitive game where the entrant firm is seeking rapid access to the market.

Ownership strategies, too, differ across the Triad. Joint ventures are the most common means of entry into the Japanese market and there is a lively dispute on the efficiency of using Japanese joint-venture partners (at home or abroad). In essence, new entrants are unlikely to gain a foothold in Japan without a local partner. However, such an arrangement is not fixed for all time and many US and European investors in Japan later increase their ownership share of an existing joint venture or add a parallel wholly-owned operation, utilising the accumulated experience (American Chamber of Commerce in Japan, 1991; Buckley, Mirza and Sparkes, 1996). This double-entry form of accessing the Japanese markets is particularly marked among European high-technology firms (Buckley, Mirza and Sparkes, 1996).

In addition to securing market penetration, FDI is used by multinationals to reduce costs. There is considerable evidence that such indirect targeting of markets via production bases in Third World countries is increasing. The use of Mexico to penetrate the US market and of North Africa, Central and Eastern Europe or peripheral EU locations to penetrate Europe is increasing. This does not seem to work in the case of Japan – in Japan a presence is necessary. Japanese multinationals use neighbouring cheaper labour countries to reduce costs of production aimed at the Japanese market as well as Europe and America. Japanese multinationals, however, have an advantage in accessing the Japanese distribution system. It is not the case that a manufacturing presence is necessary in FDI. Indeed, an optimal global location strategy will often dictate the separation of production from distribution. Coordination costs then become important and the superior management of activities can confer competition benefits (Buckley, Pass and Prescott, 1990).

INTERNATIONAL ALLIANCES

International alliances can be defined as inter-firm collaborations over a given economic space and time for the achievement of corporate goals (this is a modified version of Buckley's definition (1992, p. 912)). The essence of an alliance is that it operates across the boundaries of the firm using resources from at least two firms. Alliances can be defined locally, regionally, nationally or internationally and can operate in some defined real time or until certain goals are reached. The goals may be defined in terms of physical output, market share, technological achievement or managerial objective. It is possible that the partners to an alliance will have different, even conflicting goals. These factors make it extremely difficult to assess the success (or otherwise) of an alliance. Alliances may be reconfigured or even dissolved but this does not necessarily mean that they have failed. Indeed, one of the primary virtues of alliances is their flexibility. They can be formalised by equity holdings – joint ventures are alliances cemented by equity exchange – but non-equity alliances enable great flexibility to be built into international corporate strategy.

There has been a dramatic growth in international (strategic) alliances in recent years. Glaister and Buckley (1994) show a rising trend in UK joint-venture formation in the decade of the 1980s. This is confirmed by Table 2.8, which shows figures on the growth of strategic alliances in the Triad for the same decade. Glaister and Buckley show that the motives for joint-venture/ strategic alliance formation are very similar to those for foreign direct investment and that the strategic alliance phenomenon is best analysed as a form of direct investment.

Tables 2.7 and 2.8 show that international alliances form a key element of strategy in certain industries.[1] Financial services, other manufacturing, telecommunications and aerospace stand out as key sectors. Automobiles,

Table 2.7   Joint-venture formation by industry, 1980–9

Industry	1980	1981	1982	1983	1984	1985	1986	1987	1988	1989	Total No.	Total %
Food and drink	3	0	1	0	0	3	2	4	3	2	18	3.5
Metals and minerals	4	1	2	2	0	1	1	0	2	3	16	3.1
Energy	4	1	1	0	1	0	0	1	2	2	12	2.3
Construction	2	1	1	1	0	2	2	2	1	6	18	3.5
Chemicals	6	2	1	4	2	2	1	3	4	2	27	5.2
Pharmaceuticals	1	1	1	5	1	1	3	1	2	1	17	3.3
Computers	0	3	1	1	2	4	2	2	2	4	21	4.0
Telecommunications	2	4	7	5	3	4	10	7	7	10	59	11.3
Other electrical	1	3	4	3	5	0	1	4	1	6	28	5.4
Automobiles	2	3	3	2	3	6	5	5	6	3	38	7.3
Aerospace	6	4	4	2	4	7	7	3	7	12	56	10.8
Other manufacturing	2	8	2	5	5	7	9	6	10	13	67	12.9
Transport	1	2	0	0	0	1	1	2	2	2	11	2.1
Distribution	0	1	1	0	2	4	5	2	2	6	23	4.4
Financial services	7	7	8	4	13	5	3	6	6	12	71	13.7
Other services	6	3	4	1	1	4	1	0	7	11	38	7.3
Total	47	44	41	35	42	51	53	48	64	95	520	100.0

biotechnology and information technology have all shown rapid growth in alliance formation, particularly in US – Japanese firms (for example, Reich and Mankin, 1986) but the perceived benefits clearly outweigh the risks of opportunism in many cases.

Strategic alliances extend the ability of multinational firms to achieve their goals and they complement direct foreign investment as a corporate weapon. Alliances make it easier to access difficult, regulated and protected markets and resources. They also provide an option on entry: where a firm is undecided whether to make a full direct investment commitment, joint ventures and alliances help it to 'keep its options open' for a later, full investment commitment. (Such an approach is currently prevalent in Central and Eastern Europe.) Alliances may also be construed as signals – to competitors, customers, suppliers and other interested bodies. They may be a signal that the firm has a credible commitment to enter a particular market or segment.

Table 2.8   Growth in strategic alliance formation, 1980 – 9 (number and percentage)

Industry/region	1980–4		1985–9		Percent-age change
	Number	Percent	Number	Percent	
Automobiles	26	100	79	100	203
United States–Europe	10	39	24	30	140
United States–Japan	10	39	39	49	290
Europe–Japan	6	23	16	20	167
Biotechnology	108	100	198	100	83
United States–Europe	58	54	124	63	114
United States–Japan	45	42	54	27	20
Europe–Japan	5	4	20	10	300
Information technology	348	100	445	100	28
United States–Europe	158	45	256	58	62
United States–Japan	133	38	132	30	−0.8
Europe–Japan	57	16	57	13	−
New materials	63	100	115	100	83
United States–Europe	32	51	52	45	63
United States–Japan	16	25	40	35	150
Europe–Japan	15	24	23	20	53
Chemicals	103	100	80	100	−22
United States–Europe	54	52	31	39	−43
United States–Japan	28	27	35	44	25
Europe–Japan	21	20	14	17	−33

Source: United States Congress, Office of Technology Assessment, 1993, figure 5.3.

Alliances, therefore, are a useful complement to an international strategy based on strategic direct investement.

CONCLUSION

Strategic trade, driven by government policy in order to back national champions, has severe defects. It can work only in a limited number of sectors where retaliation is limited by the lack of a rival's response. Even then, it is politically infeasible to subsidise rent-seeking in a few firms from general tax revenue. The efficacy of 'backing winners' in the industrial policy of governments does not inspire confidence in the historical record – especially in advanced countries.

Trade is also a limited weapon in strategic games. There are swathes of industry where it is not possible to enter foreign markets by exporting, and non-tradables make up for a far larger share of the world economy than do tradable goods. Even where tradable goods exist, foreign direct investment is often a more important weapon in gaining access to foreign markets than are exports (or licensing). There is very little enthusiasm for subsidising outward foreign investment because the majority of value-added activity takes place outside the political remit of the (political) subsidiser.

In many situations, foreign direct investment is the most powerful means of penetrating foreign markets. FDI has been rising relative to world trade, output and capital formation. Intra-firm trade is also increasing rapidly as firms source intermediate goods on a worldwide basis and serve global markets. Despite the decline in tariff protection, FDI outpaces the growth of trade.

Policies on FDI worldwide are skewed. There is a great deal of effort expended on attracting inward FDI but most governments follow a policy of neutrality towards outward FDI. Tax neutrality is often an explicit objective of policy towards domestic and foreign locations.

Note

1.   Some authors have made alliances the centre of an analysis of the firm, rather than a strategic alternative. This trend was exemplified by Gerlach (1992) in entitling his book on the Japanese *keiretsu Alliance Capitalism* – although his analysis is specific to Japan. This trend is continued by John Dunning, who refers to 'the age of alliance capitalism' (Dunning, 1995). Dunning sees alliances as spreading rather like a virus through the global political economy, posing new issues of governance, regulation and competition. While alliances are not new – witness the cartel movement of the Western economy in the interwar years – they are salient in key sectors of the world economy. However, it is currently claiming too much to see alliances as replacing the unitary firm as the dominant player in competition, innovation and production. Intercor-

porate ties are important and growing but remain one strategic choice among many in the mosaic of competition and cooperation facing multinational firms.

References

American Chamber of Commerce in Japan (ACCJ) (1991) *Trade and Investment in Japan* (Tokyo: ACCJ).

Bairoch, Paul (1993) *Economics and World History* (Brighton: Wheatsheaf).

Bairoch, Paul (1994) 'Globalisation, Myths and Realities – One Century of External Trade and Foreign Investment', in R. Boyer and D. Drache (eds), *The Future of Nations and the Power of Markets* (Toronto: University of Toronto Press).

Brander, J.A. and B.J. Spencer (1985) 'Export Subsidies and International Market Share Rivalry', *Journal of International Economics*, 18, 83–100.

Buckley, P.J. (1992) 'Alliances, Technology and Markets: A Cautionary Tale', in P.J. Buckley, *Studies in International Business* (London: Macmillan).

Buckley, P.J. (1994) 'Comment on Investment and Trade by American European and Japanese Multinationals Across the Triad', in M. Mason and D. Encarnation, *Does Ownership Matter – Japanese Multinationals in Europe* (Oxford: Clarendon Press).

Buckley, P.J. and M. Casson (1976) *The Future of the Multinational Enterprise* (London: Macmillan).

Buckley, P.J. and M. Casson (1981) 'The Optimal Timing of a Foreign Direct Investment', *Economic Journal*, 861, 55–94. Reprinted in Buckley and Casson (1985) *The Economic Theory of the Multinational Enterprise* (London: Macmillan).

Buckley, P.J., H. Mirza and J.R. Sparkes (1987) 'Direct Foreign Investment in Japan as a Means of Market Entry: The Case of European Firms', *Journal of Marketing Management*, 2, 241–58.

Buckley, P.J., H. Mirza and J.R. Sparkes (1993) 'The Development of European Direct Investment in Japan', A Report to the Japan Foundation, University of Bradford.

Buckley, P.J., H. Mirza and J.R. Sparkes (1996) 'Contrasting Perspectives on American and European Direct Investment in Japan', *Business Economics*, 31 (1) (January), 42–8.

Buckley, P.J., C.L. Pass and K. Prescott (1990) 'Foreign Market Servicing by Multinationals: An Integrated Approach', *International Marketing Review*, 7, 25–40.

Buckley, P.J. and K. Prescott (1989) 'The Structure of British Industry Sales in Foreign Markets', *Managerial and Decision Economics*, 10, 189–208.

Buckley, P.J. and G.E. Smith (1994) 'An International Comparison of the Structure of Foreign Market Servicing Strategies', *International Business Review*, 3, 71–94.

Casson, M. *et al.* (1986) *Multinationals and World Trade* (London: George Allen & Unwin).

Casson, M. (1990) 'Entrepreneurial Culture as a Competitive Advantage', *Research in Global Business Management*, 1, 139–51.

Dunning, John H. (1993) *The Theory of Transnational Corporations* (London: Routledge).

Dunning, John H. (1995) 'Reappraising the Eclectic Paradigm in an Age of Alliance Capitalism', *Journal of International Business Studies*, 26, 461–91.

Flowers, E.B. (1976) 'Oligopolostic Reactions in European and Canadian Direct Investments in the United States', *Journal of International Business Studies*, 7, 43–55.

Gerlach, Michael L. (1992) *Alliance Capitalism: The Social Organisation of Japanese Business* (Oxford: Oxford University Press).

Glaister, K. and P.J. Buckley (1994) 'UK International Joint Ventures: An Analysis of Patterns of Activity and Distribution', *British Journal of Management*, 5, 33–51.

Graham, E.M. (1978) 'Transatlantic Investment by Multinational Firms: A Rivalristic Phenomenon?', *Journal of Post Keynesian Economics*, 1, 82–99.

Graham, E.M. (1990) 'Exchange of Threat between Multinational Firms as an Infinitely Repeated Non-cooperative Game', *The International Trade Journal*, 4, 259–77.

Graham, E.M. (1992) 'The Theory of the Firm', in P.J. Buckley (ed.), *New Directions in International Business* (Aldershot: Edward Elgar).

Holmes, P. (1995) 'European Industrial Policy and Subsidiarity after Maastricht', University of Rennes I, mimeo.

Horstmann, E.J. and J.R. Markusen (1987) 'Strategic Investment and the Development of Multinationals', *International Economic Review*, 28, 109–21.

Krugman, P. (1987a) 'Is Free Trade Passé?', *Journal of Economic Perspectives*, 1 (2) (Fall), 131–44.

Krugman, P. (1987) 'Market Access and Competition in High Technology Industries: A Simulation Exercise', in H. Kierzkowski (ed.), *Protection and Competition in International Trade* (Oxford: Blackwell).

Krugman, P. (1990) *Rethinking International Trade* (Cambridge, MA: MIT Press).

Krugman, P. (1994) *Peddling Prosperity* (New York: W.W. Norton & Company).

Reich, R.B. and E.D. Mankin (1986) 'Joint Ventures with Japan Give Away Our Future', *Harvard Business Review*, 64 (2), 78–86.

World Investment Report: Transnational Corporations and Integrated International Production (1993) (New York: United Nations).

3 Government Policy Responses to Strategic Rent-Seeking Transnational Firms*

STRATEGIC RENT-SEEKING BY FIRMS AND GOVERNMENTS

The main actors in the world economy are firms. Firms seek to maximise world profits and thus to appropriate the rents arising from their proprietary assets. These include technology, management, knowledge, organisational abilities and other internalised proprietary assets (Buckley and Casson, 1976, 1985; Magee, 1977). By denying others access to these internalised assets, transnational corporations (TNCs) earn rents that enable them to reinvest in the next generation of proprietary assets, or 'ownership advantages' (Dunning, 1980), thus enabling a dynamic competitive path to emerge over time (Buckley, 1983).

This process does not take place in a vacuum. Other firms are attempting to create proprietary assets through research-and-development activities (R&D), acquiring skills (including management) and bidding away assets from rival firms. Much of the game theoretical analysis of inter-firm rivalry takes the asset structure as given, but in practice a major part of strategy will be to bid away key resources from rival firms. Another major part of business strategy is to retain key assets by locking them into company structures (Buckley, 1983).

A further important part of the environment is the existence of national governments. Government policies play an important part in fostering and hindering the preferred business strategies of firms. A fundamental role of government is to seek to appropriate some of the rents earned by (transnational) firms. The interests of government are here twofold: to appropriate rents from foreign TNCs that have spin-offs for their citizens (political constituents); and to appropriate rents from their home-country-based TNCs wherever they operate. These policies have wide implications for TNCs, for the operation of the world economy and for the spatial location of economic

---

*Originally published in *Transnational Corporations*, vol. 5, no. 2, August 1996, pp. 1–17.

activity. The old description of government policies in a global economy as 'the struggle for the world product' must be modified to the more accurate 'the struggle for a share of the world's appropriable rents'.

The classic case for government intervention rests on two conditions of market failure being present: monopoly and externalities. The argument from monopoly rests on the interventionist being able to enforce a price equal to marginal costs and thus to eliminate private rents. Even in this case, the result is not unequivocal because there is an argument that monopoly, via the reinvestment of these private rents, enables more rapid innovation than other forms of market structure. The innovation stimulating effect of monopoly is much disputed, but what is less open to dispute is the ability of monopolists (*qua* large firms) to spread the *results* of R&D (even if it is not actually undertaken by them) over the largest potential output. This might be a reason to tolerate a monopoly *after* an innovation.

In order to justify intervention, market failure must be associated with informational problems, otherwise transaction costs would not prevent a market solution on the lines of the Coase theorem (the polluter pays). As we shall see, these informational constraints are crucially important for the possibility of effective implementation of government policies (Buckley, 1996).

THE FOREIGN MARKET-SERVICING STRATEGIES OF TRANSNATIONAL CORPORATIONS

The foreign market-servicing strategy of a firm is the set of decisions determining which production plant(s) should be linked to which specific foreign market(s), and the methods or channels through which this should be implemented. The three main generic types of strategy are: trade (exporting or importing); licensed sales (foreign licensing out, importing foreign technology); and foreign direct investment (FDI). The foreign market-servicing decision is a complex one, both theoretically (Buckley and Casson, 1985) and in practice (Buckley and Pearce, 1979, 1981, 1984; Buckley and Prescott, 1989).

Thus, on a cross-sectional, point of time basis, the total foreign sales (*TFS*) of a company is made up of exports (*X*), licensed sales abroad (*L*) and sales arising from FDI.

$$TFS = X + L + I$$

The amounts of these elements can be measured at a point of time, over time and in particular markets. It is possible to aggregate these elements at national level, using an ownership criterion for investment to give the total foreign sales of a particular country (Buckley and Prescott, 1989; Buckley and Smith, 1994). There is of course an inward analogue – sourcing into a particular market is made up of the sum of imports (M), sales arising from foreign licensees and the sales financed by inward FDI.

At the most simplified level, trade can be differentiated from the other two methods of foreign market servicing by the location effect, as the bulk of value-adding activity takes place in the home country, whereas the other two methods transfer most of the value-adding activity to the host country. Similarly, licensing can be differentiated from the other two forms by the externalisation effect. Licensing represents a market sale of proprietary assets by a firm. In trade and investment, such activities are internalised (Buckley and Casson, 1976). Broadly then, the internalisation and location effects separate the three generic forms of market servicing:

Internalisation effect

$$TFS = X + L + I$$

location effect

In practice, these simple differentiations are highly complex. Cross-section analyses of market-servicing strategies are point-of-time snapshots of dynamic processes. The individual modes are often complementary, not substitutes. For example, FDI in a market often increases demand for the firm's products via a 'presence effect' (Buckley, Newbould and Thurwell, 1988) which means that other products in the firm's range can be profitably exported. These elements, and the important fact that each of these modes of doing business abroad contains a wide variety of sub-modes, means that government policy towards foreign market-servicing strategies, both inward and outward, needs to be extremely well targeted and sensitive.

GOVERNMENT POLICIES ON TRADE, TECHNOLOGY EXCHANGE AND FOREIGN DIRECT INVESTMENT

There has been a strong tradition of writing on government policy towards TNCs. Much of it, however, takes the TNC as monolithic and fails to disaggregate the effects, consequences and policy challenges of the different forms of foreign market-servicing by the firm. It is argued here that a simplistic 'firms versus governments' stance on political economy is inadequate, and indeed dangerous in view of the differential effects of strategic rent-seeking by TNCs as exemplified by their foreign market-servicing stance.

Raymond Vernon's classic *Sovereignty at Bay* (1971a) argument posed the issue of the role of TNCs in the global economy in a particularly challenging fashion. In *Multinational Enterprise and National Security* (1971b), Vernon examines the 'nature of the multinational enterprises' as: national contributors, national challengers, trojan horses, and as hostages. The issue of power versus sovereignty is always to the fore in Vernon's writings, and his work has been influential in setting the policy agenda. This article contends that Vernon's concerns can be better understood, and the application of each of these concepts (contributor, challenger, trojan horse, hostage) can be best understood by putting the market-servicing strategy (inward and outward) explicitly into the policy matrix.

John Dunning's work has the notion of market failure very much at its core (see Dunning, 1993, pp. 313–14). Thus, his analysis is entirely consistent with the underlying premise of this analysis, that TNCs, as strategic rent-seekers, will pursue consistent policies to achieve this objective and that rational policy responses from governments are required. John Dunning (1991) traced the development of government policy from confrontation to cooperation and, by tracing the type of market imperfection which he believes to be prominent at a given historical stage, implicitly derives rational policy responses. This chapter is at once more crude and more sophisticated than Dunning's analysis. It is more crude in that it ignores interactions between government and TNCs (for the purposes of clear exposition); but it is more sophisticated in that it points to policy responses according to the type of rent-seeking strategy used by TNCs.

The nature of interactions between governments and TNCs is developed further by John Stopford and his various collaborators. John Stopford's early work (Stopford and Wells, 1972) saw governments as a constraint on the strategy of TNCs. A later study of *Britain and the Multinationals* (Stopford and Turner, 1985) saw the 'new politics' emerging in which constraint became coexistence and eventually cooperation. This developed in *Rival States, Rival Firms* (Stopford and Strange, 1991) to the view that TNCs and governments might be colluding in order to acquire world market share. This chapter steps back from such interactions between governments and TNCs and sees governments as independent of firms. It is possible to develop the present analysis to take account of such perceived interactions, but this would require resetting the policy matrix which is set up here in a rational response mode.

It was shown above that the foreign market-servicing strategies of TNCs are dynamic, complex and sensitive to changes in the environment, including policy changes. Table 3.1 shows the policy matrix at its most crude. It simply plots the three forms of foreign market-servicing strategy into and out of a country.

If one now returns to the discussion of government policy, one can begin to map policy decisions on to the various forms of foreign market-servicing decisions. The context of this discussion needs to be remembered: it is that government attempts to appropriate rents in a world of imperfect markets. Government thus has the task of designing a policy matrix which obtains a good share of rents from foreign TNCs and from home-owned TNCs wherever they operate. Governments thus require a clear vision of their strategic interest in rent-seeking before the design of a policy matrix can commence.

Table 3.1   Foreign market-servicing options: inward and outward

	Trade	Technology trade	FDI
Inward	1 Imports	2 Technology imports	3 Inward FDI
Outward	4 Exports	5 Outward technology licensing	6 Outward FDI

The national perspective on deriving rent in a world of TNCs requires attention to a rather more sophisticated matrix than that presented in Table 3.1. Each of the cells contains differentiated selements which may require policy adjustments.

In the trade cells (1 and 4), it is necessary to differentiate between final goods, intermediate goods and capital goods. Final or consumption goods do not form an input into the further production process, but intermediate and capital goods do. It may not therefore be in the best interest of government to limit the importation of intermediate and capital goods. Often, a policy of import substitution attempts to exclude final goods through tariffs, quotas or non-tariff barriers in order to foster local industries (the so-called 'infant industry' strategy). It may be necessary to allow intermediate and capital imports, however, as inputs into building up the infant. (In other words, a high effective tariff on final goods may require low – or zero – nominal tariffs on intermediate and capital goods imports into the production process.)

A variant on this theme is the strategic trade argument. From the point of view of the individual firm, exports can be a strategic weapon to gain access to a foreign market. When this is cast as a two-person game with national champions contending for a share of the international market, then government subsidies can alter the payoffs and under certain restrictive assumptions can lead to gains in national welfare, in the form of payoffs to individual firms of the home national ownership, in the post-subsidy game.

However, as Mark Casson (1990) pointed out, strategic trade policies suffer from the same difficulty as adversarial and business strategies: they can be imitated, and the results of the imitation can be disastrous. Classic strategic trade policy under which government subsidises 'national champions' (Brander and Spencer, 1985; Krugman, 1987b) can provoke foreign governments into matching the subsidies. This can result in escalation of threat and counter-threat, as each government guarantees the credibility of its national champion's threat to spoil the rival's market. Only when slow response or poor liquidity of the foreign rival causes it to exit the industry is a permanent gain likely to be achieved. The analogy with protectionist 'beggar-my-neighbour' policies is strong. Whilst a subsidised or protected firm may sometimes gain, domestic consumers and taxpayers will normally lose. This explains rent-seeking lobbying for government intervention to protect or subsidise putative 'national champions' (or infant industries).

This analysis has so far left aside the political feasibility of the 'tax generally and subsidise specifically' policy combination. In the United States, this is severely constrained by the budget deficit, and in the European Union it is constrained by the lack of a powerful centralised body. In addition, observation suggests that the ability of governments to pick winners (national champions) is severely limited. Institutional failure may be regarded as greater than market failure.

In addition, Paul Krugman (1994) made a powerful argument that trade based on comparative advantage is a non-zero-sum game. It is from this viewpoint that he labelled the notion of national competitiveness as a meaningless concept. In reviewing the arguments based on externalities and strategic trade considerations for interventionist policies, Krugman (1987a) concluded that the optimal policy is so sensitive to technological and behavioural parameters that the results of intervention are uncertain even in areas where externality and monopoly arguments abound (e.g. semiconductors). The information available to government policy-makers will be biased – not least by lying on the part of rent-seekers: 'We have a sadder but wiser argument for free trade in a world whose politics are as imperfect as its markets' (Krugman, 1987a, p. 30).

Just as the division of trade into the simple 'final, intermediate and capital goods' categories complicates the issues of government policy, so one should look more closely at licensing. Two categories of technology trade could, with profit, be differentiated. These categories concern product and process technology. It can be argued, by analogy with trade, that process technology represents an input into the production process, whilst product technology (brand names, etc.) aligns with finished product. In fact, this is far too crude an assumption and it serves to illustrate further the complexities of government intervention in a globalising world economy. Even with this crude bifurcation of technology licensing, government policy would seek to encourage the out-licensing of product technology and discourage the out-licensing of process technology whilst stimulating the acquisition of foreign process technology but dampening demand for foreign product technology. This would ensure the appropriation of rents from brand names and product technology exported whilst reducing the rent paid for foreign product technology. The inputs of process technology into domestic activity would not be discouraged. Again, this policy mix illustrates the need for micro-intervention and highlights the huge information needs required for an optimal policy mix.

Finally, one needs to examine FDI. The best way to characterise both inward and outward FDI is by motive underlying an investment. Three key motives can be distinguished: market-seeking investment that attempts to use investment to penetrate foreign markets and maximise market share; resource-seeking investment aimed at securing supplies of key inputs, notably natural resources; and efficiency-servicing investment that attempts to reduce the overall costs facing a TNC, notably in seeking non-tradable inputs, the most important of which is labour.

Again, strategic rent-seeking issues are to the fore in examining company strategy and government policy. It might be argued that outward market-seeking investment might be encouraged whilst inward market-seeking investment might be penalised. This would serve to allow domestically owned firms the maximum access to market shares abroad and at home, and therefore to available rents. Resource-seeking investment might be encouraged in an outward direction, to secure supplies for national firms, but inward resource seeking might be penalised. The third motive for FDI – efficiency seeking – poses problems for the rational rent-appropriating government. It may be expedient to limit or penalise outward efficiency-seeking investment *if* the government believes that a domestic investment is a feasible alternative. However, if that is not the case, then to restrict outward FDI may have negative effects on the ability of home country TNCs to accumulate rents. Inward efficiency-seeking investment may be regarded as increasing the welfare of citizens (by increasing wage rates, providing employment, increasing exports), but there have been policy proposals in various countries to restrict such investment in favour of higher order (higher value-adding) activities, but again the substitution possibilities are largely unknown. This section on FDI has shown that the interrelationships between the particular foreign investment and the rest of the economy need to be known in order to design an optimal policy. In particular, the vertical (value chain) relationships are important in the firm's strategy and therefore in rational policy responses (Casson *et al.*, 1986).

The arguments of this section are summarized in Table 3.2, which builds upon Table 3.1 by differentiating types of foreign market-servicing modes within each cell of the matrix. Trade is divided by stages in the production process, technology transfer by type (product and process) and FDI by motive. A complex array results.

Table 3.2   Foreign market-servicing options by subtype, inward and outward

	Trade		Technology trade		FDI	
	1		**2**		**3**	
Inward	(*a*)	Final goods Imports	(*a*)	Product technology imports	(*a*)	Market-seeking inward FDI
	(*b*)	Intermediate goods imports	(*b*)	Process technology imports	(*b*)	Resource-seeking inward FDI
	(*c*)	Capital goods imports			(*c*)	Efficiency-seeking inward FDI
	4		**5**		**6**	
Outward	(*a*)	Final goods exports	(*a*)	Product technology exports	(*a*)	Market-seeking outward FDI
	(*b*)	Intermediate goods exports	(*b*)	Process technology exports	(*b*)	Resource-seeking outward FDI
	(*c*)	Capital goods exports			(*c*)	Efficiency-seeking outward FDI

A GOVERNMENT POLICY MATRIX

After this analysis of modes of foreign market-servicing subdivided by type, one can suggest a rational government policy matrix. The matrix (Table 3.3) is coded by policies either + (encourage, promote, stimulate, subsidise) or – (discourage, prevent, reduce, tax) or? where the policy depends on other variables. As can be seen, the rational policy array is formidably complicated.

If one examines the array in Table 3.3 cell by cell, one can assess each item and the policy directed to it. Beginning with cell (1), inward trade, one can observe that conventional government policies prefer to discourage the import of final goods, as they are regarded as competing with domestic products and diverting value-adding activities abroad. The classic arguments for protectionism can be trotted out in defence of a policy that restricts final goods imports. The same arguments do not apply to imports of intermediate goods and capital goods, which are regarded as inputs into the domestic production process. This is the core of the argument for 'effective protection': protecting domestic value-adding activities at a high level by having large tariffs on output and low tariffs on inputs. It is not, of course, always possible to identify inputs and outputs, and the policy of 'cheap food' can be justified by regarding food as an input into the production process (via the labour force) just as well as it can be justified on welfare and consumption grounds.

Table 3.3 Foreign market-servicing options, by subtype, inward and outward, with policy directions

	Trade		Technology trade		FDI	
Inward	**1** (a)	Final goods imports ( )	**2** (a)	Product technology imports ( )	**3** (a)	Market-Seeking inward FDI ( )
	(b)	Intermediate goods imports (+)	(b)	Process technology imports (+)	(b)	Resource-Seeking inward FDI (+)
	(c)	Capital goods imports (+)			(c)	Efficiency-Seeking inward FDI (?)
Outward	**4** (a)	Final goods exports (+)	**5** (a)	Product technology exports (+)	**6** (a)	Market-seeking outward FDI (+)
	(b)	Intermediate goods exports (?)	(b)	Process technology exports ( )	(b)	Resource-seeking outward FDI (+)
	(c)	Capital goods exports (?)			(c)	Efficiency-seeking outward FDI (?)

Cell (4) examines exports. In general, exports might be regarded as a 'good thing', earning foreign exchange to enable the purchase of imports for investment or consumption purposes. Final goods exports are clearly a benefit to a nation, but is this necessarily so in the case of exports of intermediate and capital goods? Exports that are an input into foreign production processes may be considered to embody competitive advantages that foreigners can employ. This is an argument analogous to those used to justify prevention of technology outflows.

Cells (2) and (5) concern technology trade. Imports of product technology might be disfavoured by governments as against process-technology imports. Product technology, satisfying final demand, may be seen as less acceptable than process technology, seen as a key input into the production process. A clear example of this is given in the recent liberalisation of India's technology-importing sector. 'The Bharatiya Janata Party welcomes foreign investment in infrastructure industries, though not in junk-food businesses.'[1] Although the final objective of government policy is presumably the satisfaction of consumer demand, politicians and bureaucrats will argue that it is their job to balance investment and consumption, and to postpone present consumption in favour of investment. Control of inward technology flows and FDI is one rather crude means of effecting such a strategy. Process technology can be more easily identified with investment and product technology with (frivolous) consumption. Mirror-image arguments can be put with regard to technology outflows. Process technology enables foreigners to copy, adapt and even improve on the technology employed. Product technology has fewer strategic concerns.

These issues are bound up with concerns about the *pricing* of technology. Because the value of technology is difficult to evaluate, there can be disputes about the appropriation of the rents involved. Constantine Vaitsos (1974) argued that technology recipients (generally developing countries) will overpay for technology imports, because they do not have access to full information on its value. Mark Casson (1979) argued that licensees face great information barriers in appropriating the full return from their innovations. Asymmetries in information can thus play a distorting role in discussions of policies on technology transfer. Moreover, market-based rules may be of limited use in situations where, by definition, monopolies exist. It would be possible to add a row to each of cells (3) and (6), covering 'technology-seeking FDI'. There are many instances where the motivating factor for FDI is to gain control of a particular element of foreign technology. It is possible to argue that foreign control of technology is intrinsically bad from a strategic point of view for any nation-state. But just as all people have their price, so too do all intangible public goods ('national control', 'strategic interest', 'domestic security'). So, the question really is: what is the correct price for technology, with the appropriate collective consumption good (security, control) factored into the price?

Strategies on inward FDI, too, seem to vary according to the type of investment. Market-seeking inward FDI might be regarded as negative in its impact on the rent appropriations of the domestic economy because it provides competition with domestic firms. Here, the debate is between those who favour national champions, firms that are deliberately allowed to build up a domestic monopoly or considerable market share (and are even explicitly or tacitly encouraged to do so), versus those who believe that free competition, contestability of markets and non-interventionism are preferable. This leads to huge issues of the conflict of economic philosophies underlying policy.

Resource-seeking inward DFI has traditionally often been discouraged except where the technology, marketing and distribution skills of TNCs have been overwhelming arguments to host country governments. It is usually host country governmental bodies that are the key decision-makers in this area because control of raw materials is frequently their domain. The arguments for inward FDI *have* generally been overwhelming, and many governments have been willing to appropriate their share of rents by taxing the profits of foreign-owned TNCs. There are instabilities in such an arrangement, however. The record of extracture by vertically integrated TNCs (the oil majors, copper and aluminium companies, etc.) is fraught with political turbulence. The majority of recorded expropriations of TNCs is in the extractive sector, and foreign firms need all the political skills they can amass in these areas.

Efficiency-seeking FDI arises where TNCs are seeking to lower their total costs by locating activities in their least-cost locations. This often boils down to the search for the lowest efficiency wages (wages after taking productivity differentials into account). In mass assembly industries, the phenomenon of offshore production arises where the labour-intensive stages of production are set up in a cheap labour country. The key policy issue in these circumstances for the host country is: what is the feasible alternative? Because of the success of countries with a history as offshore bases (Singapore, Thailand, Malaysia), the answer to this question has shifted significantly over time. The ability of TNCs to transfer increasingly complex activities offshore has upgraded these facilities and, through spin-offs, buy-outs and local purchases, the host economies likewise. The dynamic, rather than static benefits of efficiency-seeking FDI to the host country have swung the balance for host countries away from a policy of caution, towards a policy of welcome. The result is a struggle amongst potential host countries to attract inward FDI, and a transfer of the rent from such activities towards TNCs with activities that are relatively 'footloose'.

In the case of outward FDI, cell 6 suggests a bias in policy against outflows. The arguments here rest on a view of the alternative position: what would happen in the absence of the outflow? Is a domestic investment a feasible alternative? In the case of resource-seeking outward investment, it can be argued that there will not be a feasible alternative domestic investment as the firm concerned will be seeking resources unavailable at home for this reason; and for the reason that resources abroad will often be input into the domestic production process, outward resource-seeking FDI will be at least treated neutrally – and often actively (if covertly) encouraged. For similar reasons, market-seeking outward FDI may be viewed favourably by source country government policies. The market-servicing strategies of host country firms will often dictate a foreign location for their marketing and finishing operations. From the source country's point of view, the most effective location of these activities may stimulate jobs and total activity within their borders by increasing foreign market penetration; the loss of jobs overseas might be more than compensated for by increases in complementary (downstream) jobs in the source country. It would be difficult in these circumstances to second-guess the location decisions of TNCs. It is therefore in the area of efficiency-seeking outward FDI that the 'alternative position' argument is likely to be invoked to support policies restricting outward investment. Investment-seeking cost reductions, largely through reducing labour costs, aimed particularly at unskilled labour, often provoke accusations of 'export of jobs'. There may be a case, in specific instances, of there being a possibility of substituting capital-intensive production at home for labour-intensive production abroad, but much will depend upon the competitive position of the firm. If offshore production is undertaken in response to a threat, then the firm is unlikely to be able to go to the capital market to raise funds from a position of weakness. Moreover, after taking into account the cost of capital to the firm, a cheap labour location may remain the cheaper option. There is the further argument that location abroad of the labour-intensive stages of production allows the retention of the supporting jobs in the source country which would otherwise be lost if the firm were not allowed to invest abroad.

The key feature of Table 3.3 which needs to be noted is that there are pluses and minuses in each cell in the array. This requires a fine judgement on the part of government and therefore a considerable amount of information. Second, although the majority of entries have an unequivocal plus or minus, many of these entries are contentious and depend upon a set of largely untested assertions rather than an almost equally plausible set of alternative assertions. Third, the array is bedevilled by relationships amongst the components. Vertical relationships, in particular, muddy the waters of unidirectional causality (Casson, 1986). Finally, the dynamics of foreign market-servicing strategies affect the whole policy set. The foreign market-servicing decisions of TNCs are constantly evolving. Firms switch from exporting to licensing and/or investment according to change in the environment, their cost structure and their evolving strategies (Buckley and Casson,

1981). Consequently, it is not only the direction of government policy, but its timeliness which is crucial. Badly applied, government policy can trigger a switch in the foreign market-servicing decision which can undo the effects of its intention (tariff jumping FDI – a switch from exporting to FDI – is an important example). To complicate the picture even further, it may be suggested that different policies are required with regard to different industries and different trading partners (within trade bloc versus outside trade block partners, for example).

CONCLUSIONS

Government policies towards rent-seeking TNCs will be influenced by three sets of considerations: the underlying philosophy determining the level of intervention in the economy; the perceived national interest, as expressed in the balance of inward/outward trade and investment activity; and technical issues in policy implementation.

The underlying philosophy of governments towards TNCs differs markedly between states, but seems to have conformed to a general trend that runs from government policy as a *constant* to policy as *conflict and bargaining* to policy as *cooperation* (Boddewyn, 1992).

The balance between inward and outward flows (particularly of FDI) is also a key determinant of governmental policy posture. The virtue of this analysis is that it includes outward FDI (see UNCTAD-DTCI, chapter VII, 1995) as within the policy compass.

There are a number of technical issues of policy which are highlighted by this analysis. Amongst the most important concerns are: the balance within each cell of the policy matrix, the timing of policies with respect to the dynamics of firms evolving market-servicing strategies and the links between different elements in the firms' value chains which severely complicated a rational analysis of the impact of policies.

A fairly simple analysis of modes and submodes of the foreign market-servicing decision yields a highly sophisticated policy matrix. One must ask the question as to whether governments (any government) have the information and the skill to implement such a policy set. This is further complicated by the notion of timeliness. Policies must be designed not for a static point of time but in a situation where market servicing and sourcing policies are continually and rapidly evolving as the world economy becomes globalised.

Broadbrush policies run the risk not only of missing the target, but actually of working in a direction opposite to their intentions. For instance, any broadbrush policy within *any* cell of the matrix given by Table 3.3 will have both

negative and positive policy consequences. Micro-interventionist policies
(aimed at a subset of a cell in Table 3.3) require careful targeting and a vast
amount of information.

The rent-appropriation model of the foreign market-servicing strategies of
TNCs calls for a careful reappraisal of government policies. It is capable of
extension by inputting alternative assumptions, for instance, on interactions
between individual policies of governments and the second-order responses
of firms. The development of this framework enables a clearer policy debate
to take place on the activities of TNCs in an increasingly complex, globalising world economy.

Note

1.   Jay Dubashi, Bharatiya Janata Party, letter to *The Economist*, 2 September
      1995.

References

Boddewyn, Jean J. (1992) 'Political Behaviour Research', *New Directions in Inter-
   national Business* (Cheltenham: Edward Elgar), pp. 81–7.
Brander, James A. and Barbara J. Spencer (1985) 'Export Subsidies and Internation-
   al Market Share Rivalry', *Journal of International Economics*, 18, pp. 83–100.
Buckley, Peter J. (1983) 'New Theories of International Business, Some Un-
   resolved Issues', in Mark Casson (ed.), *The Growth of International Business*
   (London: George Allen & Unwin), pp. 34–50.
Buckley, P.J. (1996) 'Strategic Foreign Direct Investment', in Gavin Boyd and
   Alan M. Rugman (eds), *Euro-Pacific Investment and Trade* (Cheltenham:
   Edward Elgar).
Buckley, P.J. and M. Casson (1976) *The Future of the Multinational Enterprise*
   (London: Macmillan).
Buckley, P.J. and M. Casson (1981) 'The Optimal Timing of a Foreign Direct In-
   vestment', *Economic Journal*, 92, pp. 75–87.
Buckley, P.J. and M. Casson (1985) *The Economic Theory of the Multinational
   Enterprise* (London: Macmillan).
Buckley, P.J., G.D. Newbould and Jane C. Thurwell (1988) *Foreign Direct Invest-
   ment by Smaller UK Firms* (London: Macmillan).
Buckley, P.J. and Robert D. Pearce (1979) 'Overseas Production and Exporting by
   the World's Largest Enterprises', *Journal of International Business Studies*, 10,
   pp. 9–20.
Buckley, P.J. and R.D. Pearce (1981) 'Market Servicing by Multinational Manufac-
   turing Firms: Exporting versus Foreign Production', *Marginal and Decision
   Economics*, 2, pp. 229–46.
Buckley, P.J. and R.D. Pearce (1984) 'Exports in the Strategy of Multinational
   Firms', *Journal of Business Research*, 12, pp. 209–26.

Buckley, P.J. and Kate Prescott (1989) 'The Structure of British Industry's Sales in Foreign Markets', *Marginal and Decision Economics*, 10, pp. 189–208.

Buckley, P.J. and G.E. Smith (1994) 'An International Comparison of the Structure of Foreign Market Servicing Strategies', *International Business Review*, 3, pp. 71–94.

Casson, Mark (1979) *Alternatives to the Multinational Enterprises* (London: Macmillan).

Casson, Mark *et al.* (1986) *Multinationals and World Trade* (London: George Allen & Unwin).

Casson, Mark (1990) 'Entrepreneurial Culture as a Competitive Advantage', *Research in Global Business Management*, 1, pp. 139–51.

Dunning, John H. (1980) 'Towards an Eclectic Theory of International Production', *Journal of International Business Studies*, 11, pp. 9–31.

Dunning, J.H. (1991) 'Governments and Multinational Enterprises: From Confrontation to Cooperation', *Millennium*, 20, pp. 225–44.

Dunning, J.H. (1993) *The Globalization of Business* (London: Routledge).

Krugman, Paul K. (1987a) 'Is Free Trade *Passé?*', *Journal of Economic Perspectives*, 1, 2 (Fall), pp. 131–44.

Krugman, Paul K. (1987b) 'Market Access and Competition in High Technology Industries: A Simulation Exercise', in Henry K. Kierzkowski (ed.), *Protection and Competition in International Trade* (Oxford: Blackwell), pp. 128–42.

Krugman, Paul K. (1994) *Peddling Prosperity* (New York: W.W. Norton & Company).

Magee, S.P. (1977) 'Information and Multinational Corporation: An Appropriability Theory of Foreign Direct Investment', in J. Bhagwati (ed.), *The New International Economic Order* (Cambridge, Mass: MIT Press).

Stopford, John M. and Susan Strange (1991) *Rival States, Rival Firms* (Cambridge: Cambridge University Press).

Stopford, J.M. and Louis Turner (1985) *Britain and the Multinationals* (Chichester: John Wiley & Sons).

Stopford, J.M. and Louis T. Wells (1972) *Managing the Multinational Enterprise* (London: Longman).

United Nations Conference on Trade and Development (UNCTAD) (1995) *World Investment Report 1995: Transnational Corporations and Competitiveness*, Sales No. E.95.II.A.9.

Vaitsos, Constantine V. (1974) *Intercompany Income Distribution and Transnational Enterprises* (Oxford: Oxford University Press).

Vernon, Raymond (1971a) *Sovereignty at Bay: The Multinational Spread of US Enterprises* (New York: Basic Books).

Vernon, Raymond (1971b) 'Multinational Enterprise and National Security', *Adelphi Papers*, reprinted in Vernon (1972), *The Economic and Political Consequences of Multinational Enterprise: An Anthology* (Boston: Division of Research, Graduate School of Business Administration, Harvard University), pp. 85–139.

4 Strategic Motives for UK International Alliance Formation*

with Keith W. Glaister

INTRODUCTION

Over the past two decades the incidence of strategic alliance formation has accelerated (Ghemawat *et al.*, 1986; Glaister and Buckley, 1994; Hergert and Morris, 1988). Traditionally strategic alliances were used by multinational companies as a vehicle to enter the markets of developing countries that enforced restrictive conditions on foreign investment (Hood and Young, 1979). More recently firms in developed market economies have been increasingly willing to participate in cooperative ventures often with their direct competitors. The momentum for this has come from the firms themselves, which have voluntarily adopted alliances as a strategic option in response to changing market conditions rather than in compliance to exogenously enforced rules (Harrigan, 1988; Vonortas, 1990).

An alliance can be defined as an 'inter-firm collaboration over a given economic space and time for the attainment of mutually defined goals' (Buckley, 1992, p. 91). Buckley notes a number of important characteristics to this definition:

- it covers only inter-firm agreements, i.e. an alliance operates across the boundaries of a firm
- the venture must be collaborative in that there must be some input of resources from all the partners
- the alliance defined over economic time and space means that it can range from local to global, and it can be defined in real time or until certain goals are reached

---

* Originally published in *Journal of Management Studies*, vol. 33, no. 3, May 1996, pp. 301–32.

- while an alliance will be defined for the achievement of certain goals it is not necessarily the case that all partners have the same view of the objectives.

Defined in this way alliances constitute a subset of collaborative activity that excludes a number of forms of inter-firm cooperation that are not alliances. In particular it excludes buyer–seller relationships, subcontracting agreements, licensing, franchising, barter and buyback where the parties have to some degree opposing goals – the sellers to sell dear and the buyers to buy cheap. Joint ventures (JVs) do qualify, however, because they involve inter-firm collaboration, have inputs from all parties and are defined in terms of goals over a well-defined economic space (Buckley, 1992). Moreover, two classes of joint venture can be defined – equity joint ventures (EJVs) and non-equity joint ventures (NEJVs).

Killing (1988, p. 56) views EJVs as 'traditional joint ventures', which are created when two or more partners join forces to establish a newly incorporated company in which each has an equity position, thereby each expects a proportional share of dividend as compensation and representation on the board of directors. This conforms to Harrigan's (1985) analytical concept of a joint venture where she studies joint ventures as 'separate entities with two or more active businesses as partners', where the emphasis is on the 'child', i.e. 'the entity created by partners for a specific activity' (1985, pp. 2–3). EJVs thus involve two or more legally distinct organisations (the parents), each of which invests in the venture and actively participates in the decision-making activities of the jointly owned entity (Geringer, 1991). In contrast, NEJVs are agreements between partners to cooperate in some way, but they do not involve the creation of new firms. Contractor and Lorange (1988) point out that in these cases carefully defined rules and formulas govern the allocation of tasks, costs and revenues. With NEJVs, the compensation to each firm is dependent on the level of profits earned and there is at least a moderate degree of inter-organisational dependence, as is the case with EJVs (Contractor and Lorange, 1988, p. 7). All other types of cooperative arrangements, such as franchising and licensing, may be considered as contractual arrangements where compensation is not determined by profits earned and inter-organisational dependence is low to negligible. Such contractual arrangements are not considered to be joint ventures and do not form part of this study. The domain of this study therefore comprises EJVs and NEJVs which are each a sub-set of alliance activity. Alliances themselves form a sub-set of inter-firm collaborative activity. Hence this study is not concerned with all types of inter-firm cooperative activity, but only those types identified above.

A strategic alliance denotes some degree of strategic as well as operational coordination (Teece, 1992). An alliance is also strategic in the sense that strategic decisions involve long-lasting commitments as distinct from tactical decisions, which are short-term responses to the current environment (Shapiro, 1985). A joint venture is considered to be international if at least one partner has its headquarters outside the venture's country of operation or if the joint venture has a significant level of operation in more than one country (Geringer and Hebert, 1989).

There are a number of theoretical perspectives on JV formation, which range from a mainstream economics orientation (Contractor and Lorange, 1988; Hladik, 1985), the transaction cost approach (Buckley and Casson, 1988; Hennart, 1988, 1991), resource dependency (Pfeffer and Nowak, 1976), organisational learning (Hamel, 1991; Kogut, 1988), to explanations based on strategic positioning (Contractor and Lorange, 1988; Harrigan, 1985, 1988). The transition from overall theoretical perspective to the firm's strategic motives is not a straightforward one as the theoretical approaches do not map directly on to strategic motive. However, we are able to relate individual theoretical perspectives to motives and thus to test the theories, indirectly at least.

This paper has three main goals:

(1) To identify the relative importance to the UK partners of the strategic motives for the alliance formation in the context of the objective factors facing the decision-makers: the contractual form of the alliance, relative partner size, the primary geographical location of the venture activity, the nationality of the foreign partners, and the industry of the alliance.
(2) To provide a parsimonious set of strategic motives for the sample studied by means of factor analysis.
(3) To formulate and test hypotheses on the relationship between strategic motivation and the objective factors noted above.

The conclusion builds on these results and suggests conceptual developments in the theory and analysis of international alliances. To date there have been no empirical studies reported that specifically examine the strategic motivation for UK alliances with partners from developed countries and that involve a relatively large data set. This paper therefore presents new data and new empirical insights into the strategic motivation of UK alliance formation.

The rest of the paper is set out as follows. The next section considers the previous literature relating to the strategic motivation for alliance formation, relates each strategic motive to its underlying theoretical explanation and sets out the hypotheses of the study. Following that is the methodology for the study and the characteristics of the sample reported. The core of the paper presents the results and discussion of the empirical study in achieving the goals as set out above. Conclusions are provided in the last section.

THE STRATEGIC MOTIVATION FOR ALLIANCE FORMATION

Strategic Motive and Theoretical Frameworks

An explanation for the use of international strategic alliances stems from theories on how strategic behaviour influences the competitive positioning of the firm (Kogut, 1988, p. 321). A number of authors have provided several reasons for alliance formation from a strategic perspective. Mariti and Smiley (1983) identified a number of core strategic motives for joint alliance formation. Harrigan (1985) takes a broad view of the motives for strategic alliance formation, which she groups into internal benefits, competitive benefits and strategic benefits. Porter and Fuller (1986) stress four classes of strategic benefits of alliance formation in the context of the globalisation of firms and industries. Contractor and Lorange (1988) in addressing the conditions necessary for entering into a cooperative relationship take the viewpoint of one partner and examine the contribution it makes to a given venture's strategy. Several of the same motives are identified by these authors, while some of the motives overlap. The main elements of the strategic motives identified in the literature are set out below.

Risk Sharing

Strategic alliances are seen as an attractive mechanism for hedging risk because neither partner bears the full risk and cost of the alliance activity (Porter and Fuller, 1986). Alliances of this type often provide for the management of the operation by one of the partners, while the other merely contributes capital and absorbs some of the risk of failure (Mariti and Smiley, 1983). More broadly, Contractor and Lorange (1988) have identified the ways in which alliances can reduce a partner's risk. These include: (1) spreading the risk of a large project over more than one firm; (2) enabling product diversification and thus reducing market risks associated with being reliant on only one product; (3) enabling faster market entry and quicker establishment of a presence in the market, which in turn allows a more rapid pay back of investment; (4) cost subaddity, i.e. the cost of the partnership is less than the cost of investment undertaken by each firm alone. A strategic alliance can lower the total investment cost of a particular project or the assets at risk, by combining expertise and slack facilities in the parent firms.

Product Rationalisation and Economies of Scale

Where production is characterised by economies of scale and learning by doing, firms may attempt to reduce costs by expanding output to achieve these benefits. Organic growth may, however, be limited by low product demand and the costs of firm growth. External growth through horizontal merger, which is another possible way to achieve the cost-reducing benefits of larger output, involves the combination of whole firms. This poses uncertainties about the efficient operation of the larger firm following post-merger integration. Any resulting difficulties of the merger could offset the cost reduction given by a larger volume of output. Strategic alliances, in contrast, allow firms in the same industry to rationalise production, thus reducing costs through economies of scale and learning by doing, while avoiding the uncertainties and difficulties of full-scale merger (Mariti and Smiley, 1983).

Strategic alliances also reduce costs by using the comparative advantage of each partner. Where, for example, components are made by both partners in different locations and with unequal costs, production can be transferred to the lower cost location – i.e. the location which has the greatest comparative advantage – thus lowering sourcing costs. The larger volume produced in the more advantageous location also provides further reductions in average unit costs by realising economies of large-scale production (Contractor and Lorange, 1988).

Transfer of Complementary Technology/Exchange of Patents

Alliances provide strategic benefits from the exploitation of synergies, technology or other skills transfer (Harrigan, 1985). An alliance must be more than a simple inter-firm transfer of technology. It must involve a longer-term relationship. Quite often technology agreements involve transfer to a large firm with the necessary manufacturing, scale and distribution outlets, and transfer by a smaller firm that does not have the necessary manufacturing and/or marketing scale, but which benefits from the alliance through the commercial exploitation of the technology by the larger firm.

Contractor and Lorange (1988) point out that in general, alliances may be used to bring together complementary skills and talents which cover different aspects of the know-how needed in high technology industries. Significant innovations are likely to result from the fusing of these complementary skills, a result which is unlikely to be achieved by one firm acting alone. A further advantage of exchanging patents is that faster entry into a market may be possible if the testing and certification completed by one partner are accepted by the other partner's territories. An important consideration with respect to patents is that they not only provide a right to a process, they also allow the right to a territory. Often the marketing or territorial rights is the dominant strategic issue behind the formation of an alliance (Contractor and Lorange, 1988).

Shaping Competition

Strategic alliances can influence who a firm competes with and the basis of competition (Porter and Fuller, 1986). Joint ventures could blunt the abilities of competing firms to retaliate by binding potential enemies to the firm as allies. Joint ventures can defend current strategic positions against forces that are too strong for one firm to withstand. Through the combined internal resources of diverse firms, joint ventures could create more effective competitors (Harrigan, 1985). Strategic alliances may, therefore, be used as a defensive ploy to reduce competition, for example by co-opting potential or existing competition into an alliance. Alternatively, an alliance may be used as an offensive strategy, for example by linking with a rival in order to put pressure on the profits and market share of a common competitor (Contractor and Lorange, 1988).

Conform to Host Government Policy

One of the oldest rationales for strategic alliances has been building links with local companies in order to accommodate host government policy. Many governments in developing countries and the former Soviet bloc insist that access to the local market can occur only if the foreign company works in cooperation with a local partner (Beamish, 1988). These protectionist policies are not confined, however, to developing countries or to former planned economies. Japan has had what in effect is a policy of exclusion, which has been a major contributory factor in many US and European firms using strategic alliances as the most practical way of selling products in the Japanese market (Contractor and Lorange, 1988).

Host government pressure to form strategic alliances also applies in particular industries. Firms in the defence industry, telecommunications and parts of the financial services industry are often obliged by host government requirements, concerned to safeguard particular sectors of the economy, to establish links with local firms. Although large firms in the defence industry, for example, may prefer not to establish alliances with foreign firms in order to develop weapon systems, they must do so because the purchaser (i.e. the foreign government) prefers it. A side benefit is that there are fewer competitors (they are part of the alliance) when the weapons system is marketed in other countries (Mariti and Smiley, 1983).

Facilitate International Expansion

It is necessary to distinguish between the role of alliances in establishing corporate linkages as opposed to their role in corporate entry strategies (Young *et al.*, 1989, p. 19). Firms faced with foreign market entry have a wide array of entry modes to choose from (Root, 1987). Hill *et al.* (1990, p. 118) note that most of the international business literature focuses on three distinct modes of entry into a foreign market: licensing or franchising, entering into a joint venture, or setting up a wholly owned subsidiary. Each entry mode has different implications for the degree of control (i.e. authority over operational and strategic decision-making) the parent firm can exercise over the foreign operations, resource commitment (i.e. dedicated assets that cannot be redeployed to alternative uses without cost) to the foreign operation and the dissemination risks (i.e. the risk that firm-specific advantages in know-how will be expropriated by a licensing or joint venture partner) that it must bear to expand into the foreign country. The level of control is assumed to be lowest in the case of licensing, highest in the case of wholly owned subsidiaries and falls somewhere between these two extremes in the case of JVs. Resource commitment with licensing is low, high with a wholly owned subsidiary and falls somewhere between these two extremes for a joint venture. The risk of dissemination is highest with licensing, lowest with a wholly owned subsidiary and moderate in joint ventures. Hill *et al.* (1990) argue that for a given context of strategic, environmental and transaction specific variables identifying the optimal entry mode is a complex and difficult task. Further complicating the issue, they contend that a firm's choice of entry mode depends on the strategic relationship the firm envisages between operations in different countries. Hence a particular entry decision should not be viewed in isolation, but rather must be considered in relation to the overall strategic posture of the firm.

Despite the fundamental problems associated with identifying the optimal entry mode, a number of authors have noted the role that alliances may play in facilitating entry to a foreign market. For small and medium sized enterprises which lack international experience, initial overseas expansion is often likely to be a strategic alliance. A firm may, for example, have the production capability but lack knowledge of foreign markets for which it depends on its partners. Contractor and Lorange (1988, p. 15) argue that in general it is an expensive, difficult and time-consuming business to establish a global organisation and a significant international competitive presence. In this respect a strategic alliance offers considerable time savings. While Contractor and Lorange apply this argument to firms undertaking international expansion for the first time, in principle it would also seem to apply more generally to firms who already have corporate overseas expertise. The move to new foreign markets and the development of either a multi-domestic or global strategy can be facilitated by alliance formation even for firms with considerable overseas experience. Also, the speed of internationalisation may be critical given the benefits that may accrue to early entrants such as the ability to command premium prices and the possibility of gaining significant market share (Gannon, 1993). The speed of market entry may therefore be an important determinant of the choice of entry mode. Speed of entry must be balanced, however, against the associated costs and risk.

Vertical Linkages

Strategic alliances can create competitive strengths such as vertical linkages (Harrigan, 1985). Contractor and Lorange (1988) argue that alliances can be a form of vertical quasi-integration with each partner contributing one or more different elements in the production and distribution chain.

Other Motives

Harrigan (1985) explicitly considers a number of other motives for alliance formation. Strategic alliances have a competitive use in that they could consolidate firms' existing market positions. Strategic benefits arise from diversification, for example, in terms of attaining 'toehold' entries into new businesses that may be of long-term strategic importance to the venture partners. Strategic alliances also allow firms to diversify into attractive but unfamiliar business areas, thereby providing a less risky means of entering new markets. While Harrigan sets out these latter motives as strategic uses of alliances, they are subsumed by Contractor and Lorange under the general heading of 'risk reduction'.

As mentioned above, the theoretical frameworks for the explanation of alliances do not map neatly on to motives. The mainstream economics approach treats the extension of the firm by alliances as a means to obtain economies of scale and some control over inputs (vertical links) at low cost. Horizontal and vertical integration can be achieved without the costs associated with controlled capital investment. This may also have some secondary role in shaping competition. Transaction cost explanations, too, emphasise the use of alliances as a means of reducing costs – specifically the transaction costs involved in extending vertical links and in transferring technology (ne-gotiation and re-negotiation of contracts, creation of trust between partners) and the reduction of risks involved in replacing external markets by quasi-internal ones. The central thrust of resource dependency explanations is to extend the firm's domain of control – this can be proxied by vertical links and risk sharing. The implied motives of the organisational theory also in-volve the transfer of technology and exchange of patent motives and the sug-gestion from this body of theory is that international expansion is facilitated by alliances. Finally, strategic positioning theory implies that alliances are motivated by the desire to shape competition and consolidate the firm's mar-ket position. This approach also suggests that international expansion is facilitated by attention to global competitive structures.

These propositions are embodied in Tables 4.1 and 4.2. Table 4.1 classifies strategic motive according to its theoretical roots. Table 4.2 sets out in detail the strategic motives which make up an approximation to the theoretical ex-planation. To reiterate, motive does not map neatly on to theory. The motives implied are not pure or perfectly distinct. We should remember that theory builders are mainly concerned with issues other than the firm's motivation.

Table 4.1   Strategic motive and theoretical explanation

Strategic motive	Theoretical explanation
1. Risk sharing	ME, TC, [RD]
2. Product rationalisation and economies of scale	ME
3. Transfer of technology/exchange of patent	TC, OL
4. Shaping competition	SP, [ME]
5. Government policy	–
6. Facilitate international expansion	OL, SP
7. Vertical links	ME, TC, RD
8. Consolidate market position	SP

Notes:
ME = mainstream economics; TC = transaction cost; RD = resource dependency; OL = organisational learning; SP = strategic positioning.
Bracketed terms [ ] – secondary.

Hypotheses

The literature gives little indication *a priori* of what to expect in terms of the relative importance of a set of motivating factors for alliance formation. It may be conjectured, however, that the relative importance of the motives would vary with the underlying key characteristics of the sample. For the purposes of this study these characteristics have been identified as contractual from (EJV or NEJV), relative partner size, primary geographical location of the venture activity, industry of the alliance, and nationality of the foreign partner.

Table 4.2 Theoretical explanation and strategic motive

---

1. *Mainstream economics – Implied motives*
   Risk sharing
   Product rationalisation and economies of scale
   Vertical links
   (Shaping competition)

2. *Transaction cost explanations – Implied motives*
   Risk sharing
   Transfer of technology/exchange of patents
   Vertical links

3. *Resource dependency – Implied motives*
   Vertical links
   (Risk sharing)

4. *Organisational learning – Implied motives*
   Transfer of technology/exchange of patents
   Facilitate international expansion

5. *Strategic positioning – Implied motives*
   Shaping competition
   Facilitate international expansion
   Consolidate market position

Note:
Bracketed terms () – secondary

Contractual Form

There is a paucity of discussion in the prior literature dealing with the choice of organisational mode of alliance and no prior discussion of how strategic motives might differ between EJVs and NEJVs. There is often a presumption, however, that EJVs, which formally embody the creation of a new firms, represent a longer-term commitment by the parent organisations than do NEJVs, which are often viewed as more temporary organisational modes. It may also be the case that the amount of investment required in the establishment of an EJV is on average greater than that for the establishment of an NEJV and that the former absorbs more managerial time and effort than the latter. Given these potential differences it may be supposed that the fundamental motivating forces differ between the two alliance forms, with one set of motives being more prevalent for one type of alliance than another. This reasoning leads to the first hypothesis:

Hypothesis 1:   The relative importance of the strategic motivation will vary with the contractual form of the alliance.

Relative Partner Size

One firm specific variable that might condition the motives for alliance formation is firm size. For instance, size may be important in that smaller partners might be more motivated to enter international alliances in order to secure scale economies. Caves and Mehra (1986) and Hill *et al.* (1990) have argued that firm size may influence entry mode selection, with firm size acting as a proxy measure for the number of resources available. Woodcock *et al.* (1994) have noted that firm size may also produce concerns related to the bounded rationality problem in an organisation. Bounded rationality could influence top managers' perceptions of core or inimitable resources, and thus influence the motives for cooperative linkages including the entry mode selection process. As a contingency variable, therefore, relative partner size may influence the motives for alliance formation, which leads to the second hypothesis:

Hypothesis 2:   The relative importance of the strategic motivation will vary with relative partner size.

Geographical Location of the Venture

The primary geographical location of the venture activity may be in some way related to the nationality of the foreign partner or may be completely different from it. Thus a UK firm may establish an alliance with a Japanese firm in order to facilitate the UK firm's entry into the Japanese market, with the primary geographical location of the venture being Japan. Conversely the alliance may be established between the same two firms in order to provide the Japanese firm with access to the UK market, with the primary geographical location of the venture being UK-based. Alternatively both partners may form an alliance in order to penetrate a third market such as the USA, with the primary geographical location of the venture being unrelated to the nationality of the foreign partner. To the extent that UK partner firms wish to establish alliances in order to expand their activities abroad or to enter new markets quickly it would be expected that the underlying set of strategic motives would tend to vary with the primary geographical location of the venture – either UK-based or based abroad. This readily leads to the third hypothesis:

Hypothesis 3:   The relative importance of the strategic motivation will vary with the primary geographical location of the alliance.

Industry of the Alliance

There is no prior literature that provides an extensive examination of the strategic motives of alliances formation according to the industry of the venture. The prior literature on strategic motives for alliance formation discussed above has, however, been implicitly focused on the manufacturing sector, with relatively little in the literature specifically dealing with motives for alliance formation in the tertiary sector. *A priori*, several of the strategic motives appear to lend themselves more readily to alliance formation in the manufacturing sector, for example product rationalisation and economies of scale, and transfer of complementary technology/exchange of patents, than they do to alliance formation in the tertiary sector where risk sharing, shaping competition and the use of alliances to facilitate international expansion appear to be more relevant. To the extent that this is the case it would be expected that strategic motivation would vary with the industry of the alliance, which is reflected in the fourth hypothesis:

Hypothesis 4:   The relative importance of the strategic motivation will vary with the industry of the alliance.

Nationality of Foreign Partner

There is no explicit discussion in the prior literature with respect to the choice of nationality of the foreign partner in alliance formation. Partner choice will presumably hinge on the tasks to be accomplished by the venture and the particular characteristics required from a partner (Geringer, 1988, 1991), which may identify for a UK firm a potential partner of a particular nationality. (Contrast Beamish (1988) on entry into less developed markets where JVs have purposes quite different from those of developed country JVs.) To the extent that UK firms believe that partners from particular foreign nationalities can provide certain requirements of the venture, for example access to specific markets or types of technology, these partners will be chosen in preference to potential partners of a different nationality when the alliance is formed. The fundamental motive for the alliance may then be expected to vary according to the nationality of the foreign partner. This leads to the last hypothesis:

Hypothesis 5:   The relative importance of the strategic motivation will vary with the nationality of the foreign partner.

METHODOLOGY AND CHARACTERISTICS OF THE SAMPLE

Data Collection Method

This study involves UK partners of international strategic alliances with partner firms from western Europe, the United States and Japan, formed since 1980. As there is no publicly available database of UK alliance formation, a list of qualifying alliances was obtained from press announcements in the *Financial Times*. Using press announcements as a source of alliance data has several precedents (Ghemawat *et al.*, 1986; Harrigan, 1985; Hergert and Morris, 1988). It was assumed that this source represented a good approximation of the population of qualifying alliances and that any selection biases would be minimal (Glaister and Buckley, 1994). It should be noted, however, that the qualifying alliances do not include those organised through national or international government agencies, particularly European Union programmes such as ESPRIT. This was in order to ensure that the sample was derived from alliances created from the free association of firms and not those encouraged by incentives provided by external agents.

While the press announcements provide a reasonably good indication of the extend of alliance formation over the period, they are less useful when attempting to identify the strategic motivating forces. Either strategic motivation is not reported at all, or if it is reported it is not done in a comprehensive manner. In order to obtain the requisite level of detail on strategic motivation it was necessary to approach the UK partners directly. To generate data on as large a sample as possible and given time and cost constraints it was decided to administer a postal questionnaire. As an appropriate instrument was not in the public domain, a suitable questionnaire had to be compiled.

Initially a set of semi-structured interviews were conducted with a senior manager from each of eight UK partner firms that provided a good cross-section from the sample frame. Each manager possessed detailed knowledge of the strategic alliance that his firm had established. On the basis of these semi-structured interviews a postal questionnaire was devised. In order to test the questionnaire, but to avoid eliminating any of the firms from the potential sample, it was administered to a set of UK partners that had established strategic alliances in China over the 1980s. This test indicated that the questionnaire was an appropriate instrument to obtain the data required.

From the prior literature and the discussion based on the semi-structured interviews with the representatives managers, a list of 16 strategic motives was derived. These encompassed the main motives discussed previously, while elaborating on some of the risk-reducing aspects and adding the motive 'To concentrate on higher margin business' specifically identified in discussion with the representatives managers. The 16 motives in the order they appeared on the questionnaire are shown in Table 4.3. The motive of vertical linkages, or quasi-vertical integration, does not feature in the 16 motives. This motive was omitted in part because it runs against the adopted definition of an alliance provided in the introduction to this paper, which excludes buyer–seller relationships, which are reminiscent of vertical linkages. Also, vertical linkages are unlikely to be a sufficient motive for strategic alliance formation. This motive must overlap and coexist with others identified in order to make the formation of an alliance feasible. In the absence of other motives it is difficult to see why a market transaction would not be optimal. Where vertical linkages are most likely to be important is in the identification of suitable alliance partners. This aspect of strategic alliance formation was therefore considered under the heading of partner selection and is not reported here.

Table 4.3 Strategic motivation for alliance formation: motives listed by order of appearance on the questionnaire

---

(1) Spreading risk of a large project over more than one firm
(2) Sharing R&D costs
(3) Enabling faster payback on the investment
(4) Economies of scale: joint operations lower costs
(5) Production transferred to lowest cost location
(6) Enabling product diversification
(7) Enabling faster entry to the market
(8) To facilitate international expansion
(9) To concentrate on higher margin business
(10) To gain presence in new markets
(11) To maintain position in existing markets
(12) Exchange of complementary technology
(13) Exchange of patents or territories
(14) JV formed with existing or potential competitor to reduce competition
(15) JV formed to more effectively compete against a common competitor
(16) To conform to foreign government policy

The questions relating to strategic motivation were *ex post* measures of managers' perceptions of the relative value of the motives at the time of alliance formation. Respondents were asked: 'As far as *your company* was concerned, how important were the following motives for establishing the alliance?' Responses were assessed using three-point Likert-type scales (i.e. 1 = 'of no importance', 2 = 'of some importance', 3 = 'of major importance'). Prior research indicated that ordinal classification of perception was a more realistic task for respondents than use of interval or ratio measures (Geringer,

1991). It was also expected that managers would have only a limited amount of time to devote to the questionnaire, hence an easily understood Likert scale appeared to be more feasible than a potentially more precise but more complex scaling method. A three-point scale was adopted because it was felt that more numerous response categories would exceed the respondent's ability to discriminate, with the likelihood that 'noise' rather than more precise data would result. It was also considered likely that a trichotomous measure would tend to facilitate greater cooperation and return rates (Jacoby and Matell, 1971).

A total of 203 questionnaires were administered in the autumn of 1992.[1] In exchange for their participation in the study and to provide motivation and accurate responses, the respondents were assured of anonymity and were promised a summary report of the findings. After one reminder 94 usable questionnaires were returned, a response rate of 46.3 per cent.

Characteristics of the Sample

The sample is composed of 94 strategic alliances of which 64 are equity joint ventures (EJVs) and 29 are non-equity joint ventures (NEJVs). The time dimension of the study runs from 1980 to 1992 with just over 50 per cent of the alliances formed in the three years 1987 to 1989 and with 67 per cent formed in the period 1987–92. The majority of the strategic alliances (82 per cent) involve only one foreign partner, this applies equally to the subsets of EJVs (82 per cent) and NEJVs (82 per cent) with less than 9 per cent of the sample of UK firms having more than two foreign partners.

Where the alliance had more than one foreign partner the UK respondent was asked to identify the 'most important' foreign partner. Aggregating the nationality of the foreign partner in the single partner ventures and the most important partner in the multiple foreign partner ventures, the data set comprises 50 alliances (53 per cent) with partners in western Europe, principally with EU members; 25 alliances (26 per cent) with United States partners; and 19 alliances (20 per cent) with Japanese partners.

The primary geographical location of the activity of the alliance was coded as a dichotomous variable according to whether the alliance activity was wholly or partly based in the UK or was entirely located abroad. A total of 42 alliances have a UK base (30 EJVs and 12 NEJVs) with 52 alliances having a foreign base (35 EJVs and 17 NEJVs). The majority of the 52 foreign based alliances are located in western Europe (54 per cent of the total), followed by the USA (21 per cent) and Japan (17 per cent), with a relatively small number located elsewhere (8 per cent).

The industry categories of the alliances are as follows: food/drink manufacturing (6.4 per cent of the total), metal and minerals (7.4 per cent), energy (5.3 per cent), construction (4.3 per cent), chemicals (4.3 per cent), pharmaceuticals (5.3 per cent), computers (1.1 per cent), telecommunications (4.3 per cent), other electrical (4.3 per cent), automobiles (5.3 per cent), aerospace (1.1 per cent), other manufacturing (10.6 per cent), transport (1.1 per cent), distribution (5.3 per cent), financial services (24.5 per cent), other services (10.6 per cent). In total 55 (58.5 per cent) of the alliances are in the manufacturing sector (38 EJVs and 17 NEJVs) and 39 (41.5 per cent) are in the teritary sector (27 EJVs and 12 NEJVs).

The industry category of the UK parent matches the industry category of the foreign partner in 80 cases, i.e. 85.1 per cent of the alliance activity was undertaken with a partner in the same industry. The same industry category matches for: the UK partner and the alliance in 85 cases (90.4 per cent); the foreign partner and the alliance in 81 cases (86.2 per cent); the UK partner, the foreign partner and the alliance in 76 cases (80.9 per cent). In general, therefore, the strategic alliance partners are from the same industry, and the venture is formed to operate in the same industry as the partners. There are clearly exceptions, but that is the general rule. While the industry category classification used is obviously very broad it may be conjectured that relatively few ventures are being undertaken for the purpose of diversification and those that are would appear to be limited to some what similar activities. There is little evidence from the industry data at any rate that there are significant numbers of conglomerate alliances, or joint activities undertaken by firms operating in very different industries.

The absolute size of the UK or foreign partner (e.g. in terms of turnover or number of employees) was not measured but data on the relative size of each partner in the alliance was obtained by asking respondents whether their firm or the partner firm had the highest level of turnover. A total of 88 respondents were able to provide this measure, with the UK partner being the largest in 35 alliances (40 per cent) and the foreign partner the largest in 53 alliances (60 per cent).

Statistical Analysis

The hypothesis were tested by considering differences in means of the importance of the strategic motives. Given the relatively large sample size and the reasonable assumption that the sample is from a close to normal distribution, it was considered legitimate to use parametric tests of the hypothesis. Each of H1 to H5, considering the relative strength of importance of the strategic motives by the characteristics of the sample, was therefore tested by conducting two sample *t*-tests or Anova as appropriate. The nature of the data made it judicious to 'shadow' these parametric tests by equivalent non-parametric ones (Mann-Whitney U and the Kruskal-Wallis Test) as a check on their interpretation. The non-parametric tests (not reported here) confirm the findings of the parametric, tests reported below.

RESULTS AND DISCUSSION

Strategic Motivation

The rank order of the strategic motivations for the strategic alliances based on the mean measure of the importance of the motive is shown in Table 4.4. The median measure for each motive is 2. For the full set of joint ventures the median measure is exceeded by three strategic motives: 'the desire to gain a presence in new markets' (2.46), 'to enable faster entry to the market' (2.39), and 'to facilitate international expansion' (2.35). Other relatively highly ranked motives are 'to join forces against a common competitor' (1.80), and 'to maintain the existing market position' (1.69). It is clear from Table 4.4 that the highest ranked strategic motives are concerned with relative competitive positions in either new or existing markets.

The second group of motives (those ranked 6 to 11=) display several concerns. The leading motivation in the second group is the 'exchange of complementary technology' (1.60). However, most of the motives in this group are concerned with endeavours to reduce costs and risks: 'economies of scale' (1.59), 'product diversification' (1.53), 'faster payback on investment' (1.50), 'share R&D costs' (1.46), and 'spread risk of large project' (1.46). Also of importance in this group is the move 'to higher margin business' (1.50).

The third and lowest ranked group (13 to 16) include a number of disparate factors. The desire to form a joint venture in order 'to reduce competition' (1.34) is not seen as an important motive. This finding may be subject to some reporting bias in that while this motive might at least partly underpin the joint venture, respondents may be unwilling to admit to it. Consequently this might be a more important factor than indicated here. The desire 'to obtain a lower cost location' (1.28) or 'to exchange patents and/or territories' (1.25) do not feature as important motives for this sample of joint ventures, nor does the requirement 'to conform to host government policy' (1.13).

The prior literature on the strategic motives for joint venture formation provided no clear indication on which to base *a priori* expectations of the likely rankings of the motives with the exception of the need to conform to host government policy. It is hardly surprising that this motive is ranked the lowest, as the joint ventures in the sample concern the free association of companies across advanced industrial nations, and only in infrequent circumstances, for example to conform to defence industry or financial service industry requirements, would a joint venture be obliged to be formed by the government of the foreign partner.

Table 4.4   Strategic motivation for UK joint venture formation: motives ranked by mean measure of importance

Motivation	Rank	Mean	SD
Gain presence in new market	1	2.46	0.73
Faster entry to market	2	2.39	0.78
Facilitates international expansion	3	2.35	0.84
Compete against common competitor	4	1.80	0.77
Maintain market position	5	1.69	0.76
Exchange of complementary technology	6	1.60	0.69
Economies of scale	7	1.59	0.71
Product diversification	8	1.53	0.71
Faster payback on investment	9=	1.50	0.68
Concentrate on higher margin business	9=	1.50	0.69
Share R&D costs	11=	1.46	0.67
Spread risk of large project	11=	1.46	0.68
Reduce competition	13	1.34	0.60
Produce at lower cost location	14	1.28	0.56
Exchange of patents/territories	15	1.25	0.48
Conform to foreign government policy	16	1.13	0.42
N = 94			

Notes:
1. The mean is the average on a scale of 1 (= 'of no importance') to 3 (= 'of major importance').
2. SD = standard deviation.

Considering the motives in terms of their underlying theoretical explanations as discussed in the context of Tables 4.1 and 4.2, it is apparent that, for this sample of alliances, the main strategic motives are underpinned by the theories of strategic positioning and organisational learning. The first five ranked motives are concerned with improving the firm's competitive position through the use of alliances that may be characterised as most importantly allowing the UK partner firms to enter new, often foreign markets at speed and/or consolidating existing market positions particularly against competitors common to the partner firms. This set of motives is very much in line with the strategic positioning perspective of Kogut (1988) who argues that the strategic behaviour view places alliances in the context of competitive rivalry and collusive agreements to enhance market power. Strategic alliances are thus a mode of organisation which maximises profits through improving a firm's competitive position.

The leading set of motives also lend some support to the organisational learning view of alliances, particularly when it is recognised that the alliance is formed because the partner lacks the necessary requirements to undertake the venture alone. Where one firm wishes to acquire a capability that it does not have but is possessed by a second firm, such as knowledge of new markets (including knowledge of local culture), access of major buyers in new markets (for instance through well-established distribution systems), or knowledge of a particular technology and production routines, then a strategic alliance may be formed which facilitates the learning of these capabilities. Given causal ambiguity, imperfectly articulated capabilities (Barney, 1991) and tacit knowledge (Polanyi, 1958), certain capabilities can be added to the resource base only through intimate working relationships with partners (Badaracco, 1991; Ciborra, 1991; Kogut, 1988; Teece, 1992). A strategic alliance thus provides the opportunity for one partner to internalise the capabilities of the other and thereby improve its competitive position both inside and outside the alliance (Hamel, 1991).

Factor Analysis of Strategic Motivation

As noted earlier, the 16 strategic motives represent a number of overlapping perspectives. This is partly confirmed by the correlation matrix of strategic motives, which displays a number of low to moderate intercorrelations between the strategic motive categories. Because of the potential conceptual and statistical overlap an attempt was made to identify a smaller number of distinct, non-overlapping strategic motives for the sample data by means of exploratory factor analysis.[2] Factor analysis is normally employed to uncover any dimensions or structure underlying the data. Its purpose is to highlight key features that might otherwise be obscured by detail and in this way to simplify and clarify analysis. The factor analysis produced five underlying factors which make good conceptual sense and explained a total of 56.9 per cent of the observed variance, as shown in Table 4.5. The remainder of this section discusses the interpretation of each of these factors.

Factor 1: Technology development and transfer (*Technology development*). The first factor had high positive loadings on the following three strategic motives: share R&D costs; exchange of complementary technology; and, exchange of patents/territories. This first factor was therefore interpreted to be a motive related to technology development and transfer.

Table 4.5   Factors of strategic motivation

Factors	Factor loads	Eigen-value	% Vari-ance explained	Cumula-tive percent
Factor 1:		2.82	17.6	17.6
Technology development				
Share R&D costs	0.78			
Exchange of complementary technology	0.71			
Exchange of patents/territories	0.67			
Factor 2:		2.36	14.8	32.4
Market power				
Compete against common competitor	0.68			
Maintain market position	0.66			
Produce at lowest cost location	0.65			
Reduce competition	0.51			
Factor 3:		1.41	8.9	41.3
Market development				
Facilitates international expansion	0.73			
Faster entry to market	0.71			
Gain presence in new market	0.57			
Conform to foreign government policy	0.51			
Factor 4:		1.40	8.8	50.1
Resource specialisation				
Concentrate on higher margin business	0.81			
Economies of scale	0.79			
Faster payback on investment	0.54			
Factor 5:		1.09	6.9	56.9
Large project				
Spread risk of large project	0.72			
Product diversification	−0.71			

Notes:
Principal components factor analysis with varimax rotation.
K-M-O Measure of Sampling Adequacy = .6175.
Bartlett Test of Sphericity = 280.293; $p < .0000$.

Factor 2: Market power with low cost relocation (*Market power*). This factor had high positive loadings on four strategic motives: compete against common competitor; maintain market position; produce at lowest cost location; and, reduce competition. This factor was interpreted as a motive to gain market power with low cost location transfer.

Factor 3: Market development with host government influence (*Market development*). This factor had high positive loadings on four of the strategic motives; facilitates international expansion; faster entry to market; gain presence in new market; and, conform to foreign government policy. It was interpreted that this third factor reflects the nature of market development including the influence of host government policy.

Factor 4: Resource specialisation and fast payback (*Resource specialisation*). The fourth factor had high positive loadings on three motives: concentrate on higher margin business; economies of scale; and faster payback on investment. Therefore, this factor was interpreted as a motive of resource specialisation and fast payback.

Factor 5: Large project risk reduction, not product diversification (*Large project*). This factor had a high positive loading on spread risk of large project and a high negative loading on product diversification. This factor was therefore interpreted to be a motive to reduce the risk of a large project but not one related to product diversification.

As the five factors are not correlated with each other, each of these strategic motives may be pursued independently. This does not rule out the possibility, however, that particular combinations of these five factors may underline joint venture formation.

Strategic Motivation and Sample Characteristics

To further investigate the underlying nature of the strategic motivation for this sample of alliances, the analysis was developed by considering the strategic motives in terms of the characteristics of the sample. For each of the relevant characteristics of the sample under consideration Tables 4.6 to 4.8 report the means and standard deviations of the five factors and the individual strategic motives comprising each factor, the rank order of the individual strategic motives and the appropriate test statistic for comparing differences in means.

Strategic Motivations and Contractual Form

Table 4.6 shows that the rank order for the individual motives is generally consistent across contractual forms. The first five ranked strategic motives for the sample as a whole follow the same rank order for the largest sub-sample of EJVs. For the sub-sample of NEJVs, while the same five motives are highly ranked, the rank order changes somewhat, with joint ventures 'facilitating international expansion' being ranked first. The lowest ranked motives (ranked 13 to 16) for the full sample also coincide in the sub-samples of EJVs and NEJVs. There is thus a high degree of consistency between the highest and lowest ranked motives for the sub-samples. The group of middle rank, while largely consistent in terms of motives as far as EJVs and NEJVs are concerned, is, though, subject to difference in rank order. Most notably, product diversification has a higher rank in EJVs (7), than in NEJVs (12), while the sharing of R&D costs is ranked higher in NEJVs (7) than in EJVs (12).

Despite the finding of consistency in rank order, as is conjectured by hypothesis 1 (H1), it may be argued that the relative importance of the motivating factor varies between the contractual forms; for example, it could be the case that 'exchange of complementary technology' is a relatively more important motivating factor for EJVs than for NEJVs. There is, however, no support for H1. First, testing H1 for each of the five factors, Table 4.5 shows that the hypothesis can be rejected, and that the relative importance of the factors do not vary with contractual form of alliance. Second, testing H1 for each of the 16 strategic motives shows that the hypothesis can be rejected except for the motives to produce at the lowest cost location and product diversification, where the relative importance is found to vary between contractual form. Table 4.5 shows that for both of these motives the mean score of importance is higher and significantly different (at the 0.1 level or better) for EJVs compared to NEJVs.

While intuitively there is an expectation that there may be fundamental differences in motives between contractual forms of alliance, such intuition is not supported by this sample of EJVs and NEJVs. As noted earlier, the prior literature provides relatively little guidance as to the underlying differences in strategic motivation between different contractual forms of alliance, or indeed why one contractual form is chosen instead of another. In this respect it is difficult to comment on why the identified factors or so many of the individual motives do not vary with contractual form, or indeed why the motives of seeking to produce at the lowest cost location and product diversification do appear to vary with contractual form, other than to argue that for UK alliance partners these motives appear to be facilitated better through an EJV than through an NEJV. A basic conclusion from the evidence of this study, however, is that the fundamental motivating forces for alliance formation do not differ importantly by contractual form, and that whatever differing characteristics the two contractual forms may embody they are not to be differentiated in a significant manner according to the motivation for alliance formation.

Table 4.6   Strategic motivation for UK joint venture formation: contractual form and relative partner size

Motivation	Contractual form					Relative partner size				
	Group	Rank	Mean	SD	t-value	Group[a]	Rank	Mean	SD	t-value
Technology development	EJVs		0.37	0.97		UKPL		-0.23	0.94	
	NEJVs		-0.84	1.07	0.52	FPL		0.20	1.03	-2.01**
Share R&D costs	EJVs	12	1.43	0.64		UKPL	11	1.43	0.66	
	NEJVs	7	1.52	0.74	-0.55	FPL	11	1.50	0.69	-0.55
Exchange of complementary technology	EJVs	6	1.65	0.71		UKPL	7=	1.49	0.66	
	NEJVs	8=	1.48	0.63	1.11	FPL	5	1.72	0.72	-1.56
Exchange of patents/territories	EJVs	15	1.26	0.48		UKPL	16	1.20	0.47	
	NEJVs	14	1.21	0.49	0.50	FPL	14	1.28	0.49	-0.79
Market power	EJVs		0.04	1.09		UKPL		0.30	1.21	
	NEJVs		-0.09	0.77	0.68	FPL		-0.16	0.85	1.99*
Compete against common competitor	EJVs	4	1.79	0.76		UKPL	4	1.91	0.78	
	NEJVs	4	1.83	0.80	-0.24	FPL	4	1.74	0.79	1.05
Maintain market position	EJVs	5	1.72	0.78		UKPL	5	1.71	0.79	
	NEJVs	5	1.62	0.73	0.62	FPL	6	1.67	0.78	0.21
Produce at lowest cost location	EJVs	14	1.34	0.59		UKPL	10	1.45	0.74	
	NEJVs	15	1.14	0.44	1.82*	FPL	15	1.19	0.39	1.97*
Reduce competition	EJVs	13	1.37	0.65		UKPL	13	1.37	0.65	
	NEJVs	13	1.28	0.46	0.80	FPL	13	1.34	0.59	0.23
Market development	EJVs		0.03	0.99		UKPL		0.14	1.07	
	NEJVs		-0.06	1.04	0.43	FPL		-0.05	0.98	0.86
Facilitates international expansion	EJVs	3	2.31	0.88		UKPL	1	2.43	0.78	
	NEJVs	1	2.45	0.74	-0.80	FPL	3	2.30	0.87	0.71

Factor					t						t
Faster entry to market	EJVs	2	2.45	0.77	0.97	UKPL	2=	2.40	0.81		-0.20
	NEJVs	3	2.28	0.80		FPL	2	2.43	0.75		
Gain presence in new market	EJVs	1	2.48	0.69	0.36	UKPL	2=	2.40	0.69		-0.57
	NEJVs	2	2.41	0.83		FPL	1	2.49	0.77		
Conform to foreign government policy	EJVs	16	1.15	0.44	0.96	UKPL	15	1.25	0.61		1.86*
	NEJVs	16	1.07	0.37		FPL	16	1.06	0.23		
Resource specialisation	EJVs		0.03	1.04	0.52	UKPL		0.01	1.12		-0.07
	NEJVs		-0.07	0.91		FPL		0.33	0.95		
Concentrate on higher margin business	EJVs	9	1.52	0.66	0.49	UKPL	7=	1.49	0.70		-0.41
	NEJVs	10=	1.45	0.69		FPL	8=	1.54	0.67		
Economies of scale	EJVs	8	1.60	0.70	0.30	UKPL	6	1.69	0.79		0.85
	NEJVs	6	1.55	0.74		FPL	8=	1.54	0.67		
Faster payback on investment	EJVs	10	1.51	0.71	0.17	UKPL	7=	1.49	0.70		-0.40
	NEJVs	8=	1.48	0.63		FPL	8=	1.54	0.69		
Large project	EJVs		-0.06	1.00	-0.86	UKPL		0.14	0.90		1.07
	NEJVs		0.13	0.99		FPL		-0.85	1.06		
Spread risk of large project	EJVs	11	1.46	0.69	0.09	UKPL	12	1.40	0.60		-0.64
	NEJVs	10=	1.45	0.69		FPL	12	1.49	0.72		
Product diversification	EJVs	7	1.63	0.72	2.11**	UKPL	14	1.34	0.59		-2.10**
	NEJVs	12	1.31	0.66		FPL	7	1.64	0.73		
N	Equity JVs = 65; Non-equity JVs = 29					UK partner largest = 35; Foreign partner largest = 53					

Notes:
The mean for the factors is the mean of the factor scores; the mean for the individual motives is the average on a scale of 1 (= 'of no importance') to 3 (= 'of major importance').
$* p < 0.1;$ $** p < 0.05;$ $*** p < 0.01.$
[a]UKPL = UK partner is largest; FPL = foreign partner is largest.

The finding of the general uniformity in the rank order of strategic motivation between EJVs and NEJVs, and the lack of support for H1, as noted, indicates a degree of consistency between strategic motives for EJVs and NEJVs. In light of this the remainder of the hypotheses (H2 to H5) are tested by pooling all of the alliances and ignoring the distinction between contractual form. This pooling procedure appears to be warranted given the relatively minor differences in strategic motives between the contractual forms.

Strategic Motivation and Relative Partner Size

The rank order by the relative partner size is shown in Table 4.6 (where UK-PL denotes that the UK partner is the largest and FPL denotes that the foreign partner is the largest). The ranking of the individual motives shows a high degree of consistency according to relative partner size, apart from the motive of product differentiation which is ranked much higher in alliances where the foreign partner is largest (7) compared to those alliances where the UK partner is the largest (14).

At best there is only weak support for hypothesis 2 (H2) in that for two of the five factors – Technology development and Market power – there is a significant difference in the mean of the factors scores (at the 0.1 level or better), with the mean factor score of Technology development being significantly higher for alliances where the foreign partner is largest, while the mean factor score of Market power is significantly higher for alliances where the UK partner is largest. However, there is no significant difference in the means of any of the individual motives that comprise these factors, apart from the motive to produce at the lowest cost location (a component of the Market power factor), which is found to be of greater importance in alliances where the UK partner is the largest. On the basis of these findings it may be argued that in relative terms smaller UK firms are linking up with larger foreign firms in order to pursue R&D at lower cost and to gain from the technological know-how of the larger foreign partner. At the same time it may be argued that in relative terms larger UK partners are linking up with smaller foreign partners in order that the UK partners may better shape and consolidate their competitive environment and gain access to lower cost locations. It should be stressed however that these conclusions are highly tentative given the rather weak statistical support for H2.

Strategic Motivation and Location of the Alliance

The rank order of the strategic motivation according to the primary geographical location of the alliance activity is shown in Table 4.7 (where UK indicates that the alliance activity is based wholly or partly in the UK while Abroad indicates that the activity of the alliance is located entirely outside the UK). The four highest ranked motives are the same despite the location of the alliance activity, although there is some slight difference in rank order according to the location of the alliance. There is a degree of variation, however, in the rank order of several of the strategic motives according to the location of the alliance.

Table 4.7 shows that there is moderate support for hypothesis 3 (H3). Two of the five factors – Technology development and Market development – show significant differences in means of factor scores (at the 0.05 level or better), with the mean of the factor score of Technology development significantly higher for alliances based in the UK, while the mean of the factor score of Market development is significantly higher for alliances based abroad. Two of the three individual motives comprising the Technology development factor, i.e. the motives to share R&D costs and the exchange of complementary technology, have means which are significantly different (at the 0.1 level or better), with both motives being more important for alliances based in the UK than for alliances based abroad. Three of the four individual motives comprising the Market development factor, i.e. the motives of facilitating international expansion, faster entry to the market and to conform to foreign government policy, have means which are significantly different (at the 0.01 level or better), with all three motives being more important for alliances based abroad than for alliances based in the UK. Table 4.7 also shows that the motive to obtain a faster payback on investment is significantly more important for alliances based abroad than for alliances based in the UK.

The finding that the Market development factor and two of the factor's constituent motives (faster entry to the market and to facilitate international expansion) are more important for foreign-based alliances is relatively unsurprising. This is particularly the case for the motive 'facilitating international expansion' where it is to be expected that this motive would be relatively more important for foreign-based alliances. The finding that the Technology development factor, and the constituent elements of sharing R&D costs and exchanging complementary technology, are relatively more important for UK-based alliances is perhaps a reflection of the need for UK firms to invite foreign partners to be involved with local ventures that the UK firms would either find too expensive to pursue alone or could not pursue for lack of the appropriate technology, while these concerns are less of a motivating force for UK firms involved in alliances based abroad. Table 4.8 also shows that the motive to conform to host government policy was of no importance for all of the UK-based alliances but that this motive is clearly of some importance to UK firms with ventures abroad. As noted in the literature

Table 4.7 Strategic motivation for UK joint venture formation: location of alliance and industry of alliance

Motivation	Location of alliance					Industry of alliance				
	Group	Rank	Mean	SD	t-value	Group[a]	Rank	Mean	SD	t-value
Technology development	UK		0.23	1.09		Man		0.18	1.06	
	Abroad		−0.19	0.88	2.05**	Tert		−0.25	0.85	2.23**
Share R&D costs	UK	7	1.62	0.73		Man	9	1.60	0.76	
	Abroad	12	1.33	0.59	2.10**	Tert	12	1.25	0.44	2.76***
Exchange of complementary technology	UK	6	1.73	0.73		Man	6	1.72	0.73	
	Abroad	9=	1.48	0.64	1.79*	Tert	8=	1.41	0.60	2.31**
Exchange of patents/territories	UK	15	1.33	0.57		Man	15	1.32	0.55	
	Abroad	16	1.17	0.38	1.56	Tert	14	1.12	0.34	2.18**
Market power	UK		0.07	1.14		Man		0.23	1.09	
	Abroad		−0.05	0.88	0.60	Tert		−0.33	0.74	2.93***
Compete against common competitor	UK	4	1.88	0.80		Man	4	1.95	0.76	
	Abroad	4	1.73	0.74	0.93	Tert	4	1.59	0.75	2.26**
Maintain market position	UK	5	1.76	0.85		Man	5	1.80	0.75	
	Abroad	6	1.63	0.69	0.79	Tert	5	1.54	0.76	1.65
Produce at lowest cost location	UK	13=	1.36	0.66		Man	14	1.41	0.66	
	Abroad	15	1.21	0.48	1.22	Tert	16	1.08	0.27	3.46***
Reduce competition	UK	12	1.38	0.66		Man	13	1.43	0.66	
	Abroad	13	1.31	0.54	0.58	Tert	13	1.20	0.47	1.99**
Market development	UK		−0.44	0.81		Man		−0.09	1.09	
	Abroad		0.36	0.99	−4.34***	Tert		0.14	0.85	−1.17
Facilitates international expansion	UK	3	2.00	0.88		Man	3	2.25	0.87	
	Abroad	1	2.64	0.69	−3.82***	Tert	2=	2.48	0.79	−1.35

Faster entry to market	UK	2	2.14	0.81	-2.87***	Man	2	2.32	0.79	-0.99
	Abroad	2	2.60	0.69		Tert	2=	2.48	0.76	
Gain presence in new market	UK	1	2.33	0.75	-1.48	Man	1	2.40	0.76	-0.92
	Abroad	3	2.56	0.70		Tert	1	2.54	0.68	
Conform to foreign government policy	UK	16	1.00	0.00	-3.05***	Man	16	1.15	0.45	0.50
	Abroad	14	1.23	0.55		Tert	15	1.10	0.38	
Resource specialisation	UK		-0.09	0.95	-0.77	Man		0.17	1.03	2.04*
	Abroad		0.07	1.05		Tert		-0.24	0.92	
Concentrate on higher margin business	UK	11	1.45	0.67	-0.62	Man	8	1.63	0.73	2.55**
	Abroad	8	1.54	0.67		Tert	10=	1.31	0.52	
Economies of scale	UK	9=	1.50	0.60	-1.08	Man	7	1.70	0.76	2.13**
	Abroad	5	1.65	0.79		Tert	8=	1.41	0.59	
Faster payback on investment	UK	13=	1.36	0.58	-1.89*	Man	12	1.50	0.66	0.15
	Abroad	7	1.61	0.75		Tert	6=	1.48	0.72	
Large project	UK		-0.07	0.99	-0.57	Man		0.06	1.11	0.73
	Abroad		0.05	1.01		Tert		-0.08	0.82	
Spread risk of large project	UK	9=	1.50	0.67	0.54	Man	10=	1.56	0.74	1.89*
	Abroad	11	1.42	0.70		Tert	10=	1.31	0.57	
Product diversification	UK	8	1.60	0.73	0.77	Man	10=	1.56	0.74	0.52
	Abroad	9=	1.48	0.70		Tert	6=	1.48	0.64	
N		UK = 42; Abroad = 52						Manufacturing = 55; Tertiary = 39		

Notes:
The mean for the factors is the mean of the factor scores; the mean for the individual motives is the average on a scale of 1 (='of no importance') to 3 (='of major importance').
* $p < 0.1$; ** $p < 0.05$; *** $p < 0.01$
[a] Man = alliances in the manufacturing sector; Tert = alliances in the tertiary sector.

review for some ventures, for example in the defence industry, utilities and financial services, there may be a need to conform to foreign government regulations and the principle of this motive appears to be confirmed for the foreign-based alliances in this sample.

Strategic Motivation and Industry of the Alliance

To facilitate the ranking and statistical testing of the strategic motives by the industry of the alliance, the latter was categorised in the conventional way by distinguishing between the manufacturing and tertiary sectors in the following manner:

Manufacturing: food and drink; metals and minerals; energy; construction; chemicals: pharmaceuticals; computers; telecommunications; other electrical; automobiles; aerospace; other manufacturing.

Tertiary: transport; distribution; financial services; other services.

Table 4.7 shows that the ranking of strategic motivation by industry group (where Man signifies alliances in the manufacturing sector and Tert signifies alliances in the tertiary sector) displays a high degree of consistency for the highest ranked motivating forces. Although there is some slight difference in rank order between the industry groups, to gain a presence in new markets, faster entry to the market, to facilitate international expansion, to compete against a common competitor and to maintain market position are the five most important forces motivating alliance formation in each of the industry groupings. There is, however, some degree of difference in the rank order of several of the middle group of motivation factors across the industry categories.

There is reasonable support for hypothesis 4, with the mean of the factor scores being significantly different for three of the five factors (at the 0.1 level or better) – Technology development, Market power and Resource specialisation, with the mean score for each factor being higher for alliances in the manufacturing sector. All three of the individual motives constituting the Technology development factor, i.e. the motives to share R & D costs, the exchange of complementary technology and the exchange of patents/territories, have means significantly higher (at the 0.05 level or better) for alliances in the manufacturing sector compared with alliances in the tertiary sector. Three of the four motives constituting the Market power factor, i.e. to compete against a common competitor, to produce at the lowest cost location and to reduce competition, have means significantly higher (at the 0.05 level or better) for alliances in the manufacturing sector compared with alliances in the tertiary sector. Two of the three motives constituting the Resource specialisation factor, i.e. to concentrate on higher margin business and economies of scale, have means significantly higher (at the 0.05 level or better) for alliances in the manufacturing sector compared with alliances in the tertiary sector. Table 4.7 also shows that the mean for the motive to spread the risk of a large project is significantly higher (at the 0.1 level) for alliances in the manufacturing sector than for alliances in the tertiary sector.

As noted above, for each of the motives that vary in importance with the industry of the alliance the motive is relatively more important for ventures in the manufacturing sector than for tertiary sector ventures. For some of the motives this is not particularly surprising, in particular the Technology development factor, and the individual motives to exchange complementary technology, share R&D costs, produce at the lowest cost location and exchange patents/territories appear in principle to be a set of motivating forces more pertinent to the manufacturing sector than to the tertiary sector. It is interesting to note that the other motives that vary with the industry of the alliance, in particular the Market power factor, and the individual motives to compete against a common competitor, to maintain position in existing markets, concentrate on higher margin business and to reduce competition, may be viewed as a set of largely defensive motives designed to consolidate and protect the UK firms' positions in existing markets. Given that this set of motives is relatively more important for alliances in the manufacturing sector than it is for motives in the tertiary sector it may be conjectured that alliance formation in the manufacturing sector is more a reactive response to competitive pressure than is the case for alliance formation in the tertiary sector.

Strategic Motivation and Nationality of Foreign Partner

The strategic motivation for alliance formation by nationality of foreign partner is shown in Table 4.8. There is a high degree of consistency in terms of rank order for the highest ranked and lowest ranked groups of strategic motives as far as the nationality of the foreign partner is concerned. Although there are some minor differences in rank order between foreign partners, to gain a presence in new markets, faster entry to the market and to facilitate international expansion are ranked as the three leading strategic motivating factors for alliances with partners in each of western Europe, the USA and Japan. There are, though, some noticeable differences in rank order for several of the middle group of motivating factors. The search for economies of scale is ranked higher for alliances with western European partners (5=) than with partners from the USA (10) or Japan (9). The motive to share R&D costs figures more prominently with partners in the USA (5) than with partners in western Europe (12=) or Japan (12=). Finally, faster payback on investment appears to be a more important motivating force for alliances with partners from Japan (5=) than with partners from either western Europe (9=) or the USA (12).

Table 4.8 Strategic motivation for UK joint venture formation: nationality of the foreign partner

Motivation	Group	Rank	Mean	SD	F-ratio
Technology development	WE		−0.06	0.92	
	USA		0.19	1.09	
	Japan		−0.09	1.08	0.67
Share R&D costs	WE	12=	1.40	0.60	
	USA	5	1.68	0.80	
	Japan	12=	1.31	0.58	2.05
Exchange of complementary technology	WE	7	1.60	0.70	
	USA	6	1.60	0.70	
	Japan	5=	1.58	0.69	0.01
Exchange of patents/territories	WE	15	1.26	0.44	
	USA	14=	1.24	0.52	
	Japan	14=	1.21	0.53	0.07
Market power	WE		0.09	0.97	
	USA		−0.08	1.16	
	Japan		−0.12	0.86	0.43
Compete against common competitor	WE	4	1.84	0.73	
	USA	4	1.92	0.90	
	Japan	7=	1.52	0.61	1.59
Maintain market position	WE	5=	1.68	0.74	
	USA	7=	1.56	0.76	
	Japan	4	1.89	0.80	1.05
Produce at lowest cost location	WE	14	1.28	0.53	
	USA	14=	1.24	0.59	
	Japan	12=	1.32	0.58	0.10
Reduce competition	WE	12=	1.40	0.64	
	USA	13	1.32	0.56	
	Japan	14=	1.21	0.53	0.71
Market development	WE		0.11	1.04	
	USA		−0.17	0.91	
	Japan		−0.07	0.99	0.73
Facilitates international expansion	WE	2=	2.38	0.85	
	USA	3	2.32	0.80	
	Japan	3	2.31	0.88	0.06

		Rank	Mean	SD	F
Faster entry to market	WE	2=	2.38	0.78	
	USA	1=	2.36	0.75	
	Japan	1=	2.47	0.84	0.13
Gain presence in new market	WE	1	2.50	0.70	
	USA	1=	2.36	0.75	
	Japan	1=	2.47	0.77	0.30
Conform to foreign government policy	WE	16	1.22	0.55	
	USA	16	1.00	0.00	
	Japan	16	1.05	0.22	2.76*
Resource specialisation	WE		0.06	1.16	
	USA		−0.12	0.79	
	Japan		−0.01	0.80	0.27
Concentrate on higher margin business	WE	8	1.56	0.70	
	USA	11	1.44	0.65	
	Japan	10=	1.42	0.60	0.43
Economies of scale	WE	5=	1.68	0.79	
	USA	10	1.48	0.59	
	Japan	9	1.47	0.61	0.95
Faster payback on investment	WE	9=	1.52	0.67	
	USA	12	1.40	0.64	
	Japan	5=	1.58	0.76	0.41
Large project	WE		0.02	0.94	
	USA		−0.07	1.09	
	Japan		0.04	1.08	0.07
Spread risk of large project	WE	11	1.44	0.64	
	USA	9	1.52	0.77	
	Japan	10=	1.42	0.69	0.14
Product diversification	WE	9=	1.52	0.67	
	USA	7=	1.56	0.82	
	Japan	7=	1.52	0.69	0.02
N			WE = 50; USA = 25; Japan = 19		

Notes:
The mean for the factors is the mean of the factor scores; the mean for the individual motives is the average on a scale of 1 (= 'of no importance') to 3 (= 'of major importance').
*$p < 0.1$
Scheffe test: No two groups significantly different at the 0.05 level.

Despite these apparent differences in importance reflected in the ranking of the strategic motives, Table 4.8 shows that there is no support for hypothesis 5. None of the factors has mean factor scores that are significantly different (at the 0.05 level or better) between the partner groups, nor are the means of the individual motives significantly different (at the 0.05 level or

better) between the partner groups, although the mean of the motive to conform to foreign government policy is significantly different (at the 0.1 level).
In general the important motives for strategic alliance formation differ little
across the nationality of the foreign partners, although there is some difference in rank order for several of the middle group of motivation forces. Nevertheless, the relative importance of each strategic motive is independent of
the nationality of the foreign partner for this sample of alliances. The evidence of this study indicates, therefore, that the underlying strategic motivation for alliance formation and the relative importance of these motives for
the UK partners is not fundamentally related to the nationality of the foreign
partner. The driving force of alliance formation for UK partners on the basis
of the evidence in this study clearly suggests that the same forces appear to
have been at work in driving alliance motivation across the nationality of the
foreign partners.

CONCLUSIONS

This paper is the first attempt to identify, classify and explain the key motives
for international strategic alliance formation by UK firms over a substantial
period of time. Its use of a relatively large sample size strengthens the findings.

The paper identifies the main strategic motives for alliance formation by
UK firms with partners from western Europe, the USA and Japan as intrinsically linked to the market and geographical expansion of the firm. Alliances
are seen primarily as means of gaining a significant presence in a new market,
enabling faster entry to the market and achieving greater international market
penetration. This suggests that, conceptually, the nature of alliances and their
motives should be compared with foreign direct investment, the closest alternative means of achieving these objectives. This is reinforced by the finding
that alliances are often designed to shape competition in terms of building entities of sufficiently critical mass to beat off challenges from a common competitor and to maintain both local and global market share. This suggests that
the competitive analysis implications of alliances are crucial. However some
of the often suggested motives for alliance formation found in the literature,
in particular aspects of risk reduction associated with new projects (for example, to achieve faster payback on investment, share R&D costs and spread
the risk of a large project), appear not to be particularly important motivating
factors. Nor do efforts to reduce production costs associated with the motives
of economies of scale and the desire to produce at a lower cost location. The
finding that the exchange of complementary technology is relatively import-

ant, while the exchange of patents and/or territories covered is not important suggests that it is the learning and dynamic benefits of the *process* of cooperation which are crucial, not the exchange of outcomes. Again, this is an important finding in terms of future conceptual development.

Due to the potential for conceptual or statistical overlap among the 16 strategic motives, factor analysis was employed to produce a set of distinct, non-overlapping strategic motives. This analysis produced five non-overlapping factors which explained almost 57 per cent of the observed variance in the sample data. Conceptually these factors appear to be valid, encompassing motives that may be broadly configured as technology development, market power, market development, resource specialisation and large project completion.

The most important set of motivating factors are robust in the sense that they predominate across a range of sample characteristics: contractual form of the alliance, relative partner size, the primary geographical location of the alliance, the broad industry group of the alliance and the nationality of the foreign partner. The ranking of the least important motives is also robust in this sense. The ranking of the middle group of strategic motives is less consistent and does tend to vary with the characteristics of the sample.

Tests of hypotheses 1 to 5 indicate that the relative importance of the motivating factors vary most significantly with the industry of the alliance, to a moderate extent with the primary geographical location of the alliance and to a modest extent with the relative size of the parent firms. While the variation in importance of several of the strategic motives appears to be fairly readily explicable, the reason for the variation in importance is not always apparent. Further investigation of the relative importance of the strategic motives between industries, in the context of the primary geographical location of the venture, and in terms of the relative size of partners, would help in providing a deeper understanding of the way in which strategic motives vary across these characteristics.

This paper suggests some further conceptualisation is called for. The findings suggest that alliances are largely utilised as competitive weapons in the battle for global (and national) market share. In this respect the analysis should pay attention to the choice between foreign direct investment and alliances. This choice is crucial and can be supported by reference to the analysis of foreign direct investment in future conceptual development. This must be combined with a view of alliances as mutual learning devices in which the process of learning is critical. Sharing of outcomes is less important than participating in the process. Both of these findings suggest that the dynamics of alliance formation are vital. Analytical techniques which only capture static benefits are unlikely to convey the full picture of strategic alliances.

Notes

1. To ensure good quality responses, telephone contact was made with each UK partner to ascertain the name and position of the most appropriate senior manager in the organisation to whom the questionnaire was personally addressed. The questionnaire cited the alliance referred to in the *Financial Times* of which the UK firm was a partner, but invited the respondent to complete the questionnaire with respect to another alliance with which they were more familiar, providing the foreign partner(s) was from western Europe, the USA or Japan, and that this alliance had been formed since 1980. The request for information on the alliance with which the respondent had the most detailed knowledge was designed to improve the quality of the data. In total, 18 respondents chose to do this; of these, 15 respondents provided data on alliances formed in the 1990–2 period. The sample therefore contains data on strategic alliances that were not in the original sample frame, and in particular includes alliances that were formed post-1989. The benefit of this is that respondents provided data on more recent alliances, hence obviating the danger of memory decay. Moreover, the respondents have self-selected to report on the alliances that they know most about. Given the detailed nature of the questions asked it is unlikely anyone without a full knowledge of the alliance and interest in the research topic would have returned the questionnaire.

   The analysis of the press announcements indicated that there were 277 separate UK firms recorded as having been involved in the formation of strategic alliances over the 1980s. Of these, several had either gone out of business or been taken over and restructured, so it was not possible to contact them. Other firms had moved location and could not be traced. In some of the firms contacted there was no longer anyone in employment with sufficient knowledge to provide the depth of answers the questionnaire demanded. This left a total of 203 UK firms. Several of these firms had a record of more than one alliance. While data on each of these alliances would clearly have enriched the study it was not considered feasible to attempt to administer a questionnaire for each alliance recorded for multi-alliance firms. To do so would have entailed either sending multiple questionnaires to one manager having a detailed knowledge of several alliances, or else sending a questionnaire to several different managers in one firm, each of whom would report on a different alliance. Both procedures were deemed to be potentially damaging to the response rate and the decision was made to investigate only one alliance for each of the multi-alliance firms. For these firms the alliance identified on the questionnaire was the one most recently established and which telephone contact with the named senior manager indicated that they had most knowledge of.

2. Factor analysis is a statistical technique used to identify a relatively small number of factors that can be used to represent relationships among sets of many interrelated variables. In order to judge how many factors best represent the underlying structure of a data set it is usual to inspect the eigenvalues. Eigenvalues greater than 1.0 indicate that the factor explains more of the variance in the data than a single variable. A potential limitation of this technique for this study is that whereas ordinal level data was obtained from the questionnaire, the technically correct input should be interval or ratio-level data.

Although the Likert-type response categories used to measure the importance of the strategic motives were technically ordinal, they may be appraised as sufficiently approximating interval-level data to warrant the use of factor analysis. The use of interval-approximating ordinal level data as input for factor analysis has been supported by a number of researchers (for example, Nunnally, 1978) and has been used by Geringer (1988) in the analysis of partner selection criteria in joint ventures. It is necessary, however, to exercise a degree of caution when interpreting the results.

References

Badaracco, J.L. (1991) *The Knowledge Link: How Firms Compete Through Strategic Alliances* (Boston, MA: Harvard Business School Press).

Barney, J.B. (1991) 'Firm Resources and Sustained Competitive Advantage', *Journal of Management*, 17, 99–120.

Beamish, P.W. (1988) *Multinational Joint Ventures in Developing Countries* (London: Routledge).

Buckley, P.J. (1992) 'Alliances, Technology and Markets: A Cautionary Tale', in P.J. Buckley, *Studies in International Business* (London: Macmillan).

Buckley, P.J. and M. Casson (1988) 'A Theory of Co-operation in International Business', in F.J. Contractor and P. Lorange (eds), *Co-operative Strategies in International Business* (Lexington, MA: Lexington Books).

Caves, R.E. and S.K. Mehra (1986) 'Entry of Foreign Multinationals into US Manufacturing Industries', in M.E. Porter (ed.), *Competition in Global Industries* (Boston, MA: Harvard Press).

Ciborra, C. (1991) 'Alliances as Learning Experiments: Co-operation, Competition and Change in Hightech Industries', in L.K. Mytelka (ed.), *Strategic Partnerships: States, Firms and International Competition* (London: Pinter Publishers).

Contractor, F.J. and P. Lorange (1988)'Why Should Firms Co-operate? The Strategic and Economics Basis for Co-operative Ventures', in F.J. Contractor and P. Lorange (eds), *Co-operative Strategies in International Business* (Lexington, MA: Lexington Books).

Gannon, M. (1993) 'Towards a Composite Theory of Foreign Market Entry Mode Choice: The Role of Marketing Strategy Variables', *Journal of Strategic Marketing*, 1 (1), 41–54.

Geringer, J.M. (1988) *Joint Venture Partner Selection: Strategies for Developed Countries* (Westport, CT: Quorum Books).

Geringer, J.M. (1991) 'Strategic Determinants of Partner Selection Criteria in International Joint Ventures', *Journal of International Business*, 22 (1), 41–62.

Geringer, J.M. and L. Hebert (1989) 'Control and Performance of International Joint Ventures', *Journal of International Business*, 20 (2), 235–54.

Ghemawat, P., M.E. Porter, and R.A. Rawlinson (1986) 'Patterns of International Coalition Activity', in M.E. Porter, (ed.), *Competition in Global Industries* (Boston, MA: Harvard Business School).

Glaister, K.W. and P.J. Buckley (1994) 'UK International Joint Ventures: An Analysis of Patterns of Activity and Distribution', *British Journal of Management*, 5 (1), 33–51.

Hamel, G. (1991) 'Competition for Competence and Inter-Partner Learning with International Strategic Alliances', *Strategic Management Journal*, 12, 83–103.

Harrigan, K.R. (1985) *Strategies for Joint Ventures* (Lexington, MA: Lexington Books).

Harrigan, K.R. (1988) 'Joint Ventures and Competitive Strategy', *Strategic Management Journal*, 9, 141–58.

Hennart, J.F. (1988) 'A Transactions Cost Theory of Equity Joint Ventures', *Strategic Management Journal*, 9, 361–74.

Hennart, J.F. (1991) 'The Transaction Costs Theory of Joint Ventures: An Empirical Study of Japanese Subsidiaries in the United States', *Management Science*, 37 (4), 483–97.

Hergert, M. and D. Morris (1988) 'Trends in International Collaborative Agreements', in F.J. Contractor and P. Lorange (eds), *Co-operative Strategies in International Business* (Lexington, MA: Lexington Books).

Hill, C.W.L., P. Hwang and C.W. Kim (1990) 'An Eclectic Theory of the Choice of International Entry Mode', *Strategic Management Journal*, 11, 117–28.

Hladik, K.J. (1985) *International Joint Ventures: An Economic Analysis of US–Foreign Business Partnerships* (Lexington, MA: Lexington Books).

Hood, N. and S. Young (1979) *The Economics of Multinational Enterprise* (London: Longman).

Jacoby, J. and M.S. Matell (1971) 'Three Point Likert Scales Are Good Enough', *Journal of Marketing Research*, 8, 495–500.

Killing, J.P. (1988) 'Understanding Alliances: The Role of Task and Organizational Complexity', in F.J. Contractor and P. Lorange (eds), *Co-operative Strategies in International Business* (Lexington, MA: Lexington Books).

Kogut, B. (1988) 'Joint Ventures: Theoretical and Empirical Perspectives', *Strategic Management Journal*, 9, 319–32.

Mariti, P. and R.H. Smiley (1983) 'Co-operative Agreements and the Organization of Industry', *Journal of Industrial Economics*, 31 (4), 437–51.

Nunnally, J.C. (1978) *Psychometric Theory*, 2nd edn (New York: McGraw-Hill).

Pfeffer, J. and P. Nowak (1976) 'Joint Ventures and Interorganizational Interdependence', *Administrative Science Quarterly*, 21, 398–418.

Polanyi, M. (1958) *Personal Knowledge: Towards a Post Critical Philosophy* (Chicago: University of Chicago Press).

Porter, M.E. and M.B. Fuller (1986) 'Coalitions and Global Strategy', in M.E. Porter (ed.), *Competition in Global Industries* (Boston, MA: Harvard Business School).

Root, F.R. (1987) *Entry Strategies for International Markets* (Lexington, MA: D.C. Heath).

Shapiro, C. (1985) 'The Theory of Business Strategy', *RAND Journal of Economics*, 20 (1) (Spring), 125–37.

Teece, D. (1982) 'Towards an Economic Theory of the Multiproduct Firm', *Journal of Economic Behavior and Organization*, 3, 39–63.

Teece, D.J. (1992) 'Competition, Co-operation and Innovation', *Journal of Economic Behavior and Organization*, 18, 1–25.

Vonortas, N.S. (1990) 'Emerging Patterns of Multinational Enterprise Operations in Developed Market Economies: Evidence and Policy', *Review of Political Economy*, 2 (2), 188–220.

Woodcock, C.P., P.W. Beamish and S. Makino (1994) 'Ownership-Based Entry Mode Strategies and International Performance', *Journal of International Business Studies*, 25 (2), 253–73.

Young, S., J. Hamill, C. Wheeler and J.R. Davies (1989) *International Market Entry and Development: Strategies and Management* (Hemel Hempstead: Harvester Wheatsheaf).

5 International Technology Transfer by Small and Medium-Sized Enterprises*

INTRODUCTION

This paper attempts to summarise the key issues involved in the international transfer of technology by small and medium-sized enterprises (SMEs). It focuses on what is new in the area and relies for its empirical evidence largely on the UNCTAD report on small and medium-sized transnational corporations (UNCTAD, 1993).

After a brief review of the role of SMEs in the world economy, the paper examines theoretical approaches to the internationalisation of SMEs; attempts to reconcile internationalisation approaches to globalisation; examines the technology transfer strategies of SMEs; and focuses on types of technology transfer and managerial strategies. The last section provides conclusions.

SMALL AND MEDIUM SIZED ENTERPRISES IN THE WORLD ECONOMY

Small and medium sized enterprises (SMEs) (here the working definition of a company with less than 500 employees is used) play an important role in the world economy as employment generators, as innovators and as exporters. They are important job generators because they tend to be more labour-intensive than larger firms, and as well as internal growth of SMEs, much job creation is the result of small business start-ups. The extent of innovation by SMEs, as opposed to large firms, is controversial and it is clear that their exporting potential is generally less than the proportion exported by large firms. Nevertheless SMEs have a crucial role to play in developing and transferring certain types of technology, and where there is a satisfactory niche for small firms they can play a critical role in technological advances.

In terms of their international role, it is clear that SMEs account for a relatively small proportion of world foreign direct investment, but this pro-

*Originally published in *Small Business Economics*, vol. 9, no. 1, February 1997, pp. 67–78.

Table 5.1   United States: shares of parent firms and foreign affiliates of small and medium-sized transnational corporations in those of all transnational corporations, by industry of parent firms, 1988 (percentage)

Industry	Foreign affiliates				
	Number of parent firms	Number	Assets	Sales	Employment
Primary	40.6	6.1	5.7	0.1[a]	6.9
Agriculture, forestry and fishing	66.7	15.6	4.5	3.2	10.3
Mining and petroleum	38.0	5.8	5.7	0.1[a]	6.5
Manufacturing	19.8	3.3	0.8	0.8	1.1
Food, beverages and tobacco	19.2	1.3	0.2	0.3	0.3
Textile products and apparel	23.5	8.9	3.9	3.1	6.5
Lumber, wood and paper products	17.2	3.8	1.1	1.1	0.9
Chemicals and allied products	17.6	2.2	0.7	0.6	0.6
Primary and fabricated metals	24.8	6.4	1.7	2.3	2.1
Machinery, except electrical	25.0	5.7	1.2	1.2	1.8
Electrical and electronic equipment	21.3	4.7	2.6	3.4	2.6
Transportation equipment	8.0	0.5	–	0.1	0.2
Other manufacturing	17.1	3.0	0.8	1.0	1.1
Services	39.9	12.8	4.1	3.2[a]	3.1[a]
Wholesale and retail trade	44.7	30.4	11.3	4.3[a]	4.5
Finance (except banking), insurance and real estate	59.4	4.6	2.2	2.2	1.0
Hotels and other lodging places	20.0	21.2	23.0	–	–
Construction	27.6	7.0	8.7	3.0	0.6
Transportation, communication and public utilities	13.6	5.4	0.6	0.7	0.7
Other services	23.2	7.6	4.1	3.6[a]	4.6[a]
All industries	28.3	5.5	2.7	3.4	1.9

[a] Excludes data that are suppressed to avoid disclosure. Thus, the figures are underestimated.

Sources: Based on special tabulation of United States TNCs by firm size by United States Department of Commerce at the request of United Nations Conference on Trade and Development, Programme on Transnational Corporations. UNCTAD (1993) p. 66.

portion is growing. Global figures for SME FDI as a proportion of the total are unavailable (UNCTAD, 1993). Some information is available on a national basis, however. Unfortunately each major source country keeps the information on a different basis and uses a different definition of 'small' (or SME). This makes aggregation impossible. Representative figures for USA (Tables 5.1 and 5.2), show some important regularities. However TNCs are measured, they represent a high proportion of outward investment in terms of numbers in each of these major source countries (28.3 per cent of parent firms investing abroad in the USA – 5.5 per cent of all foreign affiliates – in 1988, 39.8 per cent of equity investment in Japan in 1991, 66.3 per cent of foreign investors in the UK in 1981, 74 per cent of all transnational corporations in Sweden in 1987, and 60.2 per cent of all Italian transnational corporations and 28.8 per cent of foreign affiliates in 1987). However, when we look at SMEs' contribution to aggregates such as foreign assets, sales or employ-

Table 5.2   United States: shares of foreign affiliates of small and medium-sized transnational corporations in those of all transnational corporations, by host country, 1988 (percentage)

Country	Number of affiliates	Assets of affiliates	Sales of affiliates	Employ- ment of affiliates
Developed countries	5.7	2.0	2.5	1.7
Canada	9.1	2.1	1.9	1.9
Europe	5.3	1.2	1.8	1.6
Japan	4.8	–	–	1.6
Others	3.4	–	–	1.4
Developing economies	4.7	4.9	8.0	2.6
Africa	5.2	2.7	4.4	2.9
South and East Asia	5.8	9.9	17.6	4.2
Hong Kong	8.0	5.1	5.1	9.7
Philippines	4.4	–	–	3.4
Republic of Korea	3.1	–	–	–
Singapore	5.3	–	–	2.6
Taiwan Province of China	6.0	2.5	5.4	5.1
Latin America	3.8	3.1	1.8	1.7
Argentina	1.3	0.2	0.3	0.4
Brazil	3.5	0.6	0.8	0.8
Colombia	3.4	1.0	1.0	2.0
Mexico	2.8	2.2	1.7	1.4
Venezuela	3.0	1.5	1.7	–
Middle East	8.4	6.1	11.7	7.1
All countries	5.5	2.7	3.4	1.9

Sources: Based on special tabulation of United States TNCs by firm size by United States Department of Commerce at the request of United Nations Conference on Trade and Development, Programme on Transnational Corporations. UNCTAD (1993) p. 67.

ment, the picture changes dramatically. For the same years as given above, SMEs accounted for 2.7 per cent of foreign assets, 3.4 per cent of foreign sales and 1.9 per cent of foreign employment for the USA, 0.8 per cent of the book value of foreign direct investment of the UK, 2 per cent of employment in Swedish-owned foreign affiliates and 7.4 per cent of employment, 6.2 per cent of turnover in Italian transnational companies.

The UNCTAD survey did show foreign direct investment by SMEs to be growing rapidly. Table 5.3 shows that they are rapidly becoming more international.

Table 5.3   Distribution of foreign-direct-investment cases by small and medium-sized enterprises, by period

Country/industry	Number of invest- ments surveyed	Distribution by period (percentage)					
		Before 1949	*1950–9*	*1960–9*	*1970–9*	*1980–9*	*1990–2*
By home country							
Japan	142	–	1	5	25	55	15
United States	24	8	–	4	42	37	8
Europe	57	–	–	7	23	51	19
All countries	225	1	–	5	27	52	15
By industry of parent firm							
Primary	5	–	–	20	–	80	–
Manufacturing	156	1	–	6	29	49	15
High-technology industries	33	6	–	6	21	55	12
Medium-techno- logy industries	71	–	–	4	37	44	15
Low-technology industries	52	–	–	10	23	52	15
Services	67	–	1	1	24	57	16
All industries	228	1	–	5	27	52	15
By host country							
Developed countries	129	2	–	5	27	51	15
United States	42	–	–	5	21	64	10
Europe	72	1	–	6	29	46	18
Others	15	7	–	7	33	40	13
Developing countries	99	–	1	5	26	53	15
South and East Asia	91	–	1	5	26	54	13
Others	8	–	–	–	25	38	38
All countries	228	1	–	5	27	52	15

Sources: Based on the United Nations Survey. UNCTAD (1993) p. 54.

We should also note that SMEs which do internationalise tend to be larger, more capital rich, more productive and profitable and to have a higher export ratio than SMEs in general (Table 5.4). This is unsurprising, but it does pro-

Table 5.4   Comparison of some features of small and medium-sized manufacturing transnational corporations with small and medium-sized manufacturing enterprises in general

Features	Small and medium-sized TNCs[a]	SMEs in general
Size		
Average sales world-wide (millions of dollars)	89	3.3[b]
Average number of employees in home country	286[c]	30[b]
Average number of employees world-wide	515[c]	–
Average capital world-wide (millions of dollars)	42	0.3[d]
Average value added world-wide (millions of dollars)	28	1.3[b]
Labour–capital ratio (= number of employees/capital in millions of dollars)	13	58[d]
Labour productivity (= value added in millions of dollars/numbers of employees)	0.06	0.04[b]
Capital productivity (= value added/capital in millions of dollars)	0.5	1.8[d]
Export ratio (= exports/sales, percentage)	22	15[e]
Profit ratio[f] (= profits/sales, percentage)	7.9	4.2[d]

[a] Based on 62 firms for average sales worldwide, 47 firms for the average number of employees in home country and worldwide, 57 firms for average capital worldwide, 39 firms for average value-added world-wide, 55 firms for labour–capital ratio, 39 firms for labour productivity and for capital productivity, 56 firms for export ratio and 47 firms for profit ratio.
[b] Based on the data of Australia, Austria, Canada, France, Germany, Ireland, Japan, New Zealand, Norway and United States in table I.1, UN Survey.
[c] There are a few firms with more than 500 employees in home country. These firms, however, employed fewer than 500 employees at the end of the 1980s, the criteria year in the United Nations Survey. These firms' data are included.
[d] Only Japanese SMEs.
[e] Data of France, Italy, Netherlands and Norway in table 1.5, UN Survey, are used.
[f] Defined here as income (sales minus costs) before taxes divided by sales.

Sources: Based on the United Nations Survey, tables 1.1 and 1.5; and Ministry of Finance, *Zaisei Kinyu Tokei Geppo (Monthly Report of Fiscal and Financial Statistics)*, no. 462 (Tokyo, Ministry of Finance Printing Bureau, October 1990). UNCTAD (1993) p. 86.

duce a curious statistical artifact – SMEs which internationalise rapidly cease to be SMEs (on any of the definitions used)!

SMEs show a strong preference for non-equity forms of technology transfer such as licensing (rather than FDI). SMEs from advanced countries also concentrate their investments more in other advanced countries rather than in less developed countries (LDCs). In fact, their investments are locationally clustered near to the source country to a larger degree than large multinational companies (MNCs). This may be the result of limited horizons, risk aversion and the influence of 'psychic distance' (Hallen and Wiedersheim-Paul, 1979) which all bear heavily on SMEs. Internationally oriented SMEs also tend to be industrially concentrated, specialising particularly in locationally bound services and manufactured and capital goods (UNCTAD, 1993).

It is against this background that the international technology transfer activities of SMEs needs to be set.

THEORETICAL APPROACHES TO INTERNATIONALISATION BY SMEs

In a previous paper (Buckley, 1989), I reviewed the analysis of the internationalisation of SMEs under four generic headings: the economics of the firm's growth; internationalisation and evolutionary approaches to growth; the 'gambler's earnings hypothesis'; and the corporate decision-making approach. There is no point in reviewing each of these in detail again; instead, this paper attempts to synthesise the key issues and update the arguments.[1]

Several key arguments can be abstracted from the literature.

First, there is an important relationship between the firm and the market. There is a crucial relationship between the firm's size and overall market size. In one polar case, we can envisage a small firm attempting to grow (internationalise) in a 'big-firm' industry, i.e. an industry where optimal scale is large in relation to market size. This poses problems in terms of resource acquisition, notably capital and management skills. In the other extreme case, there are industries with few economies of scale where many small firms prosper. Industries requiring a wide range of specialist intermediate inputs, in particular, present a small firm in equilibrium with a small market. Thus we can make a distinction between absolute smallness and relative smallness. The role of small firms in filling a niche market has been noted as a key attribute of Third World multinationals whose key competitive advantage is their skill as versatile users of flexible equipment (Wells, 1983). There is a case to be made that the current 'downsizing' and moves towards 'lean production' and outsourcing mean greater opportunities for smaller firms to fill new supply niches. Table 5.5 shows the view that SMEs who have already internationalised have of the problems or opportunities given by small size. It was felt to be more of a constraint than an advantage in R&D, finance and recruitment of skilled employees. However, small scale was more often seen as an advantage than a constraint in economies (or diseconomies) of scale, overseas marketing and distribution and information capacity. These factors give clues to the types of industries, contexts and markets in which SMEs' internationalisation is likely to be successful. Where local skills are needed, small scale is a positive advantage and information processing is required (speedily), then SMEs are likely to feel more confident of success.

Table 5.5   Shares of small and medium-sized transnational corporations that think that firm size constitutes a constraint or an advantage for foreign direct investment[a]

Category associated with foreign direct investment	Constraint	Advantage	No difference
Research and Development	27	19	44
Finance	35	19	40
Recruitment of skilled employees	26	22	45
Economies/diseconomies of scale	21	26	45
Overseas marketing/distribution	27	42	29
Information capacity	23	32	35

[a] Based on 108 company responses.

Sources: Based on the United Nations Survey. UNCTAD (1993) p. 136.

Second, there are several important constraints on the international activities of SMEs. Perhaps the most important of these are internal constraints. Two key issues here are shortages of capital and of managerial skill. In raising capital, a small firm faces a 'catch-22' problem – how to raise finance without disclosing its competitive advantages (in particular its proprietary technology). These institutional difficulties of capitalising knowledge are compounded by the necessity to retain (family) control. The shortage of skilled management in SMEs is often a more serious problem. Small firms, typically, do not have specialist executives to manage their international operations, nor do they possess a hierarchy of managers through which complex decisions can be filtered. Decision-making is likely to be personalised, involving *ad hoc*, short-term reckoning based on individual perception and prejudice (this is not unknown in large multinationals!). A shortage of management time leads to the firm taking short cuts without a proper evaluation of alternatives. Information costs bear heavily on small firms, and attempts to avoid or reduce these costs, for instance by making no serious attempt to evaluate a potential agent or joint venture partner, can be disastrous. The horizons of small firms are limited by managerial constraints and there is little 'global scanning' of opportunities. Therefore, when an opportunity presents itself, it is often seized without proper evaluation. Given this problem, why does the firm not recruit management from outside the firm? One problem is the desire of family-owned companies to retain control inside the family circle; the other is the difficulty in obtaining specialist knowledge of how to evaluate outsiders. Lack of these crucial evaluation skills constrains recruitment and makes endemic the burden on management. Consequently small firms with inexperienced managers can behave in a naive fashion, particularly outside their normal cultural milieu. They can be politically naive because they lack public relations skills, lobbying power and the sheer economic muscle of larger firms.

The role of risk and uncertainty is an important one in determining SME internationalisation patterns. It is likely that the proportion of resources committed to a foreign direct investment will be greater than for a large, diversified multinational. Failure is thus more costly. This can interact with information costs in a negative way – in that costly information collection will not be undertaken. Thus 'short cuts' or spurning of opportunities can result. Alternatively, owner managers often act on impulse and are often greater risk-takers than more 'managerialist' entrepreneurs. The rather erratic financial behaviour of SMEs may also be explained by these factors. The 'gambler's earnings hypothesis' highlights an important empirical phenomenon – a small initial foreign investment eventually leading to a large payback of profit in the form of dividends. An explanation is given by analogy with ploughing and harvesting. A period of ploughing may be set by the firm (say 5 to 7 years). In this time the foreign subsidiary is given a great deal of freedom of action. After that the foreign subsidiary either generates a stream of income for the next project (the next ploughing) or it is sold off to obtain a return on the capital. The short decision-making horizon arises because of the restricted capital and management capacity. Thus a target rate of return and/ or payback period are discovered by trial and error.

Fourth, we need to pay attention to the dynamics of growth in the industry. Large multinational firms often have highly sector specific expansion routes. This leaves niche markets or 'interstices' for SMEs to exploit. These niches are often in 'small firms industries' or exist as a fringe in 'large firm industries'. SMEs may thus be 'pulled' into foreign markets by large firms requiring suppliers or 'pushed' abroad by increasing competition in home markets. The flexibility of SMEs in adjusting to external conditions needs to be set against their vulnerability to radical change in technological, political, institutional and competitive conditions. The role of SMEs will vary over the life-cycle of an industry. In the early stages, numbers of small firms will vie for position. As the industry matures, economies of scale become prevalent and only a few will survive. In the decline phase, established competitors will face a threat from new entrepreneurial, innovating SMEs (Vernon, 1966, 1979).

Table 5.6 shows the relationships between SMEs and multinational firms both from the point of view of the SME's growth and in relation to its foreign direct investment. The relationship, of course, varies according to the type of industry, even when such broad industry groupings as these are used.

INTERNATIONALISATION, GLOBALISATION AND SMEs

The motivation for SMEs to make foreign direct investments is remarkably orthodox. The three key motives which we observe for multinational companies – market seeking, resource seeking and efficiency (low cost) seeking investments – are all present in the list of motivations for SMEs as they are for multinationals (Buckley, 1995). In terms of market-related motivations, seeking growth in local markets is mentioned by 50 per cent of the firms, strengthening competitive capacity by 27.3 per cent, access to third country markets by 24.4 per cent and information gathering by 20.6 per cent. Low cost labour is mentioned by 14.5 per cent and securing raw materials by 11.2 per cent. This leads to a discussion of the overall strategies of SMEs in reaching foreign markets. Table 5.7 shows the degree of internationalisation of SMEs in the UN Survey. SMEs in services were the most highly internationalised in terms of their FDI presence, followed by medium-technology industries, whilst low-technology industries had the highest proportion of exports to total sales followed again by medium-technology industries. It is possible to contrast internationalisation with globalisation. Internationalisation is the term normally used for the gradual, sequential incremental approach described in Scandinavian literature (Johanson and Wiedersheim-Paul, 1975; Johanson and Vahlne, 1977) and by the studies carried out at Bradford (Buckley, Newbould and Thurwell, 1988; Buckley, Berkova and Newbould, 1983). In contrast, the globalisation approach suggests that firms can reach foreign markets in a simultaneous fashion – by a 'big bang'.

Casson (1994) has attempted to synthesise these approaches by examining internationalisation as a corporate learning process. He posits a model where the cost of acquisition of information about a market generates a set-up cost of entry. The sequential approach to entry hinges on the exploitation of systematic similarities between markets. Because of such similarities, experience acquired in one foreign market is of potential relevance to another. If

Table 5.6 Shares of small and medium-sized transnational corporations that think
their relationship with large firms is important in their growth and foreign direct
investment, by area of relationship and industry[a] (percentage)

Industry	Area of relationship with large firms				
	Customers/ suppliers	Information concerning technical development	Financial services	Advisory services	Marketing/ distribution
Firm's growth					
Manufacturing	37	25	5	7	30
High-technology industries	67	40	–	7	40
Medium-technology industries	26	20	3	3	26
Low-technology industries	35	23	10	13	29
Services	39	17	6	11	22
All industries	37	21	6	9	26
Foreign direct investment					
Manufacturing	16	7	6	9	15
High-technology industries	33	13	7	13	27
Medium-technology industries	14	6	3	3	9
High-technology industries	10	6	10	13	16
Services	8	14	3	6	11
All industries	13	9	5	7	13
Both firm's growth and foreign direct investment[b]					
Manufacturing	14	7	2	5	11
High-technology industries	33	13	–	7	27
Medium-technology industries	11	6	–	–	6
Low-technology industries	6	6	6	10	10
Services	8	11	3	6	8
All industries	11	8	2	5	10

[a] Based on 123 small and medium-sized TNCs.
[b] Answer to this is also included in separate responses to firm's growth and FDI.

Sources: Based on the United Nations Survey. UNCTAD (1993) p. 81.

foreign markets were all totally different from one another, then nothing
learnt in one market would have any significance for another. However,

if markets are very similar, then a globalisation pattern – a single discrete simultaneous entry into all markets – becomes feasible.

Table 5.7   The degree of internationalisation of small and medium-sized transnational corporations (percentage)

Industry	Proportion of exports to total sales	Proportion of FDI to total assets
Manufacturing	22	5
High-technology industries	10	5
Medium-technology industries	19	11
Low-technology industries	28	3
Services	14	20
All industries	18	15
Number of companies observed	81	66

Sources: Based on the United Nations Survey. UNCTAD (1993) p. 88.

In a sequential approach, decisions about entering the second market are deferred until the first has been entered because this provides an option value which strengthens the case of sequential entry when some markets are only marginally profitable. However, this model assumes that each market is investigated before the local marketing strategy is determined. This can be contrasted with purely experimental learning where the market is entered *without* systematic investigation and learning results from responding to mistakes. The decision to learn by experience, Casson suggests, depends 'first and foremost on the confidence of the management, and on the costliness of mistakes, and only peripherally on the issue of sequential entry' (1994, p. 15). Thus there is a key trade-off between exploiting economies of scope in knowledge (maximised by a sequential strategy), and the gains from exploiting profitable market opportunities without delay (a simultaneous entry globalisation strategy).

Casson's piece is also illuminating on the issue of uncertainty. He suggests that there are two varieties of uncertainty facing the internationalising firm: uncertainty about the state of the market (how similar it is to the home market and other previously entered markets); and the cost of collecting information to overcome this problem. The cost of collection depends on the type of market which is not known in advance. The cost of 'mistaken entry' may well be below that of systematic investigation; thus, making mistakes may be a rational way of expansion!

Table 5.8 shows the nature of the relationship between the foreign affiliate of the SMEs in developing countries and the parent firm. SMEs parallel multinational firms except that they are more conservative in conglomerate diversification abroad.

Table 5.8   Production relationship between foreign affiliates in developing countries and their parent firms[a] (percentage)

Kind of production relationship	Affiliates of small and medium-sized TNCs in developing countries	Affiliates of large TNCs in developing countries
Horizontal relationship		
Producing the same products as parent firm with the same technology	66	64
Producing the same products as parent firm with different or modified technology	23	29
Varietal relationship		
Turning raw materials into semi-manufactured products	15	19
Turning semi-manufactured products into final products	28	23
No relationship		
Producing completely different or unrelated products	10	14
Number of companies observed	79	129

[a] As some of the affiliates are engaged in different lines of production, there is more than one production relationship. Therefore, total adds up to more than 100.

Sources: Based on the United Nations Survey. UNCTAD (1993) p. 99.

TECHNOLOGY TRANSFER STRATEGIES OF SMEs

The UNCTAD study of technology transfer (UNCTAD, 1993) found that SMEs, like MNEs, transferred technology internationally that was overwhelmingly from their parent firms. They are not thus unbiased conduits but are vehicles for the international projection of parent-firm-driven technology (98 per cent of affiliates – UNCTAD, 1993, p. 106). Table 5.9 shows that SMEs do carry out a considerable amount of in-house R&D and that this is largely conducted in the home country. The most common vehicle for international transfer is via a joint venture with a host country company. Because SMEs have a constraint on their in-house set of capabilities (Penrose, 1959), joining with others enables international expansion to become profitable by adding to those pre-existing capabilities. A narrower range of technology is transferred through SMEs than through MNEs; particularly lacking are transfers of management technology and marketing technology. This may be partly due to the mode of transfer joint ventures – it may also result from the lack of development of these technologies in SMEs in general.

The UNCTAD survey shows that the means of technology transfer in SMEs is much less formalised than in MNEs. This is related to their management style and the crucial constraints referred to above. The channel of written instructions is used much less in SMEs than in MNEs, partly because of lack of personnel to codify the technology and partly because many of the skills in SMEs are acquired through personal experience. Sending technical experts abroad to aid in technology transfer is much more difficult for SMEs (the high opportunity cost of technical personnel is crucial here) and written instructions are used much less frequently. There is also less (expenditure on) specialised technical training to aid in the transfer. Only 40 per cent of foreign affiliates of SMEs had technical training other than on-the-job training, compared with 70 per cent for large firms (UNCTAD, 1993, p. 109).

Typically, therefore, on-the-job training plus the supply of machinery and parts which embody the technology is the crucial transfer mechanism in SMEs. Manuals and technical handbooks are used by a minority of SMEs and even blueprints and drawings are only utilised in 51 per cent of cases.

Efforts are made to adapt technology to host country conditions. Key factors causing adaptation are scale differentials, different factor endowments and gaps in technological capabilities between source and host countries. However, the UNCTAD survey found that a lower percentage of SMEs than MNEs made efforts to adopt their technology (77 per cent against 86 per cent). Several reasons can be adduced for this dissemination: (1) the lower level of technological mastery in SMEs; (2) the reliance of SMEs on the experience of skilled technicians (including owners) and the custom order nature of technology in SMEs that reduces the need to formalise adaptation efforts (i.e. the tacit component of technology is higher in SMEs); (3) barriers to adaptation (e.g. poor local supplies) are greater for SMEs than MNEs; (4) adaptation may divert very scarce resources away from activities at home; and (5) the technologies transferred by SMEs may be inherently more suitable to LDCs than that of large companies – thus there is a reduced need to modify SME technology.

Table 5.9 Research-and-development activities by small and medium-sized transnational corporations (percentage)

Country/industry	Proportion of small and medium-sized TNCs that carry out R&D	Proportion of small and medium-sized TNCs that have a specialised R&D department	Proportion of small and medium-sized TNC that have R&D facilities abroad	Ratio of total R&D expenditures to sales	Ratio of R&D expenditures abroad to total R&D expenditures
		By home country			
Japan	66	34	7	10	4.3
United States	69	56	31	2.0	4.1
Europe	76	52	36	2.3	6.1
All countries	70	43	17	1.5	5.0
		By industry			
Manufacturing	81	55	18	2.0	5.0
High-technology industries	86	64	7	2.4	8.7
Medium-technology industries	85	59	24	2.2	3.5
Low-technology industries	74	44	19	1.0	5.2
Services	43	20	10	0.3	7.5
All industries	70	43	17	1.5	5.0
Number of companies observed	109	109	109	56[a]	46[b]

[a] Ten out of 56 small and medium-sized TNCs report zero R&D expenditures.
[b] Thirty-four out of 46 small and medium-sized TNCs report zero R&D expenditures.

Sources: Based on the United Nations Survey. UNCTAD (1993) p. 96.

TYPES OF TECHNOLOGY TRANSFER BY SMEs

Three types of technology may be picked out as appropriate for international transfer by SMEs: small-scale technologies, labour-intensive technologies, and specialised high-technology know-how.

In the first case, we can refer back to our earlier discussion of the firm and the industry. SMEs may be operating in industries where efficient scale is reached at a small volume of output relative to the total demand for the product. Thus the industry can accommodate a large number of SMEs. Second, there are industries where efficient scale is reached only at a large volume of production but demand still remains unsatisfied. Perhaps this is due to discontinuities in technology. One or two large plants of efficient scale do not satisfy demand, but unsatisfied demand is insufficient to attract a new entrant. Thus a fringe of SMEs fill unsatisfied demand. Third, SMEs can operate alongside large firms where there are not huge cost penalties in operating below efficient scale. Here SMEs may use a different production mode – specialising in made-to-order, custom built or small batch production.

These three situations are very different. Technologies transferred in the first and third situations will be viable alternatives to MNE technology. In the second situation, the risk is that SMEs will possess an inferior or second-best technology which will be vulnerable to not only technological change but also to changes in the competitive structure of the industry. Over time, the rate of decline of costs with respect to scale will be critical to the viability of SME-transferred small-scale technology.

In the case of labour-intensive technologies, it is obvious that SMEs operate in the most labour-intensive sectors – notably services – and therefore they may be more suited to the international transfer of more labour-intensive technologies. Here a distinction must be made between *processes* which are labour-intensive and collections of activities (as in normal industry and firm accounting) which are labour-intensive. It has long been observed that labour-intensive stages of production are relocated in cheaper labour locations (Vernon, 1966), but this is mainly the prerogative of large, well-organised multinational firms. The relatively internationally unsophisticated SMEs are not in a position to reconfigure their activities globally and it is usually the whole of productive activities which are relocated.

Third, new technologies are transferred internationally by SMEs; examples include biotechnology and microelectronics. We should also be wary of assuming that new technology aligns perfectly with industry (or even strategic group) divisions. Much new technology is disguised within traditional industries. SMEs face a general problem of capitalising in-house knowledge. They therefore need external funding to develop and spread their innovatory developments. Going to the market can be risky, so firm-to-firm deals are often chosen to extend their range. Equity (joint ventures) and non-equity (licensing deals, alliances) routes are often used as a means of leveraging technology in a way which appears less risky than normal market capitalisation.

MANAGERIAL PROCESSES IN SMALL FIRMS AND TECHNOLOGY TRANSFER

Chen and Hambrick (1995) found (in a study of airlines) that the small firms tended to be more active than large ones in initiating competitive moves, but in contrast large firms seemed to be more responsive when attacked. This is consistent with the flexibility and rapidity in strategy often ascribed to small firms. With regard to action visibility, small firms were more likely to be more low-key and even secretive. The authors characterise actions as follows: 'it appears that small airlines tend to hold their fire, calculating well-developed, visible responses; large airlines act quickly but in rather straightforward, unexciting ways' (p. 474). Hence the title of the paper: 'Speed, stealth and selective attack: how small firms, differ from large firms in competitive behaviour'.

This stereotype of small firms as fast-moving opportunists may not be generalisable across industries or across cultures. Steinmann, Kumar and Wasner (1981) found that German medium-sized firms in the USA followed a rather cautious, managerialist approach to internationalisation. Briemann (1989) found that smaller British firms invested in search of new markets, whereas German firms were more concerned with securing existing market positions.

The multinational research project on the international transfer of technology by small and medium-sized enterprises (Buckley *et al.*, 1997) found that industry, national host and source country factors influenced the form and nature of technology transfer but that idiosyncratic management influences were strong in SMEs.

CONCLUSION

All the evidence suggests that SMEs will not, in aggregate, be the major suppliers and transferrers of technology in the world economy, but they can fill crucial niche roles. The success of these niche roles will be partly determined by the key relationship between firm size and industry size and by SMEs being able to ride the dynamic of the industry. A second important success factor is the skill of management in SMEs in being able to spot and to take opportunities in situations where resources are scarce and information is expensive.

The mechanism of transfer of technology in SMEs seems remarkably orthodox. In general, technology developed by the parent is transferred via an international network which relies rather heavily on joint ventures, alliances and licensing links rather than on foreign direct investment. The key international transfer mechanism is on-the-job training in the host country.

The key technologies transferred are efficient small-scale technology, specialised custom built or small batch production technologies and 'opportunistic transfer' of technologies which in the long run will be more suited to larger firms. Managerial processes must play to the strengths of SMEs including their ability to be flexible and to make rapid strategic moves.

Note

1. Key references for each approach are:
    (a) Economics of the firm's growth: Penrose (1959), Buckley and Casson (1976).
    (b) Internationalisation and evolutionary approaches: Buckley, Newbould and Thurwell (1988), Nelson and Winter (1982), Vernon (1966), Buckley and Casson (1981).
    (c) Gambler's Earnings Hypothesis: Barlow and Wender (1955), Penrose (1956).
    (d) Corporate decision-making approach: Aharoni (1966).

References

Aharoni, Yair (1966) *The Foreign Investment Decision Process* (Boston: Harvard University).

Barlow, E.R. and I.T. Wender (1955) *Foreign Investment and Taxation* (Englewood Cliffs, NJ: Prentice-Hall).

Briemann, Norbert (1989) 'A Comparative Study of Foreign Investment Decisions by Small and Medium Sized British and German Manufacturing Companies', unpublished Ph.D. thesis, Manchester Business School.

Buckley, Peter J. (1989) 'Foreign Investment by Small and Medium-Sized Enterprises: The Theoretical Background', *Small Business Economics*, 1, 89–100. Reprinted in Buckley and Ghauri (eds) (1993).

Buckley, Peter J. (1995) *Foreign Direct Investment and Multinational Enterprises* (London: Macmillan).

Buckley, Peter J., Zdenka Berkova and Gerald D. Newbould (1993) *Direct Investment in the U.K. by Smaller U.K. Firms* (London: Macmillan).

Buckley, Peter J., Jaimie Campos, Hafiz Mirza and Eduardo White (eds) (1997) *International Technology Transfer by Small and Medium Sized Enterprises* (London: Macmillan).

Buckley, Peter J. and Mark Casson (1976) *The Future of the Multinational Enterprise* (London: Macmillan).

Buckley, Peter J. and Mark Casson (1981) 'The Optimal Timing of a Foreign Direct Investment', *Economic Journal*, 91, 75–87.

Buckley, Peter J. and Pervez N. Ghauri (eds) (1993) *The Internationalisation of the Firm* (London: Dryden Press).

Buckley, Peter J., Gerald D. Newbould and Jane Thurwell (1988) *Foreign Direct Investment by Smaller U.K. Firms* (London: Macmillan) (previously published in 1978 as *Going International – The Experience of Smaller Companies Overseas* (London: Associated Business Press)).

Casson, Mark (1994) 'Internationalisation as a Learning Process: A Model of Corporate Growth and Geographical Diversification', in V.N. Balasubramanyam and David Sapsford (eds), *The Economics of International Investment* (Aldershot: Edward Elgar).

Chen, Ming-Jer and Donald C. Hambrick (1995) 'Speed, Stealth and Selective Attack: How Small Firms Differ from Large Firms in Competitive Behaviour', *Academy of Management Journal*, 38, 453–82.

Hallen, Lars and Finn Wiedersheim-Paul (1979) 'Psychic Distance and Buyer–Seller Interaction', *Organisation, Marknad och Samhalle*, 16, 308–24. Reprinted in Buckley and Ghauri (eds) (1993).

Johanson, Jan and Jan-Erik Vahlne (1977) 'The Internationalisation Process of the Firm – A Model of Knowledge Development and Increasing Foreign Market Commitments', *Journal of International Business Studies*, 8, 23–32. Reprinted in Buckley and Ghauri (eds) (1993).

Johanson, Jan and Finn Wiedersheim-Paul (1975) 'The Internationalisation of the Firm – Four Swedish Case Studies', *Journal of Management Studies*, 12, 305–22. Reprinted in Buckley and Ghauri (eds) (1993).

Nelson, R. and S. Winter (1982) *An Evolutionary Theory of Economic Change* (Cambridge Mass: Harvard University Press).

Penrose, Edith T. (1956) 'Foreign Investment and the Growth of the Firm', *Economic Journal*, 66, 230–5.

Penrose, Edith T. (1959) *The Theory of the Growth of the Firm* (Oxford: Blackwell).

Steinmann, H., B. Kumar and A. Wasner (1981) 'Some Aspects of Managing U.S. Subsidiaries of German Medium-Sized Enterprises', *Management International Review*, 21, 27–37.

UNCTAD, Programme on Transnationals (1993) *Small and Medium Sized Transnational Corporations: Role, Impact and Policy Implications* (New York: United Nations).

Vernon, Raymond, (1966) 'International Investment and International Trade in the Product Cycle', *Quarterly Journal of Economics*, 80, 190–207.

Vernon, Raymond (1979) 'The Product Cycle Hypothesis in A New International Environment', *Oxford Bulletin of Economics and Statistics*, 41, 255–67.

Wells, Louis T. (1983) *Third World Multinationals: The Rise of Foreign Investment from Developing Countries* (Cambridge, Mass: MIT Press).

Part II

Foreign Investment in Vietnam and Japan

6 Joint Ventures in the Socialist Republic of Vietnam: The First Six Years*

FOREIGN INVESTMENT IN VIETNAM

December 1993 saw the sixth anniversary of Vietnam's current foreign investment law (FIL), promulgated in December 1987 as a key element in the country's economic reform program, *doi moi*. The FIL itself has been praised for its liberal stance on permitted forms of foreign direct investment (FDI), and the executive body established to oversee its enactment – the supraministerial State Committee for Cooperation & Investment (SCCI) – has gained recognition for its refreshingly flexible and pragmatic approach toward investors. In turn, this has been rewarded with intense Asia Pacific and European business interest, and the beginnings of a significant inflow of foreign capital. As of December 1993, approved FDI inflows totalled over US$7.5bn, and 1994 alone should witness a further US$3.5bn in pledged flows. (In August 1994, the total figure for pledged FDI inflows exceeded the US$10bn mark, recording the one thousandth FDI licence one month later.) For an avowedly socialist, less developed country, which until mid-1993 endured international economic censure under a multilateral lending veto, as well as an increasingly redundant US-led investment and trade embargo (Freeman, 1993), this has been no mean feat. The last remnants of the US embargo were lifted in February 1994. So why have overseas investors expended time, capital, and energy on this emerging host country market, which, as we shall see, provides some challenging hurdles for foreign firms?

A key attraction of Vietnam has been its location at the centre of the Asia Pacific 'economic hot-house'. Vietnam is remarkably fortunate to find itself nestled just below China's dynamic Guangdong province, with a lengthy coastline exposed to the trade routes between Japan, the 'Asian Tigers', and Southeast Asia's community of rapidly developing states. (Indeed, Vietnam is

*Originally published in *Journal of Asian Business*, vol. 10, no. 3, 1994, pp. 1–10.

scheduled to gain full membership of ASEAN in late 1995). This apart, Vietnam offers a number of significant, intrinsic host country qualities, including:

(a) A relatively cheap, diligent, and fairly well-educated and skilled workforce. The minimum permissible wage at an FDI project is currently US$35 per month, although even lower salaries do occur. Literacy is high in Vietnam, and years of economic adversity have helped create an adept workforce.

(b) A market of over seventy-one million people (the most populous country in mainland Southeast Asia), with a youthful demographic profile, and discerning consumer tastes, particularly notable in the South.

(c) Mineral and agricultural wealth, which is currently under-exploited. Coal exports are significant, and Vietnam's total rice exports are only exceeded by those of Thailand and the US. Much-touted offshore oil and gas reserves could prove to rival Australia's.

These host country qualities – among numerous others – are further buoyed by a popular external perception that Vietnam's economic potential (and grim determination to succeed) may be sufficient for the country to replicate the growth curves displayed by South Korea, Taiwan, Singapore, and more recently, some of the ASEAN states and southern China.

However, it must be remembered that the salient realities of Vietnam's current host country environment remain challenging. Bureaucracy and red tape abound; the infrastructure (road, rail, power, telecommunications, etc.) is in total disrepair, and further exacerbated by Vietnam's elongated shape; land and property law is confused and confusing; the cost of office rental in Hanoi and downtown Ho Chi Minh City rivals central Bangkok; petty corruption is evident; market data is poor, made worse by a large 'parallel economy'; conflicting demands are made on foreign investors by the provincial and national authorities, and even between ministries; there is inadequate commercial law enveloping the FIL; the north and the south of the country are markedly different markets in many ways, making market penetration from a single hub difficult. With this spectrum of intimidating host country hurdles, a foreign investor must first be sure that a joint venture (JV) is the right mode of FDI and that further hurdles will not arise *within* the JV between partners: business life in Vietnam is hard enough without internal disputes.

JOINT VENTURES IN VIETNAM

Although a variety of FDI forms are permitted under Vietnam's FIL – including wholly foreign-owned projects, business cooperation contracts, and a new build–operate–transfer format – the JV form of FDI has tended to dominate as the most popular form of FDI thus far. Around 70–80 per cent of all FDI projects in Vietnam have been JVs. One major reason for this has been that, at least until late 1992, JVs were favoured by the SCCI. Indeed, with a few specific exceptions, only those FDI projects which introduced new technology, located in remote regions, invested in neglected industrial sectors, played an important role in national economic development, earned significant levels of convertible currency, or displayed some other particularly favourable attribute were likely to gain SCCI approval to undertake the other FDI forms. Typically, the SCCI has judged that JVs maximise the exposure of the local business sector to foreign capital, technology, skills, managerial expertise, and the various other non-financial inputs of FDI. In response, foreign partners have often claimed to embrace the JV form as a way of showing faith in local talent, and a desire to fully collaborate on the mutual benefits of a successful JV project. But there is more than just altruism, or host country coercion, behind the foreign partners' decision to adopt the JV form, and a degree of synergy between partners can be discerned.

Although JVs can now be established with local private enterprises, most local partners have tended to be state enterprises – controlled either at national level (i.e., line ministries) or provincial level (commonly the local people's committee) – as these still dominate the Vietnamese industrial community and tend to enjoy larger distribution networks, and when relevant, export quotas. A JV must have its own charter and perform as a separate legal entity, and is regarded in Vietnamese law as a 'juridical person'. The foreign partner's equity contribution must be no less than 30 per cent of the legal capital. The full capital contribution may include: cash, technology transfer, plant, and machinery. The local partner's capital contribution may include: cash, natural resources, plant, right of use of land, machinery, and services. Typically, the local partner's contribution is largely made up of land use rights, sometimes at an inflated value. With the exception of some major JV projects, the maximum duration of the contract and licence was until recently 20 years (50 years in exceptional circumstances). In early 1993, this was revised up to 50 years (70 years in exceptional circumstances). The JV company is controlled by a management board, normally comprising representatives of the various partners in proportion to their capital contributions. Dissolution of the JV before its contracted termination date requires the unanimous approval of the board, and must be reported to the SCCI. A partner that has caused premature dissolution as a result of defaulting on its obligations must indemnify the other partner(s) for losses incurred. To better understand the issues involved, let us turn now to two specific JV case studies in Vietnam.

TWO CASE STUDIES

The subject of Case Study A is a lubricant blending plant and marketing JV, located in Ho Chi Minh City. The foreign partner's relations with Vietnam began in the early 1980s, when the company began to import marine lubricants, and grew to meet most of Vietnam's sea-going shipping demand. Payment was made in convertible currency – at a time when many importers had to undertake complex countertrade deals – without the use of letters of credit; transactions operated on trust, evolving into what one representative of the foreign partner termed 'a nice little business'.

In 1987, the local partner – a regional downstream oil company based in Ho Chi Minh City – approached the future foreign partner concerning a potential lubricating JV project, but this failed to evolve, due largely to the lack of a tenable FIL. In 1989, however, following a reassessment of Vietnam's investment environment (and new FIL), the foreign partner commenced negotiations with the local partner, and the SCCI. Both the negotiations and subsequent licence approval were protracted, and included the input of the national government, because of the project's deemed importance and the complexities of its import-substitution demands. As a consequence of the extra delays and demands entailed, the lubricant plant proposal became, in the words of one active participant, 'a problem project', and its pursuance was in jeopardy. In 1990, the JV was established to produce and market lubricants for use in Vietnam's road and rail traffic, and to replace lubricant imports that had previously been sourced from the Soviet Union.

The JV agreement stipulates a 60 per cent capital contribution from the foreign partner, and 40 per cent from the local partner. The original memorandum of understanding had envisaged a 70/30 per cent split respectively, but following negotiations with the SCCI, this was altered to the existing division. The foreign partner supplied money and equipment, while the local partner provided use of land and new buildings, infrastructural support, and locally-provided equipment where feasible. Under the terms of the JV agreement, the foreign partner enjoys a royalty fee for its technology expertise and use of the well-known brand name. The JV was granted a two-year tax holiday, commencing from the first year of cumulative profit, and thereafter a corporate tax rate of around 18 per cent. Partly in order to protect technology transfer, under the JV agreement, the local partner is not permitted to establish any other lubricant project. The foreign partner's trade name is registered and respected under Vietnamese law, although it was conceded by the company that Vietnam's legal system is 'an unknown entity'. (It was reported in the local press that both this JV and another lubricant JV had encountered counterfeit product, with local retailers in the capital substituting low-grade lubricants in recycled packaging.)

The construction of the blending plant was on the site of the local partner's existing refinery installation, with a capacity allegedly able to meet around 25 per cent of Vietnam's total lubricant demand, although this figure has been questioned by competitors. The new blending plant was regarded by the foreign partner as a small, pilot plant and the capital equipment was purpose-built for Vietnam's requirements. Construction of the blending plant was completed well ahead of schedule, using local labour and a Vietnamese engineer. Although an expatriate engineer visited regularly during the construction period to assess progress, all day-to-day engineering activity was undertaken by local professionals. The foreign partner believed this to be 'a good job', adding that 'perfection is impossible in Vietnam'.

All the inputs for the lubricant are imported, and paid for in convertible currency, yet the lubricant product is marketed domestically in local currency (the Vietnamese *dong*). As a recognised import substitution project – 'adding value by blending locally using local labour and infrastructure, thus reducing the foreign currency requirements per given unit of product' – the JV was granted permission to convert dong into convertible currency through a variety of legal means, including membership in the local foreign exchange centre. In the words of the foreign partner's regional manager, 'we are freely able to convert dong into hard currency to pay for raw materials, [the few] expatriate salaries, etc....We have had no problems in this area.' An ability to exchange dong for convertible currency was included within the initial JV agreement and SCCI investment licence. There is no intention for the JV to produce for export, as the small scale of the blending plant negates the low labour costs on the international market.

In addition to the blending plant and offices in Ho Chi Minh City, the JV subsequently opened an office and distribution centre in Hanoi. Other regional distribution centres may follow, although at present the rest of the country is covered through local agents. The distribution network established by the JV comprised a single distributor in each province, using a feeder delivery system of trucks. This network was established solely by the JV company, starting from nothing. In 1992, just three expatriate staff and fifty local employees were employed by the JV, but this grew to well over one hundred in 1993. The foreign partner largely manages the JV and, as one representative phrased it, 'calls the tune' at the blending plant. The managing director claimed the JV was making a profit after just one year, having expected profitability to be achieved after three years. The JV was said to be doing more business in one month than the foreign partner had previously been able to import to Vietnam in one whole year, and was enjoying around 75 per cent of the packaged lubricant market in Vietnam in 1993, accounting for 15 per cent of the total market for lubricants in the country.

The JV's short-term future strategy in Vietnam will be focused on the attainment of consistent production at its blending plant. Simultaneously, the JV will attempt to expand and consolidate its distribution network throughout the country. In the words of the foreign partner's managing director, the JV company is 'committed to the long-term growth of the Vietnamese economy and our medium-term objective is to secure at least a 25 per cent share of the lubricants market'.

Case Study B involves a thread spinning and dyeing JV project, also located near Ho Chi Minh City, awarded an SCCI investment licence in mid-1989, after less than six months of negotiations. (The local partner was one of three state enterprises introduced to the foreign partner by the relevant line ministry.) Prior to the JV agreement, the local partner had enjoyed a creditable degree of business success and financial stability; far from automatic in the country's state sector. While still under the control of the ministry, the local manager commented that his organisation had progressed from being an 'enterprise' to a 'company', responding to market forces in order to attain a profit. The JV format was chosen as the mode of FDI for three reasons: previous JVs by the foreign partner had proved successful in the relatively parallel investment environment of China; there existed a suitable local partner; and this form of FDI was deemed to be most compatible with the host country's economic development priorities.

The JV agreement was initially for a duration of just ten years, with 75 per cent ownership by the foreign partner and 25 per cent by the local partner. The latter's capital input was in the form of factory space at the rear of the local partner's existing complex. The foreign partner supplied machinery; dyed yarn as working capital; and convertible currency for repairing the plant, installing machinery, acquiring vehicles, and funding other support operations. The JV agreement and licence were amended in early 1991, extending their duration to twenty years, and to permit the establishment of a representative office in Hanoi.

The JV's board of directors is comprised of four representatives from the foreign partner and two from the local partner. The director of the local partner also enjoys various state responsibilities. This helped ensure that the JV would gain a market for its product, by bringing it within the existing distribution network in Vietnam. The foreign partner has adopted a 'hands off' approach to managing the JV, and contrary to the trend, has no expatriate permanently located at the JV site. All day-to-day management is conducted by the local partner's representatives, under the direction of one of its two board members.

It was estimated in late 1991 that the JV had gained a full 50 per cent of the domestic market for high quality thread, most of which is used in the manufacture of garments for export, largely by private sector companies. The high quality market accounts for about 10 per cent of the total domestic market for yarn. Of total sales, approximately 30 per cent is paid for in dong, and 70 per cent in convertible currency (typically US dollars). By 1993 the JV had increased its market share to over 25 per cent of the entire market, also doubling turnover each year since 1990. Much of the JV's success in establishing a significant presence in the host country market was attributed to its system of customer service. The traditional method in Vietnam had been for customers to visit the factory personally (ordering by telephone or post was simply not contemplated), which required a letter of introduction. Even then, the order would require further time-consuming bureaucratic paperwork in order to be processed. Payment would have to be assured in advance, and the customer would then have to collect the product. The JV, however, encouraged its customers to place orders by phone and provided a direct delivery service to transport the product within a few hours in Ho Chi Minh City, or within a few days nationally.

Toward the end of 1992, the JV established a second thread spinning and dyeing plant in Hanoi. This arose from the local partner's take-over of a Hanoi sewing factory (also its main competitor in Vietnam). The JV used this as an opportunity to expand its own operations in Vietnam, riding piggyback on the local partner's expansion.

JOINT VENTURES: A PROPOSED SHORT-LIST OF CONSIDERATIONS

While one should avoid generalisations about the complex process of FDI activity in Vietnam, a few 'pros and cons' of the JV format have begun to emerge from the experience of investors, and as illustrated by the two case studies discussed above.

Some pros:

(1)   In a country where personal contacts remain important, a local partner's role in market penetration can be incalculable. Despite recent moves toward a market economy, state enterprises still enjoy national distribution networks, in most cases. Some state enterprises are headed by influential state representatives, and JVs may be able to harness such connections. Enterprises under national ministries or provincial

committees tend to make particularly useful JV partners. In case study A, the local partner had helped with bureaucratic hurdles and recruitment of local staff, and adopted a discreet yet supportive stance when required. As a body under the local city people's committee, the local partner also had ready access to relevant state authorities, facing no significant obstacles to the JV's establishment.

(2) In a market lacking adequate data and commercial intelligence, a local partner can provide much valuable insight, particularly into Vietnam's substantial parallel economy (informal business activity, not recorded in most official data).

(3) A JV project is more likely to enjoy the support of the SCCI than a wholly foreign-owned FDI project. JVs have also tended to enjoy preferential incentive rates and quotas.

(4) The local partner can play a useful middle role in negotiations between the foreign investor and the SCCI with regard to precise licence terms. (The flexible approach of the SCCI means that precise terms – for example, on tax rates – can be negotiated on a case-by-case basis.)

(5) A local partner can provide land use and factory space. Acquiring right of land use can be very difficult and time-consuming for foreign investors.

(6) A local partner can advise a JV on specific host country hurdles, and how to surmount them, officially or informally. As one foreign investor put it, you need a local partner 'that knows its way around and can make things happen'. While this might sound rather vague and inconsequential, the importance of this factor should not be underestimated in Vietnam's still fledgling market where the characteristic structures and transparency of a mature market economy do not apply.

Some cons:

(1) The local partner's business aptitude and financial 'health' may not be wholly evident where state subsidies continue to be used.

(2) The local partner's priorities may differ from those of the foreign partner. One issue voiced by a foreign partner to a JV was that the local firm wished to maximise the number of staff employed at the JV, at a level too high for the former. The local partner's priorities may not be solely economic. In another incident, the local partner wished to maximise exports for convertible currency, while the foreign partner's priority was maximum local market penetration. Indeed, the JV may find itself competing against other subsidiaries of the foreign partner.

(3)   The local partner may not have the same views on product quality. One foreign firm discovered its local partner marketing low-grade product from another source, packaging under the foreign partner's well-respected brand name.

(4)   The local partner's capital share may be inflated, in order to reach the ratios demanded by the FIL. (Although a foreign partner may gain from unrecognised goodwill and hidden value.)

(5)   Decision-making is likely to require an element of patience, and voting rights on the board of directors must be carefully considered.

(6)   Termination of the FDI project and withdrawal may be harder for a JV than for a wholly foreign-owned project.

With the above 'cons' in mind, there a few useful guidelines for foreign firms contemplating enacting a JV project in Vietnam, in the all-important negotiation phase (Vecchi, 1992). They include the following:

(1)   It is crucial that a suitable local partner is found for any JV in Vietnam. Time must be spent getting this right. Such intangibles as contacts, existing (and functioning) distribution networks, market knowledge, and influence are essential attributes in a local partner.

(2)   While negotiations between potential JV partners should not become protracted, it is important that both sides fully understand the commitments of a JV agreement, and the demands entailed. A foreign partner should not assume that the local partner is fully conversant with business practice. The drafting of an agreement and feasibility study can provide a useful opportunity to assess the ability of each partner.

(3)   Representatives of the local partner should be given an opportunity to visit the foreign partner's overseas plant/offices in order to gain an impression of the corporate structure they are allying with.

(4)   Prior trading or commercial links between potential JV partners may be desirable, in order to gauge compatability as part of an incremental market entry approach, but are by no means an essential prerequisite.

For those with FDI experience in China, where a far larger body of knowledge has had time to emerge, much of the above will echo the experience of JVs in this neighbouring state. Indeed, apart from the obvious differences in scale, the host country business environments of China and Vietnam are markedly similar (Freeman, 1994). It is not surprising, therefore, to witness numerous foreign investors employing old 'China hands' in their Vietnam operations. While the JV format is a useful way to harness host country contacts and knowledge – as with *guangxi* in China – in what is a highly individual market and business environment, a foreign partner must guard against the less desirable traits of the local partner permeating the JV. As a result of the SCCI's growing acceptance of other FDI forms, greater market penetration by foreign investors, and a fleshing-out of business legislation in Vietnam, JVs may begin to lose their status as the dominant form of FDI. But the advantages of a JV, as recounted above, should not be underestimated, nor overlooked.

References

Freeman, Nick J. (1993) 'United States' Economic Sanctions Against Vietnam: International Business and Development Repercussions', *Columbia Journal of World Business*, 28 (2).

Freeman, Nick J. (1994) 'Vietnam and China: Foreign Direct Investment Parallels', *Communist Economies and Economic Transformation*, Spring.

Vecchi, Sesto (1992) 'Smoothing the Way to Joint Venture Agreements', *International Corporate Law*, vol. 17, part 4.

7 Vietnam's Country Funds: An Emerging Investment Vehicle*

with Nick J. Freeman

Introduction to Country Funds

Since the early 1980s a new form of emerging market investment vehicle has appeared on the investment scene: the listed country fund. Buoyed by the thirst for exposure to the high-growth economies of the developing world, and the rapid spate of bourses opening up across the world's community of emerging markets, fund managers and other major portfolio investors have welcomed the introduction of country funds as a means by which to gain – relatively efficiently – investment exposure to these high-performing equity markets.[1] Typically, these country funds have held a fluid portfolio of shares in listed companies of the relevant country – or, in some cases, group of countries/region – determined by the fund manager, for a fee (usually defined as a percentage of net asset value (NAV)). The country funds themselves are commonly listed (although some privately placed funds also exist), providing much-desired liquidity for investors in the funds. The perceived advantages of the country funds, as viewed by Michael T. Porter, are as follows:

(1)   investors gain instant, widely diversified exposure to a market;
(2)   lower minimum investment levels;
(3)   active management of the fund by people knowledgeable of the relevant market;
(4)   listed funds typically offer liquidity and provide the accountability demanded of the relevant bourse on which they are listed;
(5)   cost-effective access of often restricted markets;
(6)   and the potential to offer attractive discounts/premiums.[2]

Points one and four above are arguably the most important single factor. With regard to point one, a recent empirical study of 32 emerging market country

*Originally published in Henri-Claude de Bettignies (ed.), *Changing Markets in Asia* (INSEAD, Paris, 1998).

funds listed on the New York Stock Exchange concluded that 'a significant diversification benefit' arose from subscribing to country funds, although offset somewhat by gains that were 'smaller than if they [the investors] had access to the originating market portfolios'.[3] Country funds therefore reduce the transaction cost of investing in an economy where they would otherwise represent a major barrier. Individual investments are pre-packaged by the fund managers into a single instrument, thereby adding liquidity and accountability.

INTRODUCTION TO VIETNAM'S INVESTMENT ENVIRONMENT

Since Vietnam opened its doors to foreign investment in December 1987, promulgating what was regarded to be one of the most liberal foreign direct investment (FDI) laws in the South-east Asia region at that time, the country has attracted a significant degree of overseas business interest. Whilst a degree of unwarranted hyperbole has surrounded this emerging market of over 72 million people, the oft-recounted macro-economic fundamentals of Vietnam prompt most observers to forecast that the country has the potential to become a major regional economic power in the next decade. In September 1994, Vietnam notched up its first 1,000 approved FDI projects, cumulatively capitalised at over US$10 billion. (See Tables 7.1 and 7.2.) The lifting of the redundant US embargo in February 1994, and the certainty that Vietnam will gain full membership of ASEAN in late 1995, also augur well.

However, numerous hurdles still need to be overcome if Vietnam is to harness its recognised, though still largely latent, potential. Crucially, the country's entire infrastructure is in desperate need of investment, domestic savings and investment rates must be increased, burdensome bureaucracy and corruption must be kept in check, a tight rein on an IMF- applauded fiscal and monetary policy must be maintained, and socio-economic strains brought about by the reform process – known as 'doi moi', or renovation – must be countered, amongst numerous other factors.

Lacking a domestic bourse in Vietnam, foreign investment has almost wholly been under the FDI format, enacting venture capital projects through joint ventures, wholly foreign-owned projects or business cooperation contracts/production sharing contracts.[4] Whilst investment proposals – of varying levels of tenability – are quite literally 'ten a penny' in Vietnam, a paucity of capital has been a major constraining factor in the country's bid to increase foreign investment inflows. Overseas investors recognise that this host country remains risky, and with the exception of major multinationals or the bold, most desire to spread the risk by taking on other foreign participants. It is in this role – as, typically non-managerial, co-investor – that Vietnam's off-shore country funds have established a presence.

Table 7.1   Approved foreign direct investment inflows (as of October 1994)

Country	Projects	Total capital (US$m)
Taiwan	172	1,900
Hong Kong	208	1,800
South Korea	93	825
Australia	46	763
France	68	732
Singapore	74	605
Malaysia	33	579
Japan	68	538
Britain	17	402
Netherlands	14	394
Switzerland	16	247
Thailand	54	225
United States	22	187
Russia	49	175
Indonesia	11	161
Canada	16	132
Total	1,093	10,300

Note: Nine FDI licences have expired and 165 have been revoked, accounting for US$89m and US$776m respectively.

Table 7.2   Approved foreign direct investment, by sector

Sector	Projects	Total capital (US$m)
Industry	481	3,800
Hotels and tourism	104	2,000
Oil and gas	27	1,300
Services	127	730
Telecomms and transport	21	637
Agriculture	74	368
Finance and banking	15	177
Aquaculture	20	60
Housing	6	26
Others (inc. EPZs)	43	441

Source: State Committee for Cooperation and Investment.

VIETNAM'S COUNTRY FUNDS: A PROFILE

Vietnam currently has four listed country funds solely focused on investments in the country. (See Table 7.3.) In addition, Vietnam enjoys a few unlisted country funds – most notably, Keppel's US$90m, 'Vietnam
Investment Fund' – and Vietnam is also represented in a small number of listed and unlisted regional funds. Most recently, in November 1994, Beta Funds
launched the US$25m 'Beta Mekong Fund', of which 30–50 per cent of this
fund's investment portfolio will be targeted on Vietnam. (This latter fund is
intending to invest across Vietnam, Laos, Cambodia, Myanmar (formerly
Burma), and Yunnan Province in PR China; an Indochina-wide remit.) Together, the four listed country funds alone have a cumulative capital resource
of over US$280m; a fairly substantial figure for a country such as Vietnam.
(See Table 7.4.) Four of the above funds have been launched on the Irish
Stock Exchange. As one country fund manager explained, these are largely
'nominal listings' – typically a demand of subscribers to the funds is that they
have sufficient liquidity through listing, although their shares trade relatively little – on a bourse that is cheaper and quicker to join than other options,
such as the Luxembourg stock exchange. Subscribers to these funds tend to
be major institutional clients, such as pension fund and other portfolio investors, looking to gain some form of long-term exposure to the Vietnam
market; they are generally not appropriate for short-term speculators or private
investors.

   As mentioned above, Vietnam still lacks a bourse, and so the managers of
these country funds have not been able to acquire shares in Vietnamese listed
enterprise, as is most common with most country funds. Instead, the fund
managers have had to assess literally hundreds of proposed venture capital
projects, in a bid to find proposals that the funds would wish to commit capital towards. But the work does not stop there. Proposals commonly have to
be adjusted, due diligence and feasibility studies must be enacted, an investment licence granted, and then the project can be established. This can take a
considerable amount of time and energy on the part of the project's investors,
including the country fund managers. Whilst the first funds might have hoped
simply to take positions on agreed foreign direct investment projects, they are
all now examining commitments to wholly local enterprises, and one fund
has also pledged to have its staff closely involved in the day-to-day management of commitments. To that extent, the fund managers have to work hard
for their fee. Always concious of having an exit route, the fund managers are
typically looking for their commitments to gain listing on a domestic or foreign bourse, as and when that avenue becomes feasible. Offshore holding

Table 7.3 Vietnam's country funds

Name	Launch	Market capitalisation (at March 1995)	Fund manager (and main offices, at March 1995)	Stock exchange listing	Maturity
Vietnam Fund	Sept. 1991	US$75.0m*	Vietnam Fund Management (Hong Kong, Hanoi, Ho Chi Minh City)	Dublin	10 years
Beta Viet Nam Fund	Oct. 1993	US$61.8m	Indochina Asset Management (London, Hanoi, Ho Chi Minh City)	Dublin	None
Vietnam Frontier Fund	June 1994	US$27.5m	Finansa Thai (Bangkok)	Dublin	10 years
Vietnam Opportunities Fund	Sept. 1994	US$83.0m	Templeton Investment Man. (Ho Chi Minh City, Singapore)	New York	None
Other funds:					
The Vietnam Investment Fund	May 1992	US$90.0m*	KV Management (Keppel Group) (Singapore, Hanoi)	Privately placed	20 years
Beta Mekong Fund**	Nov.1994	US$24.8m	Indochina Asset Management (London, Bangkok, Hanoi, Ho Chi Minh City)	Dublin	None

* After second tranche.
** According to the investment objectives of the fund, 30–50% of this fund's portfolio will be targeted on Vietnam.

Sources: Various.

companies or pre-listed 'paper companies' are being sought in order to prepare this exit route.

Table 7.4   Vietnam's listed country funds compared (as at 2 December 1994)

Country	Cumulative market capitalisation (approx. US$ millions)	Number of funds
India	2592	9
Thailand	1765	12
Mexico	1536	6
Chile	1126	4
Brazil	794	4
Philippines	430	4
Malaysia	388	4
Vietnam	*283*	*4*
Pakistan	155	2
Turkey	120	3
Argentina	105	2
Sri Lanka	67	2
Venezuela	41	1
Peru	38	1
Bangladesh	26	1
Australasia	1098	5
Eastern Europe	664	10
Sub-Saharan Africa	408	4

Source: Figures taken from *Baring Securities Closed-End Funds List*.

VIETNAM'S COUNTRY FUNDS: PAPER INVESTMENTS

It remains early days for the country funds in Vietnam. Only one fund has yet to invest more than half its total capital in projects within Vietnam. And only the eldest fund anticipated its first commitment to reach break-even point at the end of 1994. In this 'start-up' period, in order to avoid holding large quantities of cash, the fund managers have adopted various strategies to best exercise their money whilst awaiting an 'in country' commitment. One option has been to buy Vietnamese – and in some cases, other countries – debt paper. (The funds have varying degrees of flexibility as to what they can do in this regard, details of which are covered in the original placing memoranda.) One fund enjoyed marked success in acquiring Vietnamese debt paper shortly before the US embargo was lifted, which then shot up in value on news of the

President's decision. The two funds operating at that time – February 1994 – also enjoyed marked surges in their share values on the news of the embargo being lifted, although this has since been rectified to more realistic prices.

A second option, just beginning to emerge, are the various forms of bonds being issued in Vietnam; treasury bills, certificates of deposit, industry sector-related bonds, corporate bonds, and municipal bonds. Whilst it currently remains unclear to what exact extent offshore investment funds can participate in the bond market in Vietnam, the opportunity to acquire dong-denominated bonds/bills, offering 21 per cent annual interest rates, does seem attractive. (Vietnam's inflation rate was 5.3 per cent in 1993 and 14 per cent in 1994. After a trend that had seen the dong appreciate markedly against the US dollar, the dong is now being allowed to depreciate against the US dollar (and gold), to a current level of approximately 11,000 = US$1.)

A third option has been to buy shares in overseas listed companies which enjoy sizable investment exposure to Vietnam. SG Warburg's 'Indochina Warrants' – a call option on a basket of stocks of seven companies with supposedly high Vietnam-orientation – are based on this predication of Vietnam exposure 'by proxy'. (See Table 7.5.) However, relatively few overseas listed companies of any scale have significant enough exposure to the fledgling Vietnam market for their investments to impact significantly on their bottom line, and this ploy remains a rather diluted way to gain Vietnam exposure. Luks Industrial of Hong Kong, probably the most Vietnam-oriented listed company of all, only derived 7 per cent of its 1993 turnover from Vietnam operations.[5]

There are a few exceptions to this broad rule, however. Iddison Group Vietnam, which listed on the Wellington bourse in October 1994 – offering 7.5 million ordinary shares at NZ 75c (approximately US$4m) – is possibly the only overseas listed company that is wholly Vietnam-oriented. Crucially, this company still lacks an approved investment in Vietnam, but has plans to invest in poultry, gold mining and pleasure park projects. At least one of the listed Vietnam country funds took a major stake in Iddison Group Vietnam. One of the country funds also has ambitions for two of its projects to gain listings on the Sydney and Toronto bourses. Over time, we are likely to see more of these overseas listed hybrids emerge.

VIETNAM'S COUNTRY FUNDS: DIRECT INVESTMENTS

Arguably, however, 'in country' investments by the country funds, in tangible FDI projects inside Vietnam, are of more relevance to this paper. For most of the funds, the acquisition of secondary debt paper and other such portfolio holdings are simply short-term vehicles to exercise money that would otherwise remain as cash. (Subscribers in the funds do not surrender a percentage of the funds' NAV – ranging from 1.5 per cent and 2.5 per cent in the case of the Vietnam funds – to the fund managers in fees in order that the assets of the funds remain in bank accounts.) To a greater extent, the investment mandates of all the funds state that the aim is to enjoy long-term capital growth through investment in Vietnamese companies.

Table 7.5   Warburg's Indochina Warrants

Company (and activities in Vietnam)	Weighting (percentage)	Stock exchange listing
Asia Pacific Breweries (Brewing)	5	Singapore
Fraser & Neave (Brewing, and bottling soft drinks and beer)	25	Singapore
Liang Court Holdings (Property developments)	15	Singapore
Accor Asia Pacific (Hotels)	15	Sydney
Meiwa Trading (Mitsubishi) (Trading and car assembly)	5	Tokyo
Luks Industrial (Property, TV assembly, plywood, cement)	20	Hong Kong
South Sea Development (Ming Pao) (Property)	15	Hong Kong

Note: The Indochina Warrants were issued in December 1993, on the Luxembourg bourse, and will expire in December 1995.

Source: S G Warburg Securities.

Not all the country fund managers are willing to disclose their full portfolio of investments in Vietnam, which makes a comprehensive list of their commitments almost impossible to collate. However, Table 7.6 intends to give a profile of the major commitments which are thought to have taken place. (Most, although not all, of these investments have been confirmed by the respective fund managers. The authors have chosen not to identify each investment with the relevant country fund.) As Table 7.6 shows, the size of individual commitments varies widely, from less than US$0.5m to over US$10m. Most funds have strict investment restrictions preventing the managers from investing more than a fixed percentage of total assets in any one commitment. The locations of the investments also range across the country, taking in Hanoi, Ho Chi Minh City, Haiphong, Danang, Nha Trang, Hue and Dalat. The predominance of the first two locations is attributable to their positions as the state capital and business centre respectively. A sectoral breakdown of the commitments shows that property development is a major element in four of the sixteen listed investments, with consumer products, banking, garments-related operations, and (gold) mining also registering at least twice. This is not surprising, given that most fund managers partly try to minimise risk by ensuring a wide sectoral spread to their portfolios, in a bid to reduce the damaging effects of a specific industry encountering adverse events. The forms of investment are also diverse; taking a stake in planned investment projects in Vietnam dominates, but there are also debt for equity deals, overseas share issues, and domestic shareholdings being attempted. This diversity of (i) commitment scale, (ii) sectoral breakdown, (iii) host locations, and (iv) the precise investment form adopted, probably reflects the flexible approach that Vietnam demands of its country fund managers in order to enact investments, and yet also suggests that room still exists for more country funds to tap this emerging market. But as a caveat to this latter point, it should be remembered that enacting investments in Vietnam – and managing country funds pertaining to Vietnam – is far from an easy task.

The empirical evidence from this brief survey of the Vietnam country funds does appear to support Porter's thesis – and echoed by Diwan, Errunza and Senbet's (1994) study of NYSE-listed country funds – that subscribers to the funds are likely to gain a widely diversified exposure to the market. However, the Vietnam funds do not conform to the important liquidity factor; they remain broadly illiquid. Interestingly, as of late 1994, all the funds' shares were trading at premiums, ranging from around 4.5 per cent to just over 40 per cent although this may stem more from international investor sentiment towards Vietnam as a whole, than from the intrinsic, comparative merits of the funds themselves.

HURDLES TO INVESTMENT

Finally, what are the hurdles preventing the country funds enacting greater commitment activity in Vietnam? These largely stem from the nature of the country funds themselves, and the business environment in which they are attempting to work. As noted above, the Vietnam funds are not typical of the offshore country funds that most investors are familiar with, yet to a greater or lesser extent they must still conform to the same performance characteristics – and stock exchange rulings – demanded by their contemporaries. Subscribers' desire to see dividends (at least eventually) and capital growth

Table 7.6 Major commitments by Vietnam's country funds (as of November 1994)

Project	Capital invested	Date of commitment	Location	Notes
Agravina	US$0.49m	Dec. 1992	Dalat	Hong Kong agricultural project.
Apex Dalat – knitwear factory	US$1m	Late 1993	Dalat	54% stake in a joint venture.
Barlile Corp.	US$1.3m	1994	Australian holding company	Plans for dairy farming and brewing in Vietnam.
La Compagnie Générale des Zincs	US$2m	July 1994	Nha Trang	Coastal resort development.
Dragon Properties Asia	US$10.1m	June 1994	Hanoi	US$40m Singapore office and shopping development, close to the city's central Hoan Kiem lake. The local partner is Hanoi Trading Co (30%).
Huy Hoang Co. – garments and construction	US$3.91m	Dec. 1993	Ho Chi Minh City	A convertible loan to result in a 25% equity stake in the firm, when the law permits.
Iddison Group Vietnam	N.A.	October 1994	Hanoi	Listed on Wellington bourse. Various planned investments.
Indochina Goldfields	US$5m	1994	Gold mining projects throughout Indochina	Looking to list in Toronto in 1995. Has a 20% stake.

Johnson Suisse Asia	US$2m	August 1994	Hanoi	Consumer products.
Luksvaxi – cement plant	US$7m	1994	Hue	A joint venture cement plant between Hong Kong-listed Luks Industrial and a local firm.
Maritime Bank*	US$1.2m US$2.35m	1994 Jan. 1994	Haiphong Haiphong	Equity stake in local joint stock bank. As above.
Northbridge Parkview	US$10.3m	1994	Hanoi and HCM City	Residential property developments.
Viet Hoa Construction Co.	US$3.5m	Nov. 1994	Ho Chi Minh City	Property development.
Vinataxi	N.A.	N.A.	Ho Chi Minh City	Taxi company.
Vinathai – consumer products	US$3.5m	1994	Hanoi	Thai–Vietnamese joint venture.
Others:				
Bank of Tokyo 1985 restructured loans to Vietcombank	N.A.	N.A.	N.A.	
Moroccan, Venezuelan debt paper	N.A.	N.A.	N.A.	
South African bonds	N.A.	N.A.	N.A.	
Various Euro-commercial paper	N.A.	N.A.	N.A.	

*Two of the country funds have plans to invest in this Vietnamese bank.

(at a relatively speedy pace if the fund is closed-ended), without undue risk, creates demands not wholly compatible with the salient realities of investing in Vietnam, which remains a challenging business environment. The pace of decision-making in Vietnam, such as taking an investment proposal through from first initiative to enactment and profitable returns, can be lengthy. Even if the country fund managers felt able to 'push along' a project to which they have committed, most do not have the resources or volition to become involved in the day-to-day management of investments. Working in one distinct environment, yet reporting to another, must be a severe constraint on the fund managers' room for manoeuvre. Whilst the fund managers themselves would probably point to myriad other dilemmas confronting them, including finding local expertise and all the other 'in country hurdles' facing direct investors in Vietnam, this dichotomy between the two environments which they inhabit is one relatively unique to them, and to country fund managers attempting the same activities in other newly emerging markets.

CONCLUSION: LOOKING TO THE FUTURE

Looking to the future, the introduction of more Vietnam country funds is anticipated, as are more regional or sub-regional investment funds with significant exposure to Vietnam. Of course, should Vietnam establish a securities market – officially set to commence in late 1995 – then this development is likely to act as a major fillip for the existing country funds, and greatly increase the chances of further Vietnam country funds coming to the market. Not least, a domestic securities market would do much to improve the liquidity of investments by the country funds. Whilst some observers have warned that Vietnam may become over-funded, the fund managers assert there is still plenty of room, and that they rarely bump into each other. Given the continued need for capital in Vietnam, the arrival of more country funds is unlikely to lead to overcrowding, at least in the short term. As the business environment in Vietnam matures this should permit speedier and more diverse forms of investment activity open to the funds, and as the first commitments start to generate revenues, the role of the country funds and their investment portfolios are likely to be of increasing relevance in Vietnam's economic development. And regardless of the salient realities on the ground, as long as the international thirst for Vietnam exposure continues, funds are likely to be launched in order to tap into this market. These future developments should also bring greater liquidity in the shares of the funds themselves. In the words of one of Vietnam's most respected financial commentators, [country fund] investment managers have been extremely hard put to find suitable vehicles for their funds and as a result, only a small percentage of available capital has actually been invested and that in the extremely illiquid form of joint venture participations...Clearly the attraction is not the present environment but the future prospects.[6]

In addition to their role as conduits through which advanced institutional investors can gain exposure to Vietnam's high potential economic growth, the country funds play an equally important role bringing scarce capital to an emerging market in need of substantial sums of money. For those reasons alone, the Vietnam country funds should be welcomed as playing an important role in the development of the Vietnamese economy.

Notes

1. Also see Michael T. Porter, 'Closed-End Emerging Country Funds Review', in Park and van Agtmael (1993) pp. 459–74.
2. Ibid, p. 470.
3. Diwan, Errunza and Senbet (1994), p. 212.
4. See Price Waterhouse (1994).
5. Mees Pierson Securities (Asia) Limited (September 1994) *Luks Industrial Co Ltd – "Luks Great!" – Buy*, p. 3.
6. John Brinsden, Standard Chartered Bank's resident director for Indochina and Myanmar. Taken from the text of a speech entitled 'Latest Developments in Banking and Financial Services', given in Ho Chi Minh City on 25 November 1994.

References

Diwan, Ishac, Vihang R. Errunza and Lemma W. Senbet (1994) 'Diversification Benefits of Country Funds', in Michael Howell (ed.), *Investing in Emerging Markets* (Euromoney Publications) pp. 199–214.
Freeman, Nick and Sridhar Venki (1994) *Vietnam Fund Review – The Next Jewel in Asia's Crown?* (Baring Securities Limited, Country Fund Research) November.
Park, Keith K.H. and Antoine W. van Agtmael (eds) (1993) *The World's Emerging Stock Markets* (Heinemann Asia Business Reference).
Price Waterhouse (July 1994) *Vietnam: A Guide for the Foreign Investor*, 3rd edn (Price Waterhouse, Hong Kong).

8 European Direct Investment in Japan*

with Hafiz Mirza and John R. Sparkes

INTRODUCTION

In 1983–4 the authors, sponsored by The Japan Foundation, undertook a study of European affiliated companies operating in Japan.[1] The present study, also funded by the Japan Foundation, revisits most of the companies interviewed ten years ago (all but one of which are still in Japan) and includes a small number of additional companies subsequently added to the sample. The broad objective of the study was to examine the development of European direct investment over the last decade by tracking specific companies. This paper reports some of the findings.

BROAD CHARACTERISTICS OF THE SAMPLE

The twenty-one parent firms are based throughout the European Union and the former EFTA[2] and, as Figure 8.1 shows, are involved in a wide range of industries. Care was taken, in the initial study, to ensure wide coverage by source country and the size of parent firm, but the industries covered were constrained by the nature of the products and technologies most able to penetrate the Japanese market. This does not seem to have changed too much in the intervening period. For example, Ministry of Finance (MOF) figures show that 48 per cent of cumulative foreign direct investment (by value) in Japanese industry[3] was in 'chemicals', whereas the chemicals, pharmaceutical and biotechnology *firms* in our sample constitute 57 per cent of the total. The respective figures for 'machinery', the next biggest category, are 23 per cent and 19 per cent; and the only major manufacturing industries absent from our sample are petroleum and food products.

The sales of the sample firms in Japan (inclusive of local production and imports) vary from less than ¥5 billion (about a quarter of the companies) to

*Originally published in *Management International Review*, vol. 35, special issue 1.1, 1995, pp. 21–34.

nearly ¥200 billion, partly reflecting the relative size of the parent firms in Europe. A mode of between ¥21 to ¥50 billion ($200 million to $500 million) is not insubstantial and, as a result, most European firms in our sample employ at least 100 Japanese workers and, in four cases, over 1,000.[4] In most cases, however, the share of global business represented by Japan in each company's production-sales network is quite small (1–5 per cent for about half the sample); and in only 5 cases is this share over 10 per cent.

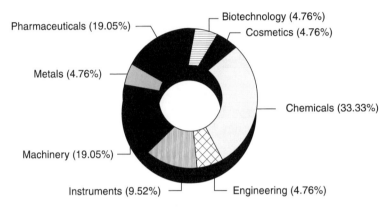

Figure 8.1   Industry of parent firms

THE EVOLUTION OF EUROPEAN MANUFACTURING DIRECT INVESTORS IN JAPAN

Most European companies have expanded employment, trade and investment in Japan since 1985, sometimes quite substantially (Figure 8.2). Arguably, this merely reflects the growth of the Japanese economy and the growing familiarity of these firms with the host environment. More interesting is the fact that much of this expansion has apparently resulted from 'subsequent entries' (new affiliates, etc.) into the Japanese market.[5] All firms were present in Japan, in one form or another, by the late 1970s; while most subsequent entries occured in the late 1980s and early 1990s (12 cases out of 20). This has resulted in a number of alterations to the dimensions and structure of European operations in Japan, especially in terms of organisational form and ownership.

Two-thirds of sample firms have changed their organisational form, about one half since our first survey in 1983–5. At entry,[6] the predominant organisational form used by most European parents (62 per cent of firms) to pensetrate the Japanese market was imports through a third party (including *sogo shosha* and *senmon shosha*), followed by the establishment of a sales sub-sidiary (19 per cent).

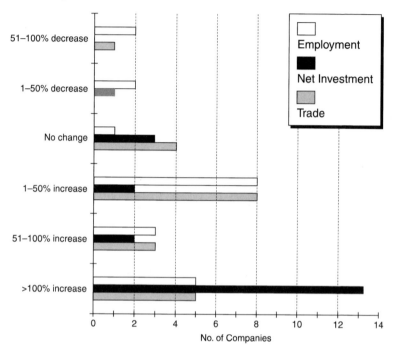

Figure 8.2 Change in parent's Japanese trade, investment, and employment since 1985

About 14 per cent of firms licensed local companies to manufacture their products; and a tiny 5 per cent manufactured locally. By and large this is at great variance with the normal post-war practice in entering a new market. In 1983–4, as our previous study showed, most of these companies were manu-facturing locally either directly or indirectly (for example by using the facil-ities of a partner). Figure 8.3 illustrates how the activities of these companies have continued to evolve. Nearly all companies continue to manufacture in Japan; 14 per cent indirectly through licensing or subcontracting. The move-ment has been in both directions and a few companies have limited their di-rect manufacturing operations in Japan for cost reasons (see next section). Only one company has ceased entirely to manufacture in Japan and has moved its production base to elsewhere in Asia. Most importantly, 71 per cent of European investors now conduct R&D in Japan as a 'main-line' activ-ity, though this is sometimes secondary to other activities. When we began this project, R&D was a minor element of most affiliates' operations.

The evolution of European activities in Japan is perhaps more vividly illustrated in terms of changes in the ownership of local affiliates. The primary ownership mode[7] at entry[8, 9] (and in 1983–4) was the 50:50 joint venture (48 per cent of firms), followed equally by minority and majority owned joint ventures (14 per cent each). Only 24 per cent of firms established a wholly-owned subsidiary at inception. The situation by 1993 was quite different. Joint ventures are primarily employed by only a third of firms, while over a third of firms have shifted to wholly-owned subsidiaries. Most of the remaining companies have a 'holding company' structure in which a subsidiary plays an intermediate role between the European parent and other affiliates in Japan. To all intents and purposes, the holding company[10] can be treated as the 'parent' of Japanese affiliates and is the strategic nucleus of each European firm's operations in the country. Sometimes the holding company is essential for rationalising a large number of historically established collaborative arrangements (especially joint ventures) between a European major and its partners in Japan.[11]

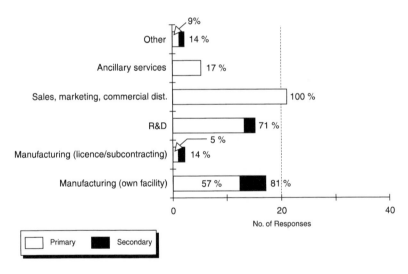

Figure 8.3 Main activities performed in Japan (per cent of companies performing activity)

THE RESTRUCTURING OF EUROPEAN OPERATIONS IN JAPAN: A PRELIMINARY ANALYSIS

The previous section has shown how European activities in Japan have evolved, restructured and been reorganised since 1983–4 (and before). A number of factors are involved in this process, of which the following are the most significant.

Evolving Strategies in Japan qua Japan

Japan has always been regarded as a difficult market to penetrate, not least because foreign companies are attempting to cross the threshold in the face of fierce local competition and a variety of other barriers. Japan is not unique in this respect, but perhaps the difficulties of entry and local operation are greater than in most other host countries. As Figures 8.4 and 8.5 show, there are still a number of inhibitors to trade with, and investment in, Japan which tend to compel overseas firms to seek a local presence in partnership with Japanese concerns. For example, 'controlled distribution systems' require an insider strategy, while 'high costs of doing business' and 'staffing problems' mean that joint ventures or other forms of collaboration with Japanese firms (which possess local knowledge and experience) may be useful. Figures 8.6

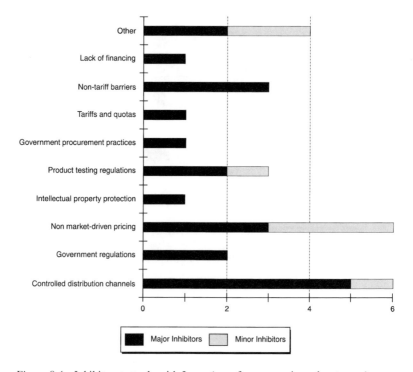

Figure 8.4 Inhibitors to trade with Japan (no. of responses in each category)

to 8.8 also underline some of the specificities which determine the particular initial stance taken by foreign investors in Japan. Consumer resistance[12] to foreign goods means that the main customers for the products of our sample firms were (and are) Japanese companies, although the lucrative local pharmaceuticals market has meant that European drugs companies are well represented and therefore 'doctors, hospitals and clinics' are major customers (Figure 8.6).[13] Figure 8.7 shows how nearly all companies have to adapt their products to Japanese conditions in terms of range, quality, marketing, prices and distribution. The net result of all this is that objectives in Japan are frequently different from those of our sample firms elsewhere (although opinion is evenly divided, as indicated in Figure 8.8). Most significantly there is a strong emphasis on market share and market leadership, implying a growth orientated, insider strategy.[14] The emphasis on sales may also link in with this tendency.

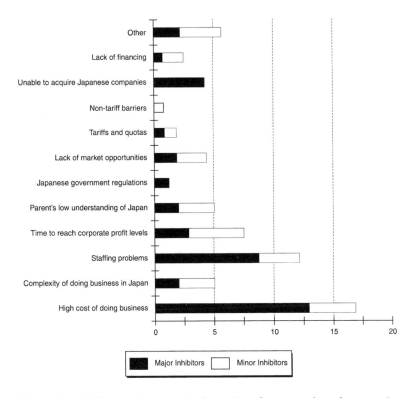

Figure 8.5   Inhibitors to investment in Japan (no. of responses in each category)

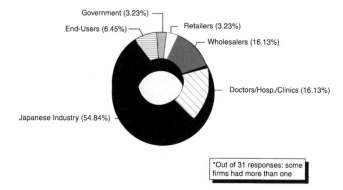

Figure 8.6   Main customers in Japan (per cent of responses*)

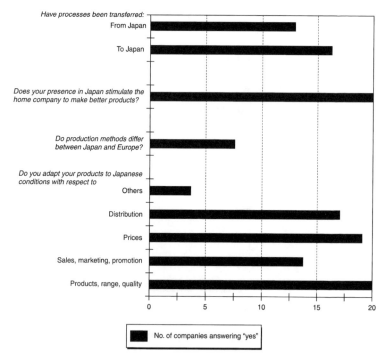

Figure 8.7   Adaptation of products and processes

The implication of the above discussion is that, quite apart from government legislation, European investors deem collaborative entry into Japan (e.g. joint ventures and non-direct manufacturing) as a valuable vehicle

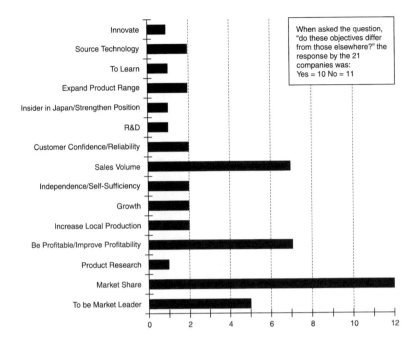

When asked the question, "do these objectives differ from those elsewhere?" the response by the 21 companies was:
Yes = 10 No = 11

Figure 8.8   Objectives in Japan (no. of responses in each category)

which reduces risk and financial burdens. This was certainly the position of most companies when we interviewed them in 1983–4. Since then, as they become recognised as insiders and more familiar with the local market and business environment, they have altered their structure to make it more suitable for their long-term strategy in Japan. Normally this has involved asserting control by increasing the European shareholding to over 50 per cent, often to the 100 per cent level. Sometimes this evolution was anticipated in the original contract between the European and Japanese partners and has proceeded amicably, but sometimes the separation (where it has occurred) has been fractious. In our view this process of initial entry and later restructuring to achieve a final preferred outcome in terms of market servicing strategy can be termed '*double entry*' and it may be useful, theoretically, to discuss such strategies in terms of 'first order' and 'second order' entry. Japan may be one of a small number of countries where such a process is the norm. Other examples may be South Korea and Turkey. Locally based holding companies may also be the hallmark of such *double entry* strategies, but it is too early to reach such a conclusion.

Evolving Strategies in an Evolving Japan

The foregoing analysis assumes that Japan is not changing – and certainly there are particular features, usually 'non-tariff barriers' such as a highly competitive business environment, cultural preferences and personnel practices, which change only in the long term[15] – but of course changes do occur and these clearly affect the strategies of foreign firms in Japan.

Most significantly, the climate for foreign investment is now deemed favourable with few restrictions on direct investment in most sectors; 76 per cent of companies believe this to be an improvement over a decade earlier (Figure 8.9) and as many as 43 per cent of companies considered this improvement to be significant. Also of interest is the fact that 62 per cent of firms believe that the investment climate will continue to improve, with only 5 per cent expecting some deterioration. The conviction that the investment climate is improving is being acted upon, 72 per cent of companies having definite plans to invest in Japan over the next five years or 'seeking opportunities'. Most of the remainder also intend to invest if the opportunity arises.

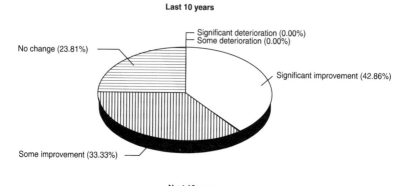

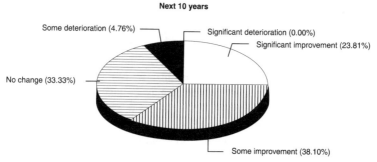

Figure 8.9 The degree to which the investment climate has changed in Japan (per cent of companies)

There are several reasons why the investment climate has changed. Government and bureaucracy restrictions on inward foreign direct investment have reduced since the early 1980s (partly because of external pressures) to the extent that there is some high profile encouragement. 1992 even saw the enactment of a special law to promote foreign direct investment in Japan and moves to establish a 'Foreign Affiliate Business Support Company'.[16] This support reduces the need to depend on a local company. The recruitment difficulties identified in our earlier study have diminished markedly[17] which makes reliance on local partners less compelling; nevertheless their advice may still be welcome to ensure stable industrial relations. Greater Japanese internationalisation and familiarity with foreign business methods has also resulted in changes in practices in Japan itself. One example is the increased acceptance of Mergers and Acquisitions (M&A) in Japan: whereas a decade ago such corporate activity would have been regarded as taboo, today it is merely frowned upon. In 1992 there were 43 acquisitions of Japanese ventures by foreign companies, a threefold increase on 1989.[18] The greater use of M&A in Japan opens up new options for new investors and this may change the pattern of initial entry. Existing investors which are already recognised as insiders are in an excellent position to further their ambitions in Japan and, certainly, some of our sample firms can be described as 'gearing up for action'.

It should also be mentioned that probably the most fundamental factor underlying the considerable change in the investment climate in Japan is the state of the economy: two recessions have hit the country since 1984 and this has resulted in major restructuring on both the commercial front and in government, business and public attitudes towards foreign companies.[19] Foreign technology is essential for the economy's reorganisation and overseas firms are valuable providers of investment and jobs, especially since Japanese companies are increasingly being forced overseas because of the relentless appreciation of the yen. This pressure is also being especially felt by those of our sample firms which export some or all of their Japanese output. One company has moved its entire production facilities to another location in East Asia and now imports into Japan. Indeed, since Japan was formerly its principal bastion in the Asia-Pacific, such a drastic reorientation has meant that, in effect, this firm has had to 're-enter' Japan: first, because the new affiliates in Japan have drastically different (import-related) duties; and secondly, because the large redundancies in Japan necessary for this restructuring has cost the firm dear in terms of its 'insider' credibility.[20] On the other hand, companies which import inputs for use in their Japanese plants have benefited from the yen appreciation; and the fact that European goods are often now regarded as being 'cheap' also helps new entrants in the consumer good sector, particularly in the light of rapidly changing consumer attitudes toward the purchase of overseas products.

World Trends

One has also to examine external dynamics to understand changes in European strategies in Japan. One major factor is the 'regionalisation' of the world economy which requires companies to reassess their position in each of these new 'blocs'. Another is the dramatic rise of East Asia (especially the Newly Industrialising Economies, China and ASEAN) as manufacturing powerhouses on Japan's doorstep. This expansion is partly linked to the yen appreciation, as Japanese companies have sought cheap production bases for (sub-contracted) imports into Japan and exports further afield.[21] Other foreign companies, mainly from the West and the overseas Chinese business communities, are clearly also investing large amounts into East Asia and thinking twice about their operations in Japan (if any). One company in our original sample which *declined to be reinterviewed* may have refused because of a large-scale pull-out from Japan.

European Trends

Although a subset of world trends, these clearly affect our sample companies very directly. Again regionalisation, manifest in the establishment of the Single European Market, the European Economic Area etc., is a key factor, especially because of the restructuring needed to fend off competition from European and non-European firms.[22] Suffice it to say that the impact of restructuring in the parent firm on the Japanese affiliates can be tremendous. In one case a firm we had interviewed in 1984 had been taken over by a competitor. As a result, the activities of the Japanese affiliates of both formerly separate parent companies had to be combined with considerable influence on the local organisational structure. In another case, one of our sample firms had merged with another company in Europe, but at a later stage de-merged. The net result of this process, however, was the loss of virtually all Japanese activities by our sample firm. The original firm had therefore effectively to re-enter Japan, but with the advantage of retaining some of its employees (and experience-base) from its previous affiliates in Japan. In a country where business is conducted on the basis of relationships this advantage is not inconsiderable.

CONCLUDING REMARKS

This paper has briefly examined the changing strategies of European Manufacturing Direct Investors in Japan over the last ten years. Although the sample is small, tracking the changing characteristics of existing companies in Japan offers valuable insights into how to service a distinctive and complex market. Some explanations for the evolution of European strategies have been offered, but further analysis is required before definitive conclusions can be drawn. There also seems to be some scope for using the experience of European investors in Japan to refine international business theory so that 'double entry' strategies in Japan and elsewhere can be understood and predicted.

Notes

1. Buckley *et al.* (1984).
2. The country breakdown is, 2 firms from Belgium, 4 from Denmark, 3 from France, 3 from Germany, 1 from Italy, 2 from Netherlands, 1 from Sweden, 2 from Switzerland and 3 from the United Kingdom.
3. Based upon figures released by the MOF on 5 June 1992 and including all investments to 31 March 1992.
4. Of course these employees are usually spread over a number of affiliates or subsidiaries owned by the parent firm in Japan.
5. The MOF figures mentioned earlier support this view since reinvestments by all foreign companies in Japan were only about 10–12 per cent of quite small total FDI inflows into the country.
6. In some cases this was pre-war.
7. Most parent firms, of course, have more than one affiliate in Japan, but for ease of analysis the discussion focuses on *either* the mode of ownership most commonly employed by each firm *or* the mode of the dominant affiliate.
8. 'Entry' in this context differs from that employed above. In the earlier discussion 'entry' meant the year when a company first began to sell its products in Japan. 'Entry' with reference to *ownership* relates to when a company first set up a *direct* presence in Japan.
9. It must be borne in mind that prior to 1980 most FDI into Japan was highly restricted and wholly-owned ventures were seldom permitted.
10. Usually the holding company owns the (European) shares of other affiliates.
11. Within this rationalisation there is also a tendency to move from joint ventures to wholly-owned subsidiaries: the holding company plays a key role in arranging this.
12. This is changing, of course (see below in this section), and the customer profile reported in Figure 8.6 may well be less typical for newer entrants.
13. The role of doctors in the drug industry, for example, is unusual in Japan. See Mirza *et al.* (1993).

14.   For more on this see Mirza *et al.* (1989).
15.   See Mirza *et al.* (1989), ibid.
16.   See International Business Affairs Division (1992).
17.   See also British Chamber of Commerce (1991).
18.   Source: KPMG Peat Marwick, Tokyo Office.
19.   See Mirza *et al.* (1990).
20.   The picture is also complicated by restructuring in the European parent company.
21.   See Tejima (1993).
22.   See Buckley *et al.* (1991).

References

British Chamber of Commerce in Japan (1991) *Human Resources in Japan: Strategies for Success* (Tokyo).

Buckley, Peter J., Hafiz Mirza and John R. Sparkes (1984) *European Affiliates in Japan: A Comparative Study of Corporate Strategy and Planning by European Firms and Their Affiliates in Japan* (Tokyo: The Japan Foundation).

Buckley, Peter J., Hafiz Mirza and Kate Prescott (1991) 'The Single European Market and Pacific Futures', *The Pacific Review*, 4, 4.

International Business Affairs Division, MITI (1992) *Measures for Promoting Foreign Direct Investment in Japan* (Tokyo).

Mirza, Hafiz, Peter J. Buckley and John R. Sparkes (1989) 'Swimming Against the Tide? The Strategy of European Manufacturing Investors in Japan', in Kazuo Shibagaki, Malcolm Trevor and Tetsuo Abo (eds), *Japanese and European Management: Their International Adaptability* (Tokyo: University of Tokyo Press).

Mirza, Hafiz, Peter J. Buckley and John R. Sparkes (1990) 'New Multinationals for Old? The Political Economy of Japanese Internationalisation', *Japan Forum*, 2 (2).

Mirza, Hafiz, Peter J. Buckley, Christopher L. Pass and John R. Sparkes (1993) 'Government–Industry Relations in Japan: Some Contrasts with the UK and Europe', *International Business Review*, 2 (1).

Tejima, Shigeki (1993) 'Future Prospects of Japanese FDI in the 1990s', paper presented at the workshop on 'OECD Foreign Direct Investment Relations with Dynamic Non-Member Countries', Paris, 12–13 July.

9 Contrasting Perspectives on American and European Direct Investment in Japan*

with Hafiz Mirza and John R. Sparkes

INTRODUCTION

CONCERN in the United States, and increasingly in Europe, with regard to barriers facing foreign companies in Japan has heightened interest in the trade and investment climate for foreign firms seeking greater access to the Japanese market.

The trend of foreign investment between the United States and Japan has been towards greater imbalance. Between 1980 and 1990, US direct investment in Japan rose by 210 per cent from a minimal level in 1980 to $19.3 billion in 1990. This pales in comparison with Japanese investment in the United States, which grew steadily from $4.2 billion in 1980 to $70 billion in 1990. In comparison, Japanese investment in Europe over the decade increased from $4.7 billion to $45 billion, exceeding the flow of European investment into Japan by a ratio of 25:1 (EBC, 1992).

The American Chamber of Commerce in Japan (ACCJ) has periodically studied the issue of foreign investment in Japan. The most recent study, 'Trade and Investment in Japan: The Current Environment' (prepared by A.T. Kearney, June 1991), was undertaken at a time when the United States and Japan had completed a series of talks, the Structural Impediments Initiative, on the basic structures of their respective economies and had recorded the first attempts towards implementing the negotiated agreements.

The basis of the ACCJ study was a postal questionnaire sent to 1,200 American companies in both the United States and Japan to which 340 responses were received, 293 from Japan and forty-seven from the United States. In addition, thirty-five interviews were conducted with senior managers of US companies in Japan perceived as competing successfully there; and forty-nine interviews in the United States, principally with companies perceived as unsuccessful.

---

*Originally published in *Business Economics*, vol. 31, no. 1, January 1996, pp. 42–8.

The authors have similarly been studying European foreign direct investment in Japan since 1983. The first study, 'European Affiliates in Japan', was submitted to the sponsors, The Japan Foundation, in December 1984. The most recent report, 'The Development of European Direct Investment in Japan', was submitted to the Japan Foundation in December 1993.

Our study differs in many respects from the ACCJ study, particularly in that it has concentrated on the progress of the same cohort of companies over the entire period. The sample is significantly smaller than that of the ACCJ study, comprising twenty-one companies drawn from nine European countries. All have been surveyed through a structured, interview-based questionnaire, and senior management of *both* the European parent company and the Japanese affiliated company or companies has been interviewed.

The scope of the ACCJ study included both manufacturing and service sectors of the economy, whereas our study has concentrated entirely on the manufacturing sector (although some of these perform a service function as part of their activity in Japan). In consequence, the companies in our study sell mainly to industrial consumers rather than directly to final consumers.

Of the total number of survey responses received in the ACCJ study, 205 were from companies identified as manufacturing. Of these, the largest single grouping was chemicals and allied products, followed by electrical and electronic equipment, pharmaceuticals and industrial and commercial machinery. Three of these four categories are strongly represented in our sample, electronic equipment less so.

In tracing the development of European direct investment in Japan through our longitudinal study, the decision was made, in agreement with the American Chamber of Commerce in Japan, to replicate some of the questions used in the American survey in interviewing European companies and their Japanese affiliates. This paper uses the responses to some of those questions to contrast perceptions in the United States and Europe regarding investment barriers for foreign firms in the Japanese market.

CONCEPTUAL BACKGROUND

The theory of foreign direct investment (FDI) tells us that foreign direct investment will take place when there are net advantages of internalising markets between activities located in different national economies (Buckley and Casson, 1976; Buckley, 1988). This combination of internalisation factors and location factors gives a framework for analysis of the pattern, direction and timing of foreign direct investment (Buckley and Casson, 1981). The normal motives behind FDI can be collapsed into three: market-related reasons, cost-related reasons and attempts to control raw materials. This general framework needs modification in order to allow for special factors, including industry specific and host country specific conditions (Buckley, 1988). In the case of Japan, these are pronounced.

Japan is the weakest link in the pattern of investment between the 'Triad' (Europe, North America and Japan). The paucity of inward investment into Japan contrasts with its strong performance as an outward investor. Several key elements explain this imbalance.

First, if we examine the motives behind FDI into Japan, several special features emerge. The third motive – the search for control of raw materials and basic inputs – does not apply to a resource-poor country like Japan. The second motive – the attempt to reduce costs by FDI – again has no application because Japan is a high-cost country. In particular, labour costs are high and land costs make cost reduction impossible across the range of activities. Location factors therefore disfavour Japan. Indeed the two motives of cost reduction and the search for raw materials explain Japan's *outward* investment to other areas of the world, notably to other Asian economies.

This leaves us with one key motive for FDI in Japan – to achieve market access. Japan is a high income country with a large domestic market. On the face of it, FDI should be attracted to such a location. Here however, it is not *location* factors that disfavour Japan as a target for FDI, it is *internalisation* factors. The costs facing foreign firms in internalising markets (for intermediate products and labour services) are uniquely high. The cultural barriers faced by Western firms are very high. Difficulties in language, customs and business procedures increase the costs of entry and of internalised operations in Japan. Compared to the difficulties of simply selling in Japan, these barriers are significant. In addition, Japanese market penetration *by any means* is difficult for outsiders because of cultural barriers (buyer behaviour), the distribution system and artificial barriers, such as stringent Japanese standards and norms.

Second, the labour market in Japan is difficult to enter for foreign firms. Japanese workers have a respect for powerful indigenous employers that is atypical amongst advanced countries. Japanese workers trust long-established, large employers and distrust 'unknown' new foreign entrants. This attitude is a hangover from the (largely mythical) lifetime employment system. Poaching of workers is frowned on in Japan, and labour mobility between companies is low. Even in Joint ventures, the loyalty of the Japanese workers is largely towards the Japanese parent rather than the joint venture itself. The difficulty of building an internal labour force is another barrier to internalisation in Japan.

Third, Japanese companies are closely interrelated in both horizontal and vertical *keiretsu*, which means that vertical and horizontal links are not 'up for grabs' by foreign investors. It is thus difficult for foreign firms to build a bridgehead or niche from which to establish a secure supply base to a major purchaser. This barrier to entry by internalisation is significant. Because banks are closely linked into the *keiretsu* structure, financing may be more difficult for a foreign entrant than in countries with more open financial markets.

Fourth, takeovers are extremely difficult in Japan because of the closely held nature of Japanese companies and the cultural stigma of selling a company. Entry has to be by building from scratch. The preferred method of entry of many European and US companies in FDI is by acquisition. Where this is not possible, further barriers are raised.

An examination of the traditional methods of entry by Western companies illustrates these points. Generally, companies enter advanced country markets by exporting to these markets, then by either licensing or direct investment, with direct investment as the last stage of development (Buckley and Casson, 1981). If export access is difficult, as in Japan, it is difficult to 'prove' the market and to justify the fixed setup costs of direct investment. In these circumstances, joint ventures may be justified as an 'option on entry'. Using the joint venture route reduces capital costs, allows the entrant to test the market and, crucially, facilitates learning. Should the venture prove to be successful, the foreign firm can then attempt a full-blown entry, in the general case by buying out the joint venture partner.

Again, the general case does not apply in the special conditions of Japan. Entry via joint ventures has been the preferred method of gaining locational access to the Japanese market. However, the transition to a wholly owned (even majority owned) stage has proved very problematic. Japanese joint venture partners are often unwilling to sell their equity stake in a successful joint venture. Their motives for entering the joint venture are usually access to technology and skills from the foreign partner, which causes dissonance as the partner's motives are usually market access driven. The loyalty of Japanese workers and managers is to the Japanese parent and generally they do not wish to see this link broken. The result is that foreign direct investors into Japan often have to make a 'two stage' entry, which again increases costs.

This situation is illustrated in Figure 9.1, which shows, for European entrants into Japan, the relevance of this 'double entry' mechanism. The first entries of our sample of companies took place in the 1950s, 1960s and 1970s. The firms were constrained to make 'second entries' in the 1970s, 1980s and 1990s. The vast majority of cases were replacing, even circumventing, their initial joint venture entries. The second direct (usually wholly owned) entry could take place, in the special circumstances of Japan, only after learning from the operation of the first joint venture entry had been thoroughly internalised.

ORGANISATIONAL CHANGE

The predominant mode of market servicing at entry used by 62 per cent of our sample of companies to penetrate the Japanese market was imports through a third party, including *sogo shosha* and *senmon shosha*. A further 19 per cent imported through a sales subsidiary. Of the remainder, 14 per cent entered via a technology agreement, licensing companies to produce their products, and only 5 per cent began by establishing a local manufacturing subsidiary.

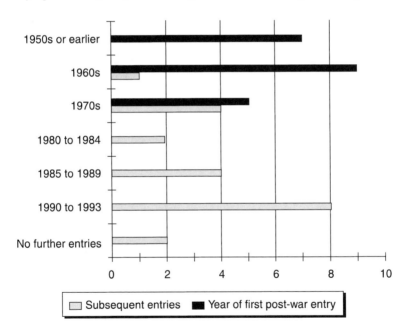

Figure 9.1 Timing of European entry into Japan (number of parent companies)

The more common form of ownership at entry was the 50/50 joint venture, represented by nearly half of the responses. Wholly owned subsidiaries accounted for nearly a quarter, the remainder being split equally between minority-owned and majority-owned joint ventures. In contrast, the preferred form of ownership at entry for US manufacturing companies in the ACCJ survey was as wholly owned subsidiaries, followed by a 50/50 joint venture.

Nearly one-third of ACCJ survey respondents indicated that their companies had changed the original form of organisation since entering Japan, 70 per cent of them (about 20 per cent of the total including non-manufacturers) from joint ventures or imports through a third party to wholly owned subsidiaries. Over half of these companies had changed organisational form since 1984. Our own survey revealed that two-thirds of European companies had changed organisational form since entry, about half since our first survey in 1983–4. These changes began in the late 1970s, but the largest group of firms changing organisational form did so more recently, nearly 30 per cent of them between 1990 and 1993.

In terms of current ownership, the situation of European affiliates in 1993 was quite different from the ownership form at entry. Wholly owned subsidiaries accounted for 38 per cent of the firms and a further 29 per cent were organised into 'holding companies' and similar complex structures in which a subsidiary plays an intermediate role between the European parent and other affiliates in Japan. Joint ventures have become very much the minority, illustrating a common tendency as companies become more securely established in the Japanese market. To all intents and purposes, the 'holding company' can be treated as the 'parent' of Japanese affiliates and is the strategic nucleus, where it exists, of each European firm's operations in the country. Sometimes the 'holding company' is essential in rationalising a large number of historically established collaborative agreements between a European major and its peers in Japan. More significantly, the 'holding company' is usually the active agent through which the second-order entry is implemented.

MANUFACTURING AND R&D

Several reasons were given for manufacturing in Japan by US and European firms. Combining those who gave it as a major and a minor reason, 63 per cent of US companies said they chose to manufacture in Japan to meet Japanese quality requirements, which was also the reason given by 67 per cent of European firms. This was especially true for US firms in the chemical, pharmaceutical and industrial machinery sectors, all of which were well represented in our European survey.

Meeting Japanese special product requirements was the second most important reason given in both surveys for manufacturing in Japan, 54 per cent of US manufacturing companies volunteering it compared with 62 per cent of European companies. Forty-four per cent of US manufacturers cited the reason for local operations as showing commitment to customers, compared with 48 per cent of European firms; and 40 per cent of US firms gave provision of a stable supply source as a reason compared with 48 per cent of European firms. These four reasons were clearly the most important for European firms, lower delivery costs and higher productivity in Japan not being rated as highly as they were by US companies. Existing legal/regulatory requirements were rated low in both surveys, although historical legal/regulatory requirements were of more concern to US firms.

Some US companies choosing not to manufacture in Japan gave as reasons the belief that they could meet quality and delivery requirements elsewhere or achieve higher productivity elsewhere. It is difficult to make a direct comparison with European firms, as the reasons apply only to those *products* that they do not manufacture in Japan. There was no uniformity in the answers with the exception of high land prices, which, in the case of both US and European firms, restricted the ability to invest in manufacturing facilities.

Seventy-one per cent of European firms in our survey had R&D facilities in Japan, a marked increase over the proportion conducting R&D activities in our earlier study in 1983–4. The attractiveness of Japan as a location for R&D facilities has increased as Japanese companies have themselves progressed in product and technology development. In both the US and European surveys, the majority of respondents again, as with manufacture, linked their reasons for undertaking R&D in Japan to their ability to meet customer needs. Fifty-nine per cent of US companies stated that the main reason they established R&D facilities in Japan was for product modification or research purposes. The corresponding European percentage, the highest for a major reason, was 48 per cent. Fifty-eight per cent of US companies did research and development in order to conduct Japan-specific market research. This compares with 43 per cent of European companies. The ability to monitor technology developments in Japan was a major reason for 25 per cent of US companies and 29 per cent of European companies. Core technology research and access to joint research opportunities were equally rated as major reasons by US responders (12 per cent) and European firms (24 per cent).

The 29 per cent of European firms choosing not to establish R&D facilities in Japan gave high facilities costs and staffing issues as the main reasons, paralleling the results of the American survey.

THE COMMITMENT AND MOTIVATION OF FOREIGN FIRMS IN JAPAN

As the conceptual section identified, the principal underlying objective of foreign investors in Japan is to achieve access to the Japanese market. It is therefore unsurprising that a close correlation exists between the views of European and US executives regarding motivations, and the same applies to the perception of inhibitions and restrictions. On the other hand, some divergences occur, partly due to the differing sample mix and partly to the different attributes and attitudes of European and US companies. For instance, in terms of parent companies' commitment to Japan, a 'strong' or 'very strong' commitment was the norm for both European (85 per cent of responses) and US companies (67 per cent). The higher commitment from European firms may well reflect the fact that these companies are entirely from the manufacturing sector, but it is worth mentioning that the commitment of US companies appears to be increasing over time. In the 1987 ACCJ study, only 62 per cent of US companies had a 'strong+' commitment; in fact the 'very strong' category increased 10 percentage points from 29 per cent to 39 per cent between 1987 and 1991. Therefore, it seems likely that US parent firms are taking the Japanese market increasingly seriously, a lesson already learned by European (manufacturing) firms.

This commitment is also reflected in the remarkable growth of sample companies' trade with, and investment and employment in, Japan since 1985 (Figures 9.2 and 9.3). In the case of investment, 62 per cent of European and

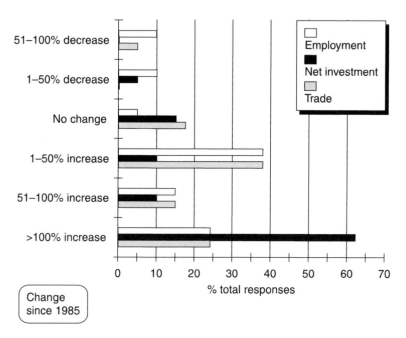

Figure 9.2 Change in European firms' trade, investment and employment with Japan

34 per cent of US respondents recorded an increase of over 100 per cent. (The higher growth in trade reflects the decline in the US dollar and consequent exports to Japan). These figures are particularly interesting, because Japan has become less competitive since 1985 and Japanese companies have been investing large amounts abroad in response. It is noteworthy that motivations for investment in Japan are stable over time for both US and European firms. For instance, 'opportunity to grow sales and profits in Japan' and 'importance of Japan in global strategy' are cited by between 50 per cent and 60 per cent of all companies for both original and sustained investment. Nearly all the motives are market access and 'local-presence' related and, because this is a long-term objective, investments are not so readily affected by shorter term shifts in economic conditions (for a fuller discussion, see Mirza *et al.*, 1989. Other motives, e.g., 'access new technology in Japan', also tend to make companies invest for the long term in Japan.

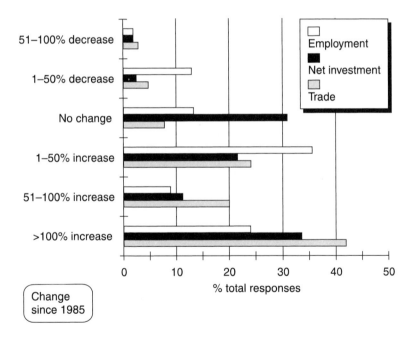

Figure 9.3 Change in USA firms' trade, investment and employment with Japan

Given a long-term perspective, it is therefore not surprising that 48 per cent of European companies had definite future investment plans in Japan, while this was the case for 13 per cent of US companies (16 per cent of US manufacturers). The proportion of companies 'seeking opportunities' or willing to invest 'if the opportunity arises' was 48 per cent for European concerns and 51 per cent for US concerns (54 per cent for manufacturers). Only 5 per cent of European firms had no investment plans, whereas the figure for US firms was 36 per cent.

INHIBITORS TO INVESTMENT IN JAPAN

There is a caveat to the previous section's discussion of the long-term related expansion of sample companies in Japan: many other European and US firms do not invest in Japan for the same reason, i.e., achieving access is difficult. It is therefore illuminating, especially for prospective investors, to examine the main inhibitors and restrictions to investment identified by companies operating in Japan.

US and European firms perceive inhibitors to investment in Japan in a markedly different way (Figures 9.4 and 9.5). This result is only partly due to the composition of the samples. Certainly, 'complexity of doing business in Japan' and 'Japanese government regulations' are probably more important to the US sample because retailers, financial institutions and telecommunication utilities are included. However, US parents generally appear less supportive than European ones; this concurs with the lower commitment mentioned earlier. Perhaps most importantly, European companies are generally less likely to perceive inhibitors to investment in Japan (Figures 9.4 and 9.5). Only with respect to staffing problems and land costs are European concerns on a par with those of US firms.

While 'general inhibitors' may dissuade new firms from investing in Japan, the investment and operating restrictions and difficulties identified by surveyed firms as specific to them and their industries *paradoxically represent a convincing case for investing in Japan*. For instance, issues such as product quality and modification requirements, *keiretsu* relationships and exclusionary or restrictive legal and business practices are probably best addressed by establishing a local presence (as discussed in the conceptual section). Having said this, it is clear that home-side difficulties, such as a short-term management outlook, lack of parent knowledge and frequent corporate strategy changes, are also significant, especially for European firms.

In contradistinction to 'general inhibitors', specific restrictions and difficulties are more likely to afflict European companies. Staffing problems, high land costs and product modification requirements are cases where differences are among the most significant. The fact that all the European firms are manufacturers partly explains their greater difficulties, but other factors are also relevant. For instance, many US firms have been in Japan longer than their European counterparts; better relationships are likely to affect factors such as access to reasonably priced land. US firms are generally better known to the Japanese population, both because of having been around longer and because of the US's postwar influence on Japan (hence a degree of 'psychic affinity'). They are thus less likely to have staffing problems. Finally, in many instances a closer concordance exists between Japanese and US standards compared with Japanese and European standards, and this will result in lower product modifications. The specific significance of each of these factors in explaining United States–European differences in perceived difficulties is hard to assess, but they do represent a viable area for further research.

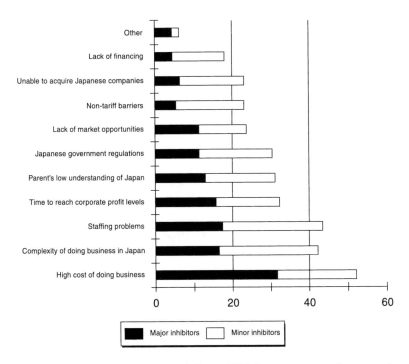

Figure 9.4   Inhibitors to investment in Japan (USA firms, per cent total responses)

Perhaps surprisingly, given the 'bad press' they receive, *keiretsu* were not regarded as being a significant retardant to effective business relationships by the majority of European and US firms. In fact, most firms (44 per cent of US concerns, 57 per cent of European concerns) said that *keiretsu* relationships did not significantly affect trade or investment in their industry sector.

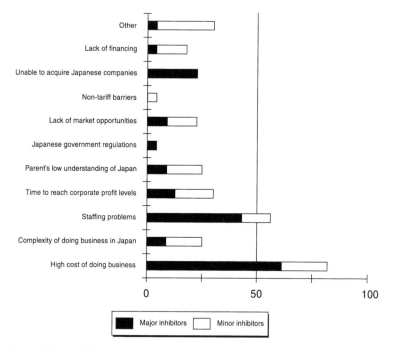

Figure 9.5 Inhibitors to investment in Japan (European firms, per cent total responses)

A number of companies with good *keiretsu* links even argued that the effect was positive (32 per cent of US concerns, 10 per cent of European ones).

SUCCESS FACTORS

Measuring success in the Japanese context is not easy, nor even obvious for a foreign-owned company. However, the European and US groups of firms have remarkably similar views on the key measures of success.

Both groups of firms place sales targets, financial targets and growth targets as the three most important success factors. European firms place market share targets next, but this is the fifth most important target for US firms as a group, behind 'brand name recognition'. European firms placed 'acquiring market and/or technological intelligence' before brand name recognition. Acquiring intelligence ranked sixth for US firms. Both groups of firms placed world-wide access to Japanese customers as the seventh ranked success factor. This remarkable agreement on measures of success is increased if we allow for the industrial differences between the two groups: US firms were more customer orientated and included service firms. European firms were selling largely to Japanese industrial buyers, so that brand name recognition would not be so important.

When asked to list the three critical factors that enable success in Japan, the US and European companies again came up with a remarkably similar list. The first three success factors on both lists are exactly the same: innovative, quality products, good local staff and support from the parent. These three must be taken as the *sine qua non* of success in Japan. Without all three factors, successful operation in Japan is impossible. In addition, a strong business reputation backed by continuously improving technology are key factors in maintaining competitiveness in the rapidly changing Japanese market. A long-term commitment is necessary, backed by knowledge of the Japanese market and respect for Japanese business traditions. Persistence and commitment are frequently occurring words in describing success in Japan.

Perhaps unsurprisingly, when asked to name foreign companies that were successful in Japan, the companies chose others within the same broad sector as themselves or the same nationality as themselves! All the companies named by US firms are US-owned, and the European companies named only Merck, Du Pont and Dow Chemicals from US ownership. Merck and Du Pont achieved the distinction of appearing on both lists of successful firms. The preponderance of chemical and pharmaceutical firms on the European list is a reflection of our sample but it is also an indication of the narrow sectoral base of European success in Japan.

CONCLUSION

There are strong *a priori* reasons to suppose that foreign direct investment in Japan will be constrained below the levels achieved in Europe and North America. Although substantiated, in part, by the empirical findings of the studies reported in this article, there is also evidence to suggest that the inhibitors to inward investment are declining. With certain notable exceptions, these barriers are not government imposed. The key problems in Japan, as perceived by the respondents, include high costs and complexity of doing business, staffing problems, some *keiretsu* relationships and the associated difficulty of acquisition in Japan. These problems are compounded by self-imposed restrictions emanating from home business practices, such as the short-term outlook of management, frequent strategy changes, the inability to meet product quality requirements in Japan and the lack of headquarters' understanding of Japanese conditions. A key finding of the authors' longitudinal study of European direct investment in Japan is that companies have made a two-stage entry: a joint venture arrangement followed by a second wholly owned facility.

References

American Chamber of Commerce in Japan (ACCJ) (1991) *Trade and Investment in Japan* (Tokyo).

Buckley, Peter J. (1988) 'The Limits of Explanation – Testing the Internalization Theory of the Multinational Enterprise', *Journal of International Business Studies*, 19 (2) (Summer) pp. 181–93.

Buckley, Peter J. and Mark Casson (1976) *The Future of the Multinational Enterprise* (London: Macmillan).

Buckley, Peter J. and Mark Casson (1981) 'The Optimal Timing of a Foreign Direct Investment', *Economic Journal*, 92 (361) (March) pp. 75–87.

Buckley, Peter J., Hafiz Mirza and John R. Sparkes (1984) *European Affiliates in Japan: A Comparative Study of Corporate Planning and Strategy by European Firms and their Affilites in Japan* (Tokyo: The Japan Foundation).

Buckley, Peter J., Hafiz Mirza and John R. Sparkes (1993) *The Development of European Direct Investment in Japan* (Tokyo: The Japan Foundation).

European Business Community (EBC) (1992) 'A Position Paper on European Investment in Japan', Investment Committee, Tokyo.

Mirza, Hafiz, Peter J. Buckley and John R. Sparkes (1989) 'Swimming Against the Tide? The Strategy of European Manufacturing Investors in Japan', in Kazuo Shibagaki, Malcolm Trevor and Tetsuo Abo (eds), *Japanese and European Management: Their International Adaptability* (Tokyo: University of Tokyo Press).

Part III

Trade Blocs, Foreign Market Servicing Strategies and International Transfer Pricing

10 Economic Integration: The Single European Market and the NAFTA and Their Implications for Canada–UK Bilateral Trade and Investment*

with C.L. Pass and Kate Prescott

INTRODUCTION

International business is increasingly being shaped by the trend towards economic integration which has engendered the establishment of large trading blocs characterised by internal free trade and common competition policies. To this extent, the world arena is now dominated by three major trading regions – the Americas (including Canada and South America), Europe (including eastern Europe) and Asia Pacific – the 'Global Triad' (Ohmae, 1985). However, while liberalisation is the essence of internal regional business transactions, it is arguable that greater protectionism and a more restricted legislative régime dominate in inter-triad trade and investment. This has profound implications for firms' international strategies where the affiliation of their domestic country to a particular economic grouping has ramifications for trade and investment in non-member countries.

This article concentrates on two individual countries, Canada and the UK, which were once tied through commonwealth linkages, but which now belong to two separate trading blocs. Therefore, while trade and investment between the two nations was based on political and cultural affinity, both countries now find themselves being subject to the external trade policies of the Single European Market and the North American trading bloc. Equally, as both countries are now affiliated to these regions, changing legislation in the new, wider, 'domestic' market is potentially effecting trade and invest-

*Originally published in *British Journal of Canadian Studies*, vol. 9, no. 2, 1994, pp. 375–400.

ment diversion away from other countries as firms are keen to concentrate on the new challenges provided at home. Consequently, it is important to look at bilateral trade and investment in the context of changing domestic as well as foreign policy. The question which this article poses is: to what extent has the creation of the Single European Market (SEM) and the North American Free Trade Agreement (NAFTA) had an impact on the historically developed business linkages between firms based in the two countries? This means assessing whether firms are concentrating more on consolidating their business in their own trading region, as well as examining changes in strategies and objectives for their international dealings in other trading blocs. Equally, the article questions to what extent the objectives of the Single European Market and the North American Free Trade area are likely to be achieved in the light of external protection between the trading blocs and continued internal barriers which detract from the achievement of homogeneous markets.

The following section provides an overview of the SEM and NAFTA – the backdrop against which firms are planning their strategies. There follows a brief description of the sampled firms – fifteen from the UK and nine from Canada – and an outline of how firms are responding to changes in international economic integration – the SEM and NAFTA in particular. The final section provides a summary and some tentative conclusions.

THE SINGLE EUROPEAN MARKET (1992)

Even after the development of the European Economic Community in 1958 and subsequent extension of the Community from six (France, West Germany, Belgium, the Netherlands, Italy and Belgium) to twelve member states (the UK, Ireland and Denmark in 1973, Greece in 1981 and Spain and Portugal in 1986), the removal of cross-border tariffs and quotas between member countries, while liberalising trade to an extent, failed to provide for real 'freedoms' of international business. Many obstacles still remained, particularly as a result of the fragmented structure of the European Community (now the European Union (EU)) bloc. Trade continued to be restricted, and costs increased in many ways: different bureaucratic requirements, border formalities, different national product requirements (particularly in terms of technological differences), different taxation régimes, company laws, restrictive government procurement practices, etc. It is difficult to calculate the cumulative cost of these controls on trade, but customs formalities, for example, have been estimated to cost up to 9 billion Ecu per annum and public procurement 40 billion. The Single European Act commits EU members to sweep away these obstacles by the progressive introduction of practices and regulations

aimed at creating a single, unified common market (DTI, 1991). Some 280
'directives' have been issued designed to harmonise products on an EU-wide
basis by '1992', although in practice the timescale involved will inevitably
extend beyond this date. Estimates of the likely gains resulting from the completion of the internal market have been made by Cecchini (1988). The total
estimate of economic gain to the EU is in the range 174–258 billion Ecu, representing some 4.3 per cent to 6.4 per cent of the EU's total gross domestic
product in 1988. A number of potential sources of efficiency gains are highlighted in Table 10.1: first, the removal of cross-border barriers to trade,
mainly customs formalities, and related delays; second, the removal of barriers to production which not only affect intra-EU trade but which also hinder
foreign entrants and thus limit competition: biased government procurement;
divergent national standards, regulations, testing and certification procedures; restrictions on services, in particular banking, insurance, house
finance, stock market and securities services in respect of cross-border solic-
iting of deposits and customers; restrictions on manufacturing, including
product specifications and standards, packaging and labelling requirements,
and tax rates. Third, cost reductions can be effected through firms more fully
exploiting economies of scale, involving restructuring their operations on a
pan-EU basis. This will be facilitated by the introduction of various measures
noted in the second category above – harmonised technical standards and
product specifications across the twelve economies. Fourth, cost reductions
can come through the elimination of business inefficiencies (and in some cases 'excess' profits) as national markets are opened up and local firms subject-
ed to greater competitive pressures.

Table 10.1   Potential gains in economic welfare for the EU resulting from the
completion of the internal market

	Billion Ecu	*% of GDP*
1. Gains from the removal of barriers affecting trade	8–9	0.2–0.3
2. Gains from removal of barriers affecting overall production	57–71	2.0–2.4
3. Gains from exploiting economies of scale	61	2.1
4. Gains from intensified competition reducing business inefficiencies and monopoly profits	46	1.6
Total for twelve member states at 1988 prices	174–258	4.3–6.4

Source: Commission of EC, 'Cecchini Report', cited in Cecchini (1988).

These estimates, of course, are subject to wide margins of error and
may well be exaggerated given that the 'directives' proposed may not be

implemented in full across the EU because of national tardiness and resistance. Moreover, 'harmonisation' is an elusive concept. Thus, the potential for achieving economies of scale through centralised production and product standardisation may prove limited. In particular, cultural differences across the twelve member states of Europe means that EU and non-EU firms need to 'customise' their products to meet customer requirements in particular national markets (Buckley *et al.*, 1992).

The achievement of these cost savings depends upon a virtuous circle of economic benefits.

(1)   The removal of barriers (physical, fiscal and technical) will allow firms to operate unhindered in a wider Europe. As they take up the opportunities of expanding their European coverage, increasing their output, they are better placed to raise the scale of their manufacturing units (closing the gap between the average scale of EU and US plants).

(2)   The lowering of barriers and the stimulus to promoting greater European expansion will intensify competition across the markets of Europe.

(3)   The combined effect of the above two issues is to reduce costs; in the first instance, greater efficiency provides the scope for cost reductions, and, in the second, competition is expected to raise price competition.

(4)   As prices fall, consumers' purchasing power will rise, which will increase demand and raise the overall volume of EU business. Despite greater levels of trade, the downward pressure on prices initiated by greater competition will stifle inflation.

(5)   Competition encourages firms to innovate and develop new technologies as a way of sustaining long-term advantages.

(6)   In turn, new technologies will expand through Europe, be produced in larger-scale units, face a downward price trend and stimulate further innovation.

Importantly, then, firms act as 'change agents' in the achievement of objectives in the Single European Market initiative. It is their reaction to changing legislation and the new opportunities which are theoretically provided by the Single Market which will determine the extent to which the overall aims of 1992 are realised. Equally, the reaction of foreign organisations to changes in proposed legislation will also have an important bearing on the future competitive environment within the EU and thus the realisation of objectives. This extends the remit beyond intra-EU trade and investment flows and questions the implications of external trade policies. The global triad which now dominates the international business arena may be regarded as analogous to an oligopolised industry: aggressively competitive actions by one party are likely to be matched by equally aggressive counteractions by others. It is therefore important for the economic groups to strike a balance between what may be beneficial protectionism and what may ultimately lead to countermeasures which are damaging to the global activities of their firms. Indeed, as many large firms continually strive to achieve a global balance in their international activities (that is, ensuring a strong presence in each of the three arms of the triad), the threat of counteractions is very real.

Consequently, the regional approach to trade liberalisation (that is, the creation of large trading blocs) may or may not lead to an improvement in world economic welfare and efficiency, for it contains an important element of discrimination against non-member countries (El Agraa, 1988). Such integration combines features of free trade and protection. On the one hand, the *trade-creating* effects of the removal of trade barriers between member countries will serve to increase welfare and efficiency *within* the bloc. On the other hand, the expansion of trade within the bloc may be at the expense of non-member countries, this *trade-diversionary* effect serving to lower other countries' welfare. The relative magnitude of these two effects determines whether the customs union is on balance favourable to worldwide allocative efficiency. Furthermore, external protectionist measures arguably stifle the realisation of true efficiency (both static – the promotion of scale economies – and dynamic – the stimulus for technological development) as they limit competition from outside the bloc. This means firms avoid adjusting to changes in international competition, consumer demand and new technologies. The latter point is particularly important in relation to the EU, which has seen an erosion of its technological base in recent decades. By restricting competition from technologically advanced countries (Japan and America in particular), Europe runs the risk of continuing to lag behind the rest of the world in its level of technological sophistication.

A further implication of protection between trading blocs is the inducement for foreign direct investment. Where companies are hampered from exporting by high tariffs and restrictive non-tariff barriers, there is a tendency for them to overcome the barriers by locating activities in the foreign market. In the run-up to 1992, therefore, high levels of inward investment into the European Union may therefore be regarded as a reaction to early fears that the Single Market will be closed to non-EU trade.

1992 AND THE UK

Although the UK has become more heavily dependent on the European Union, both economically and politically, over the years and is now firmly committed to EU institutions and policies, the benefits for the UK of EU membership have been constantly called into question. When the UK first joined the EU, it was widely believed that although the UK might suffer some 'losses', notably the extra costs of obtaining foodstuffs at CAP price levels, overall the enlargement of its 'home' market on a free-trade basis would provide massive opportunities for its manufacturing industries to expand sales and profits. Moreover, the political advantages of the EU were appealing, especially to those people who saw in the EU an opportunity to create a truly pan-European super-state which united the peoples of Europe, thereby ending forever 'tribal' warfare. The reality, however, has proved very different in the economic field. The UK has been heavily 'penalised' for its economic inefficiencies, with poor productivity, training and investment levels, rampant wage inflation and industrial disputes leading to higher costs and lack of price competitiveness.

If and when the UK rejoins the 'Exchange Rate Mechanism', the 'easy' option of restoring a loss of price competitiveness by lowering the exchange value of the pound will be considerably circumscribed. Just as serious has been the UK's general inability to compete successfully in the critical dimensions of product differentiation, sophistication and innovativeness. As a consequence, the UK is heavily in deficit to its EU trade partners. However, it is obviously simplistic to attribute the UK's current trade woes to its membership of the EU *per se*. The UK is also running substantial trade deficits with many non-member countries. Thus, the real problem of the UK's deteriorating position in the world economy at large remains one of poor competitiveness. The fact that the UK has some industries and companies which have established themselves as world market leaders on the basis of process and product innovation, high efficiency and marketing excellence (for example, Glaxo in pharmaceuticals, ICI in paint, Zeneca in pharmaceuticals, Pilkington in flat glass, British Oxygen in industrial gases) forcibly underscores this point (Buckley *et al.*, 1992).

Historically, however, trade and investment by UK firms has centred more on the North American market than those of their proximate European neighbours. The Single European Market has therefore spurred British firms into refocusing their efforts on the EU and consolidating their position in the wider European market. To this extent, 1992 has been the catalyst for redressing the global balance of business activities for British firms, many of whom felt in the past that the cultural affinity with North America provided a more advantageous platform for developing their international activities. While this could, potentially, have diverted attention away from North America, the establishment of the NAFTA has served as an important counterbalance, ensuring that many firms are aware of the need to consolidate their business in both

North America and Europe – and that the focus for the future is 'global balance'.

The UK is continually being criticised for its reluctance to embrace new EU-wide initiatives – in particular, failure to sign the Social Chapter and more recently its reservations regarding the establishment of a Single European Currency, based on fears of loss of sovereignty. Equally, it continues to reject protectionism of European markets, evidenced by a reassessment of rules on dumping, increased attention to rules of origin and a renewed effort to secure reciprocity. As the UK has traditionally been open to external competition, such protectionist measures run contrary to national policy and, arguably, EU internal policy, which keenly promotes free competition and rejects protectionism as detrimental to the promotion of efficiency. Margaret Thatcher, in her critique of the EU presented in Brussels in 1988, is quoted as saying:

> My fourth guiding principle is that Europe should not be protectionist. It would be a betrayal if, while breaking down constraints on trade to create the Single Market, the Community were to erect greater external protection. We must make sure our approach to world trade is consistent with the liberalisation we preach at home.

A liberal attitude towards inward trade and investment has been a characteristic of the UK economy during the past decade and more of Conservative rule. Indeed, inward investment (particularly from Japan and the USA) has played an important part in promoting economic activity in areas of industrial decline. Nevertheless, some critics argue that there has been a lack of clear objectives regarding the long-term gains from inward direct investment. While in the short term they have, in many cases, unequivocally directly boosted employment and indirectly promoted local business by raising demand for inputs from the local economy, the long-term advantages in terms of improving the British industrial base and potential for technology transfer are less clear. Some observers have accused the government of treating the symptoms (unemployment) rather than the problems (industrial decline) and have argued that a more substantial overall industrial vision is necessary to carry the UK economy forward into the twenty-first century.

1992 AND CANADA

Concern has been expressed by some countries that the EU will become more of a 'fortress' as a result of the Single Market initiative. This is not, however, the intent of the architects of the programme:

The Internal Market will be beneficial both to EC and to non-EC firms since they will no longer have to deal with the national and technical barriers it is to abolish; in addition, the economic growth expected from completion of the Internal Market will have favourable consequences both for the EC and its trading partners...The Internal Market Programme involves no weakening of the EC's commitment to respect its international obligations. (European Commission Progress Report, 1988, p. 8)

Inevitably, some trade frictions with non-members will arise (for example, Japanese car imports into the EU), but problems will be there with or without the internal market and may be more easily resolved if a non-EU country is dealing with a single authority rather than twelve national states.

The Canadian government, too, see '1992' as presenting an opportunity for Canadian companies to expand their European operations (see External Affairs and International Trade Canada, 1991). Europe has remained a neglected area despite the early promise of the 1976 Framework agreement and other initiatives such as cooperation agreements between Canadian provincial governments and their counterparts in the EU:

In the last decade, our exports to the EC have increased only slightly, despite a generally favourable Canadian exchange rate. In the meantime, our share of merchandise imports in the major EC markets has actually declined...the figures suggest that Canadians must be more aggressive ...and must increase their rate of investment in the EC if they are to capitalise on the opportunities offered by the development of the Single Market. (External Affairs and International Trade Canada, 1991, pp. 18–19)

In sum:

Penetration of this vast and sophisticated market will enhance any company's competitive position in the global market place. Success in the European market, however, demands an ability to respond rapidly to changing technological and business conditions. Few Canadian businesses will be able to prosper in the ec if all they do is to maintain an arms-length trading relationship. (EAITC, 1991, Executive Summary).

But how is the deeper involvement to be achieved? While mergers, takeovers and greenfield investments represent the conventional means of entering new markets, the Canadian government is currently exhorting companies to forge 'strategic alliances' (joint ventures, cross-licensing) with European partners:

Strategic alliances enable firms to position themselves in overseas markets without the huge investments that were traditionally the only alternative to exporting. Strategic alliances not only save time and money, they also enable each partner to focus on what it does best, relying on the other to provide the skills, local savvy, resources or financing necessary to achieve success. (EAITC, 1991, Executive Summary)

Strategic alliances are seen as especially useful in the context of the need to diversify and broaden Canadian involvement in the EU to include more small and medium-sized firms as well as established large firms, and are a form which is actively encouraged by the EU itself through such programmes as ESPRIT and EUREKA. Recent cases of strategic alliances involving Canadian companies include IAF Bio Chem (with Glaxo of the UK in drug research), Dowty Canada's participation in the European Airbus consortium, and Desjardins Group (with Confédération Nationale de Crédit Mutual de France in insurance and other financial services).

THE NORTH AMERICAN FREE TRADE AGREEMENT

The establishment of the Canadian–United States Free Trade area in 1989 formally recognised the trade and investment interdependency between Canada and the USA which had been very much on the increase since the Second World War. However, it may come as a surprise to note that Canada and the USA had in fact been party to a previous free-trade agreement as long ago as 1854 (Charles, 1989). This was signed by the British Government representing Canada as its colony, and remained legally binding until 1866 when the USA abrogated the agreement as a reaction to British interference in the US Civil War. In 1867, the British North American Act was passed by the British parliament, which effectively established Canada as an independent nation (although the UK monarch remains its 'nominal' head of state), and there was little popular or business support for free-trade sentiments. In fact, quite the reverse was the case as Canadian fears grew that their newly-established 'infant industries' might be eliminated by American competition.

Since 1945, Canada's trade links with the USA have increased greatly. In the 1940s, around 40 per cent of Canadian trade was with the USA; by the late 1980s, this had grown to around 70 per cent. The growing dependency of Canada on the USA as a trade (and investment) partner has not been without its detractors. Politically, the issue has blown 'hot and cold', with Liberals generally being against more formal ties with the USA, and Conservatives in recent times being more pro-USA. In the 1950s, for example, the Liberal party under Diefenbaker attempted to switch 15 per cent of Canada's trade with the USA to the UK, and again in the 1970s Trudeau, amid continuing disquiet over American dominance, developed the 'Third Option Policy' aimed at diversifying Canada's trade partners. These efforts had little impact (Papadopoulos, 1986).

A forerunner of the 1989 initiative, often cited in support of the benefits of free trade, was the 1965 Canadian–US pact on motor car manufacturing and trade ('Autopact'). Employment in the auto industry has increased twenty-fold (and now employs 132,600 Canadians). The trade effect has been dramatic: 80 per cent of the industry's output is exported to the USA, and this has led to the emergence of an overall trade surplus with the USA (Wonnacott, 1990b). Trade liberalisation was seen as a means of providing various economic benefits: real gains for consumers from reduced price distortions, greater scope for exploiting economies of scale, and a reorganisation of industries and a more efficient use of resources along the lines indicated by comparative advantage. While in principle it may be argued that multilateral rather than bilateral trade liberalisation can produce larger benefits in these respects, given the dominance of trade flows with the USA and the infeasibility of securing free trade across the board (within the current GATT Uruguay round stalemate), a free-trade treaty with the USA was seen by many as preferable to the status quo. Notwithstanding this, many Canadians have questioned the necessity of a broader-based pact with the USA as trade barriers in any case have been substantially lowered under the GATT initiatives. Eighty-five per cent of Canadian exports to the USA and 70 per cent of US exports to Canada are duty-free, while the average tariff on the remainder is only 0.7 per cent on Canadian goods and 3.8 per cent on US goods. The reality is that, for Canada, the 1989 Agreement is as much a 'defensive' response to the dangers of the spread of worldwide protectionism in general, and US protectionism in particular, as a wholehearted commitment to free trade *per se*. As Charles (1989) observed:

> the US Congress, dominated by special interest supported Democrats, was becoming more and more protectionist. Canada was also aware that 1992 in Europe may create a major trading bloc with protectionist walls about it. It feared US and Japanese retaliation. This would mean Canada, as the smallest of the Group of Seven developed economies, would be on its own against the major trading blocs. For both economic and geographic reasons, the United States was the natural trading partner with which to establish a free trade agreement.

The downside of the agreement as perceived by many Canadians is loss of sovereignty, the fear that Canada will become, *de facto*, the fifty-first state of the USA:

We built a country east and west and north. We built it on an infrastructure that deliberately resisted the continental pressure of the United States. For 120 years we've done it. With one signature of a pen you've reversed that. It will reduce us, I am sure, to a colony of the United States, because when the economic levers go, the political independence is sure to follow. (*The Independent*, 18 November 1988)

The main provisions of the Free Trade Agreement are the elimination of all tariffs between Canada and the USA, the reduction of non-tariff barriers to trade and the liberalisation of investment flows. Table 10.2 summarises the key features of the pact. A number of areas, however, are not covered by the agreement; for example, road haulage, air, rail and shipping transport, the beer industry and government subsidies to industry in general.

Various studies (summarised in Table 10.3) have attempted to quantify the benefits of free trade between Canada and the USA. These gains are estimated to accrue largely through economies-of-scale effects associated with the elimination of branch-plant duplication and more centralised production. While economies-of-scale effects were important in the automobile industry following implementation of the 1965 Autopact, similar projections in other industries may well be exaggerated given the already low levels of protection applying (Thompson, 1991).

For other trade partners of the two countries, the trade-diversionary impact of the free-trade agreement is estimated to be small. This inference is based on the relative size of existing bilateral flows between the two countries compared to trade with other countries and the low levels of overall protection. The Canada–US Free Trade Agreement has also added further impetus to inward investment by firms keen to access the North American market.

Negotiations have now been concluded which extend the Canadian–US Free Trade Agreement to include Mexico, although this has not yet been ratified by the respective governments (Nimmo, 1990; Whalley, 1990; Reitsma, 1990). Mexico, which conducts the bulk of its foreign trade with the USA and very little with Canada, originally approached the USA to secure a free-trade pact. Unlike in the case of a common market, individual members of a free-trade area can make their own trade arrangements with non-member countries. A separate bilateral trade pact between the USA and Mexico running alongside the Canadian–US FTA (a so-called 'hub and spoke' system) would have created a situation whereby only the USA would have tariff-free access to both markets, giving the USA greater bargaining power (Lipsey, 1990; Wonnacott, 1990a).

Table 10.2   The Canada–US free trade agreement

	Main provisions
Manufactured goods	Removal of all bilateral tariffs starting on 1 January 1989 over a maximum period of ten years.
Automotive	US–Canada Auto Pact continues. Canada's embargo on imports of used cars to be eliminated. Duty remissions to be phased out. To benefit from tariff exemption, at least 50 per cent of the value of goods must originate in North America.
Agriculture	Elimination of tariffs on agricultural trade within ten years and the agreement not to use direct export subsidies on bilateral agricultural trade.
Energy	Restrictions on exports of Canadian oil and gas can be imposed; however, any reduction in exports to the United States must be proportional to the total supply of oil and gas available in Canada, without price discrimination.
Banking	Canada is to eliminate restrictions on acquisition of Canadian assets by US banks. Canadian banks will receive equal treatment under US Securities laws.
Financial services	Improved access and competition; national treatment for financial institutions.
Road haulage, maritime and air transport	No change; but further restrictions ruled out.
Other services	Liberalised access to enhanced telecommunications, computer services, tourism and architectural services.
Government procurement	Exclusion of national preference on government contracts worth more than $25,000; exceptions for defence procurement.
Direct investment	Restrictions on establishing new firms relaxed; extension of national treatment.
Technical standards	Harmonisation of technical standards based on the GATT code.
Emergency action and arbitration	More stringent standards for the application of arbitration emergency safeguards. Establishment of a dispute settlements mechanism and an independent arbitration panel.

Source: External Affairs Canada (1991).

In the event, Canada became involved in the negotiations to work towards a 'pluralist' agreement giving equal access to the markets of all participants. A free-trade agreement with Mexico is not without its critics since it would

Table 10.3   Studies on the impact of Canada–US free trade

Study	Main long-run impacts	
General equilibrium models[1]		
Department of Finance	Real income	2.5%
	Scale-related cost reduction	2.1%
	Changes in real output:	
	Primary	2.1%
	Manufacturing	10.1%
Hamilton–Whalley	Real income	0.7%
Harris–Cox	Real income	8.9%
Macroeconomic models[2]		
Economic Council	Real GNE	2.5%
	Output per person	0.7%
Informetrica	Real income	3.0%
Institute for Policy Analysis	Real income	3.3%
WEFA Group	Real income	3.1%

[1] See References: Department of Finance (1988); R. Hamilton and J. Whalley (1985); R. Harris and D. Cox (1985).
[2] See References: Economic Council of Canada (1988); Informetrica Ltd (1988); Institute for Policy Analysis (1985); WEFA Group (1987).

involve two major industrial economies linking themselves with a newly industrialising country characterised by relatively low wage levels. Although in theory this should provide considerable scope for 'comparative advantage' gains, fears have centred on the possibility that low Mexican wages could induce large numbers of Canadian and US firms to close down their local plants and set up new plants in Mexico. At the present time, over half of Mexico's manufactured exports are accounted for by the subsidiaries of MNCs with mainly US parents operating out of so-called 'bond' plants along the US–Mexican border, which are given special tax and duty-free status by the Mexican government. Extending free trade 'across the board' would serve to encourage not only US and Canadian firms to locate in Mexico, but also the subsidiaries of firms from other countries. The low-wage argument, however, needs to be tempered by the fact that Mexico is a low-productivity economy with relatively high unit labour costs. At the present time, the average tariff on Mexican goods entering the USA is less than 5 per cent, with nearly half entering tax-free. From a Canadian perspective, proponents of the FTA emphasise on the one hand the extra opportunities which it provides to sell into a growing market of 80 million people where hitherto Canadian penetration has been limited, and, on the other, the downside dangers which would arise from a US-dominated 'hub and spoke' arrangement. The NAFTA–Mexico treaty provides for the removal of most duties and restrictions on trade not only in manufactured goods but also in agricultural products and services over a phased fifteen-year period.

CANADA AND NAFTA

Canada's international competitiveness has been a cause of concern for many people, a concern which has been heightened by the establishment of the free-trade agreement with the USA. Writing in 1985, Rugman commented:

> A sensible national strategy is one that builds upon the abundant resources of the nation, such that resource-intensive products will be exported. Yet Canada need not be a 'drawer of water and hewer of wood' since in today's competitive global environment it is necessary to have some value added in the trade of resources. This is achieved when corporations are organized to process and market raw material-based product lines, rather than to simply export the resources themselves. To an increasing extent Canada is already moving in this direction. (1985 p. 4; see also Rugman and McIlveen, 1985)

According to Rugman and D'Cruz (1991), Canada now needs to tap into the US resource base in a more proactive way. Whether Canada ultimately benefits from the FTA and the trade opportunities afforded by the global economy will depend on casting aside Canada's traditional 'shelter' (i.e. protectionist) mentality to one which actively embraces the US market as a platform for projecting itself into global markets and the acquisition of skills in higher-value-added products, particularly those that are knowledge-based. Rugman and D'Cruz emphasise that relying exclusively on the natural resource base of Canada to build competitive advantage, and viewing the US market merely as a set of export opportunities, will only provide a limited basis for future wealth-creation. Instead, following Porter's (1990) recipe for international success, they advocate a closer integration of Canadian business with the US resource base, support industries, infrastructure and market in order to provide a means for developing innovative new products and services that simultaneously meet the needs of Canadian and US customers and which can be used to penetrate global markets:

> The goal of this strategic approach must be to develop businesses that are capable of competing effectively through exports outside North America.

Success in the integrated US and Canadian market must be regarded only
as an intermediate step for the firm, otherwise it risks making the strategic
error of remaining content with being competitive only with its domestic
rivals and ignoring the danger of being outpaced by rivals from other parts
of the world. (Rugman and D'Cruz, 1991, p. 38)

FDI linkages are seen as a vital element in this process:

> This approach applies both to multinationals owned by Canadians and to
> foreign-owned multinationals that have a significant business in Canada
> with a global mandate and capability. In particular, this applies to busi-
> nesses of US multinationals operating with Canada as a home base...
> Canadian governments must show that they are willing to treat these for-
> eign investments as if they were 'domestic' to Canada. They must be wil-
> ling to support these businesses in their efforts to develop new, globally
> competitive products and services in the same manner and to the same de-
> gree as support is provided to Canadian-owned businesses. (1991, p. 35)

Thus, as in the UK case, multilateral free trade and unrestricted FDI is seen as
an important mechanism for improving Canada's efficiency and international competitiveness (see Rugman and Verbeke, 1990).

Porter (1991), in a recent study of the Canadian economy, noted that although Canada's abundant factor resources have been the bedrock of the
economy and allowed Canadian firms to be profitable by exporting relatively
unprocessed commodities rather than through upgrading, this together with
protectionist policies has left the economy ill-equipped for the future. Resource-based industries are vulnerable not only to depletion of resources over
time but also from the emergence of low-cost competitors. Moreover, many
of Canada's market-access-based industries (such as motor vehicles), initially spawned to overcome high tariff barriers, 'are seriously threatened by the
increasingly open trading environment. As trade barriers continue to fall,
market access no longer requires a major production base in Canada' (p. 69).
Thus, Canada should build on its existing resource advantages by developing
a more 'sophisticated' natural resource sector based on differentiation and in-
novation-based advantages. Equally, Canadian businesses need to be more
proactive in international markets, and reduce dependency on the US market.

A related competitiveness issue concerns that of the status of US 'branch
plants' in Canada. Tariff and non-tariff barriers initially forced many US and
other foreign companies to locate in Canada, supporting the traditional argument that protective barriers encourage direct investment as a substitute for
exports. Removing protectionism is likely, according to Baranson (1985), to

reverse this process, with US branch plants in Canada being replaced by more efficient plants in the USA, particularly in the south (and Mexico). However, a survey by Rugman (1987) of the twenty-one largest Canadian MNCs and the twenty-two largest US subsidiaries in Canada provides opposing evidence. Fifty per cent of the Canadian firms and 70 per cent of the US firms expected their Canadian investment to increase by between 10 and 20 per cent in response to trade liberalisation. Significantly, no firms indicated that they would give up FDI for exporting. The inference is that much US FDI in Canada is market-related, enabling firms to gain 'closeness to customer' benefits from a market presence rather than lower costs *per se*, and a continuance in some cases of a 'world product mandate' using Canada as a centralised production base for global exporting. Moreover, many 'branch plants' are no longer stand-alone operations but part of a more complex network of intrafirm activities at various stages of processing involving both horizontal and vertical specialisation, as well as final products. In these cases, as emphasised by Rugman and Verbeke (1991), trade and foreign direct investment complement each other and do not substitute for one another.

THE UK AND NAFTA

Recent preoccupation with the Single Market and the numerous directives and initiatives which are now shaping activities within the EU, coupled with important political changes in Eastern Europe, have resulted in less attention being paid to the NAFTA by industry observers and researchers. As the UK is one of the leading players in the biggest economic drama ever to be staged, it is not surprising that the NAFTA has taken a back seat. Nevertheless, this is not to suggest that firms are ignoring the implications of the NAFTA.

Earlier research by Buckley, Pass and Prescott (1992) on the competitiveness of UK firms highlighted fears that European external protectionism would be damaging to global business activities. While the opportunities and challenges provided by 1992 are being actively tackled, many firms stressed that this was only one element in a wider global strategy which embraces new opportunities in North America (brought about by the NAFTA) and Japan (which has begun to take a more liberal stance on inward trade and investment). There was therefore much evidence to suggest that international business success is increasingly being determined by achieving comprehensive global coverage (in particular, a sustainable position in each arm of the triad). One manager went so far as to suggest that the achievement of such coverage is more important than 'getting together in an incestuous huddle in Europe', which is clearly indicative of a global rather than a regional (i.e. European) mentality. The reasons underlying this assertion are based not only on the importance of spreading risk globally between the dominant world economic centres, but also on the importance of exposing the business to international technological developments which allow firms to experience the true realities of world competition, encouraging improvements in technology.

THE SAMPLE OF FIRMS

Personal interviews were conducted with managers from international companies in both the UK and Canada between January and July of 1992. This covered fifteen UK firms and nine Canadian firms, the bias resulting from the inherent time constraints on the Canadian part of the survey. Wherever possible, interviews were conducted with executive-level management, although on occasion it was only possible to talk to managers lower down the organisation.

Arising out of a survey of trade and investment data, certain industry sectors appeared to be of key importance to each economy. In particular, wood and pulp and related products emerged as a dominant sector for Canadian firms trading with the UK, and pharmaceuticals for UK firms in Canada. Alternatively, some sectors showed strong and growing bilateral trade and investment flows; this included transportation equipment, general industrial equipment and food and drink. Other sectors also showing strong reciprocal trade and investment patterns include those which are growing industries in the world economic arena, notably communications (including telecommunications and computers) as well as financial services. Finally, interviews were conducted with firms from outlying industries on the basis of major recent acquisitions and international investments. In this way, the sample of firms reflects the current developments in bilateral trade and investment for both countries.

The firms in the sample also vary greatly in size (and associated resources available for international expansion), foreign involvement (ranging from those firms with foreign turnover less than £50m generated primarily from international trade to multinational enterprises with major foreign investments and overseas turnover in excess of £200 million) and experience of international operations (a factor which is independent of size and relates to the longevity of their international dealings and consequent experience gained).

ATTITUDES TOWARDS ECONOMIC INTEGRATION

A full exposition of the findings of the research is beyond the scope of this article. What is presented here is a summary of the attitudes of managers towards closer economic integration in an attempt to understand the impact of the NAFTA and the SEM on bilateral trade and investment flows. The key focus is therefore changes in strategy brought about by integration – for, as was noted earlier, acting as 'change agents', firms have the potential to effect the realisation of benefits from economic union.

UK FIRMS AND NAFTA

The general consensus of UK firms regarding NAFTA is one of greater opportunity. Many firms feel that the long-term potential is for greater freedom to offer goods across the whole of North America, which broadens market scope and size. There was very little evidence of perceived protectionism in relation to entry into either Canada or the USA, and some firms commented on the continued differences between the two markets which the NAFTA is not expected to eliminate (in particular, continued legislative differences in financial services and cultural differences which are part and parcel of each country's historical developments).

In strategic terms, there are several organisations which maintain that a 'presence' in both markets will continue to be important in the future despite closer economic union, and it is therefore not the existence of operations in themselves, but more likely the form of these representations which will change. Therefore, for firms exporting to Canada and operating through market-based intermediaries, while some opportunities appear to exist for securing distributors who will service the whole of North America, the preferred approach is securing intermediaries in both the USA and Canada to develop business potential in each market. Alternatively, for firms with established sales/marketing subsidiaries in both markets, attempting to operate from one North American-based subsidiary in the wake of more harmonised legislation is unlikely. It is more probable that the subsidiary in one of the two markets will be replaced with a representative office to service local needs than attempts being made at cross-border business.

For firms with manufacturing facilities in both markets, a certain degree of rationalisation may be possible, although the continuation of local representation through sales/marketing offices retains priority. The major examples of firms within the sample which see possible future potential in cross-border business are those for which the replacement of indirect means of exporting with a company sales office is likely in the future. For these organisations, most of which are relatively small and lacking in resources for investment, the ability to establish single sales/marketing facilities in one market (particularly the USA) appears advantageous. There is evidence of companies outside of our sample which are not directly represented in Canada but instead use their US subsidiaries' distributors to sell into Canada. A number of UK food groups are a case in point. RHM's subsidiaries, Red Wing and Carriage House Foods, sell a range of their sauces, preservatives and peanut butter in Canada through distributors. Likewise, Dalgety uses its US catering distribution subsidiary, Martin-Bower, to service fast-food restaurant customers such as McDonald's in both the USA and Canada.

Thus, while strategies are likely to be adapted in the wake of these greater freedoms, there remains evidence of firms maintaining separate organisational developments in both markets. While some UK firms are establishing new business operations in Canada and others are consolidating existing positions, there is little evidence to suggest that these businesses will form the singular focus of their North American business. While for certain firms it provides a 'platform' for expanding into the USA, in most cases this expansion is likely to take the form of establishing separate operations (be they new distributorships, further acquisitions, establishment of sales/marketing facilities, etc.). This may be partly attributable to the size of the North American market (and, with Mexico also included, this is extended further) which makes it difficult to regard the market as a single entity. Equally, however, there remain certain barriers between the two markets which make a singular approach difficult: legislative differences arising out of historical developments in the case of financial services firms, local content rules in the case of car component manufacturing, product testing and registration for pharmaceutical companies, barriers to establishing brands in the case of food and drink companies, rates of deregulation and liberalisation in telecommunications and gas supply, different levels of indigenous competition between the USA and Canada and the continued demands of customer proximity in many sectors. It is therefore the promise of greater freedoms, along with the growing power of the region brought about by the union, which is catalysing consolidation of effort rather than 'real' economic benefits from the establishment of a single market. Most firms recognise that the market is not homogeneous, and, although there are movements which are suggesting a coming-together of legislation and practices, these will not be felt for some time. Continued discretion and a willingness to be adaptable and flexible appears prudent.

This supports earlier research on the attitudes of UK firms towards the Single European Market where the ongoing internationalisation of sales/marketing offices and subsidiaries is viewed as an important means of ensuring that sensitivity to cultural differences across the twelve member states of Europe is maintained in organisations' marketing effort (Buckley *et al.*, 1992). Therefore, while there appears to be some potential for rationalisation of businesses, this is clearly functionally-based. Larger manufacturing units may be possible in the wake of economic liberalisation permitting greater economies of scale (although the size and geographic scope of the market may dictate regionally located plants); in sales and marketing, however, there continues to be little scope for centralisation of effort as firms maintain their intentions to locate activities in each market (indeed, in some cases different states). To this end, the extent of the cost savings from the establishment of the NAFTA must surely be questioned. The experiences of UK firms in North America are likely to be paralleled by Canadian organisations for which the establishment of subsidiaries in the USA is also at issue (see 'Canadian Firms and NAFTA', below). Consequently, a degree of caution over the real economic benefits of integration is necessary.

CANADIAN FIRMS AND THE SINGLE EUROPEAN MARKET

While changes are expected to come about as a result of the Single European Market Act, the extent of these changes centres more on business consolidation rather than major strategic change. To this end, firms are more concerned about taking greater advantage of the internal freedoms promised by the Single Market and are thus keen to secure their strategic positions to take advantage of liberalisation. Once again, firms expressed a degree of caution about regarding the Single European Market as a homogeneous business centre, and parallel developments between markets are likely to continue into the future.

Where the findings here differ to those from UK firms entering Canada is in the greater attention to specific elements of new legislation. Whereas the NAFTA concerns free trade and a general move towards liberalisation, the extent of these moves and the scope of the new legislation is far less than in the European Union, where, as one interviewee put it, the changing legislation is 'all-embracing'. It is therefore the specifics of the new programme which firms are addressing in their strategic developments. For example, issues such as mutual recognition and home-country control in financial services, harmonisation of technical standards for communications firms and the longer-term issues of Nordic and eastern European country integration for the producers of wood, paper and pulp, provide the critical facets of change. Thus, although the future of the European Union is still shrouded in a lot of uncertainty (particularly with regard to recent moves by the UK government and the removal of sterling from the Exchange Rate Mechanism), the clarity of the overall objectives appears to give firms a clearer idea of the specific nature of future strategies for Europe. Rather than simple expressions of 'greater opportunities', these comments were clarified by firms which described how the key elements of the new legislation are going to impact on their business.

Another issue which deserves some comment is the concern over Europe being protectionist. While few UK firms highlighted a long-term fear of the USA raising its external barriers and making life more difficult for foreign firms, there was some hint of this among the comments of Canadian managers. Part of this may have resulted from the early 'hype' regarding the Single Market, where observers from both North America and the Pacific Rim were keen to accuse the Europeans of building a 'fortress'. This may have shaped attitudes and resulted in fears about the possibility of this becoming an eventuality. The only example of this in practice was discussed with regard to harmonisation of technology, where it is believed that the current developments are being conducted with a mind to excluding American standards. On this issue there are perhaps grounds for complaint, as the Americans have been denied access to CEN and CENELEC, the European standard-setting bodies. Thus it is difficult for US firms to make the necessary adaptations to ensure that their products meet future specifications. This rejection of any involvement is particularly galling for the USA, as the American National Standards Institute is (in theory at least) open to Europe.

Related to technology, one of the clear aims of the Single European Market is the promotion of dynamic efficiency improvements in the region's technology base. It was argued by some Canadians that the preclusion of American competition from the Single Market will hamper this development, as it means that the market will insulate itself from world technological developments. While there is a case to support this thinking, one of the most interesting findings emanating from the research relates to the changing focus on technological development which is characterising many high-tech industries. For firms which felt that they did not possess the skills to generate new technologies in-house, access to technology (either through close working relationships with suppliers or equity stakes in technology-based companies) added a new dimension to technological competitiveness and threw into relief the growing complexity and sophistication of technology on a world scale. Possibly the most surprising finding here, however, was the very high incidence of firms which alluded to joint agreements for technological development (applicable to both Canadian and UK firms) as a key element in the creation of new products and processes. Clearly, this is seen as a fundamental part of sustaining competitive advantage in highly dynamic, technology-based sectors. Interestingly, the alliances which were highlighted showed little boundary definition in the sense that they occurred between firms in the same industry regardless of parent company location. The motivations for

172 Trade Blocs, Market Servicing and Transfer Pricing

such alliances, in the main, had less to do with market entry issues and were not, therefore, entered into as a way of securing market access and market penetration in foreign countries. They were specifically centred on research and development, the joint creation of new primary technologies and joint projects to provide solutions to specific problems. Furthermore, these alliances are not restricted to competing firms in the same industry; examples arose of firms entering into joint agreements with their customers (particularly where these customers are downstream producers) and suppliers.

Given the growing cost of research and development and the growing complexity of many technologies, the benefits which accrue from joint research projects are also becoming more evident to many firms. In the first case, joint ventures permit firms to reduce their exposure to risk and facilitate resource-sharing. Second, the pooling of skills continues to take on added significance as firms specialise their business operations into areas of core strengths and therefore have a more restricted technological base on which to draw. Combining specialisms therefore offers new opportunities to derive the advantages of technological scope within the framework of business focus on the part of the individual organisation.

The effect of these alliances is the breaking-down of traditional geographic borders in favour of truly internationalised industries where shared developments and complex business linkages are supplanting the development of monopolistic advantages and patent protection. One Canadian telecommunications firm, in its company report, described this growing trend as follows:

In fact, major developments in computer and telecommunications technologies and their integration into worldwide networks have resulted in something closer to a 'global village' than anything we have ever seen before. Businesses are facing changes more extensive, more far-reaching in their implications, and more fundamental in their transforming quality than at any time since the modern industrial system was established.

The implication is that technological developments are likely to traverse economic unions as the complex patterns of international business and inter-firm linkages supplant the importance of economic trading blocs in their contribution to product development and innovation. To this extent, dynamic efficiency is likely to emanate more from global competition and international alliances than internal policies to promote technology on a regional basis. The boundaries between trading blocs and the threat of protectionism, while applicable at the level of trade and investment, are far less important in respect of changing technology.

CANADIAN FIRMS AND NAFTA

Through discussions, it became apparent that many Canadian firms felt that American protectionism was posing more of a problem to their future development than is the case in Europe. Given the vehemence with which some of these complaints were made, some discussion of the issues is essential.

Many Canadian firms were keen to highlight the problems now being experienced by Canada as a result of the North American Free Trade Agreement. For some, this centred on specific complaints about ongoing protectionism by the USA, although for others their concerns related more generally to the fact that the NAFTA was resulting in an erosion of economic activity in Canada.

Several firms commented on the impact of cheaper labour in the USA which is promoting relocation on the part of US subsidiaries. Once keen to establish manufacturing subsidiaries in Canada to overcome tariffs and taxes between the two markets, US firms are taking advantage of greater liberalisation and are retrenching out of Canada as part of their ongoing rationalisation process. While in economic terms this makes a lot of sense, the removal of large-scale activities from Canada is putting a great deal of strain on the Canadian economy, particularly in terms of employment. Nevertheless, there is little evidence of Canadian firms following suit and closing their US subsidiaries in favour of more centralised (and efficient) manufacturing units at home. Part of the reason for this is the cheap labour, although equally one may adduce the reluctance to remove activities from the US market as a reflection of continued restrictive practices, the larger scale of the US market and the ongoing need for a local 'presence' to service markets effectively.

Equally, however, while there has been much US investment in Canada, there has been relatively little Canadian investment in the USA. Consequently, the Canadians are beholden to the Americans in many business sectors, which means that they have very little bargaining power to prevent these inevitable changes. The problems associated with such relocation are, however, compounded by the fact that the NAFTA does not provide for free movements of labour. While this is understandable given concerns over the free flow of cheap Mexican labour after full integration, it does mean that it is hard for workers to follow the business. The likely impact is unequal rates of unemployment which cannot be eliminated by market mechanisms. Two managers, however, suggested that to ascribe the process of relocation solely to NAFTA is short-sighted. Relocation was taking place anyway as a result of lower wage rates and taxes, and they feel that this should give Canada the impetus to match US levels rather than being seen as a disaster which cannot be overcome. Whatever the cause of the problem, it is placing increasing pressure on Canadian firms to lower their costs and improve efficiency, as there is no cushion to stifle the blows. Arguably, this is true across the board; in today's ever-globalising markets, efficiency and competitiveness are essential regardless of whether or not governments take steps to remove tariff and non-tariff barriers. The most competitive companies in the world can effectively operate across borders with or without barriers, making the problems of facing up to free trade a lame excuse for firms' failures.

SOME TENTATIVE CONCLUSIONS

There is some obvious concern that the NAFTA will not be favourable to the Canadians in many respects, and, as by far the smaller of the two economies, there are many fears that Canada will only survive if her firms take more initiative and move aggressively towards deepening their involvement in the USA. This gives further weight to the suggestions made earlier that Canadian firms need to improve their competitiveness, lowering costs and becoming more efficient, to extend their global potential. Indeed, the idea that all of Canada's problems can be attributed to the creation of the North American Free Trade Agreement was reiterated by many managers (even where they highlighted apparent problems), who felt that it was hard to separate out the effects of the recession, free trade, the high level of the Canadian dollar and the ongoing globalisation of business sectors which is intensifying competition. To this extent, certain managers qualified their concerns by stressing that, as protectionism and the need to overcome barriers has always been a part of their business, firms simply need to adjust to the new business environment and find innovative solutions to the current problems. For several firms, part of this process is ensuring development of the business on a worldwide scale, including the balancing of activities between the major trading blocs. This broadens the perspective of business planning beyond simple concerns over the North American Free Trade Agreement and the Single European Market and extends the remit to one of global strategic planning and development. From this point of view, the general attitude of firms to economic integration and changes in the international economic order, along with important changes which are now taking place in various industry sectors outside of the framework of economic integration, also underpin current strategic thinking and determine the underlying competitiveness of organisations.

The need to improve competitiveness was also voiced by UK firms, for which research and development, innovation and greater company efficiency were high on the agenda across the range of industries as companies attempt to consolidate both their domestic and international activities.

Generally, the establishment of the NAFTA and the Single European Market, while raising the awareness of firms to develop a strong presence in their own trading areas, is not acting counter to the need to establish international operations outside of their 'home' territories. To this extent, there is much evidence of firms striving for a 'global balance' in their business activities between the major regions in the triad. Many firms alluded to the fact that this new direction in international business thinking would have happened with or without the Single European Market and the North American Free Trade Agreement. What the impact of greater economic integration has therefore been is a catalyst to the consolidation of international business effort although not the cause in itself.

The major difference identified between Canadian and UK firms centres on their regard of the traditional trading patterns between the two countries. There was evidence that Canadian firms, in various sectors, view the UK as a good base from which to service the European market and a degree of confidence about future ability to expand business out of the UK. For British firms, this kind of cross-border 'roll-out' from Canada into the USA was not so evident. For one thing, many UK firms have already established facilities in the USA, to the extent that their US operations are often more sizeable than their Canadian businesses; for another, many firms see the future potential in the USA as being far greater than in Canada, and they are therefore more likely to grow their Canadian business out of their US base. To an extent this is not surprising, given the larger scale of the US market and also the fact that many high-technology industries are centred in the USA, which means that a proximate base in America is more strategically advisable. While some concerns were voiced regarding Canadian reaction to this trend (more protectionism through non-tariff barriers and growing nationalistic tendencies), the greater freedoms offered by the NAFTA are likely to support this kind of development.

Similarly, it was suggested that the *NAFTA* will enhance trade linkages not so much by the overt removal of trade restraints between Canada and the USA (as these are already small for most sectors) but by its psychological impact, in particular getting companies to base their strategic planning on a North American scale.

Despite the greater freedoms now being offered by free trade within the major trading blocs, there remains evidence of continued protectionism. Furthermore, while free trade is embraced as offering new business opportunities around the globe, there are fears that barriers will be raised between the economic groups as bilateral restrictions reappear on a world scale. Although this has the potential to make intra-trading-bloc trade and investment more difficult, it is viewed by many firms as simply posing fresh challenges. Protected markets have always existed, and ways of overcoming the barriers have always been found. There is no evidence to suggest that this will not be the case in the future. Indeed, it may be argued that, as many global industries already transcend the major trading blocs of the world, these artificially imposed boundaries will have little impact. Many firms have already secured a strong presence in the major world markets for their goods, and for them the barriers have little significance. Additionally, the complex networks of businesses which have now emerged on a global scale mean that country and regional affiliation of firms has grown less important. This is nowhere more evident than in the area of technological development, where strategic alliances and joint research projects within industry groups remove innovation and product development from geographic limitations.

Consequently, concentrating on simple taxonomies of exporting and investment fails to highlight the important strategic developments now taking place on a world scale, developments which are not regional or country-specific but more dependent on industry-specific considerations. It is possible to suggest that the relationships now being developed between organisations, whether they be between competing firms or between manufacturers and their customers or manufacturers and their suppliers, are having a far more important impact on international business development than the artificial boundaries which are the essence of greater global economic integration. It would appear, therefore, that the major impact of integration is therefore the impetus to shore up business activities in the major economic regions rather than the promises of greater economic benefits accruing from integration itself.

References

Baranson, J. (1985) *Assessment of the Likely Impact of a US–Canadian Free Trade Agreement upon the Behaviour of US Industrial Subsidiaries in Canada* (Government of Ontario, Ministry of Industry, Trade and Technology).

Buckley, Peter J., C.L. Pass and Kate Prescott (1992) *Servicing International Markets: Competitive Strategies of UK Firms* (Oxford: Blackwell).

Cecchini, P. (1988) *The European Challenge 1992: The Benefits of the Single Market* (London: Wildwood House).

Charles, R. (1989) 'Canada–United States Free Trade Agreement: A Canadian's Personal Perspective', *National Westminster Bank Quarterly Review*, May, pp. 17–26.

Department of Finance (1988) *The Canada–US Free Trade Agreement: An Economic Assessment*.

Department of Trade and Industry (1991) *Europe 1992* (London: DTI).

Economic Council of Canada (1988) *Venturing Forth: An Assessment of the Canada–US Free Trade Agreement.*

El Agraa, A.M. (1988) 'The Theory of Integration', in El Agraa (ed.), *International Economic Integration* (London: Macmillan).

European Commission (1988) *Progress Report on the European Commission.*

External Affairs and International Trade Canada (1991) *Moving into Europe* (EAITC).

Hamilton, R. and J. Whalley (1985) 'Geographically Discriminatory Trade Arrangements', *Review of Economics and Statistics*, 68 (3), pp. 446–55.

Harris, R. and D. Cox (1985) 'Summary of a Project on the General Equilibrium Evaluation of Canadian Trade Policy', in J. Whalley (ed.), *Canada–United States Free Trade*, vol. 2 (Toronto: Research Studies, Royal Commission on the Economic Union and Development Prospects for Canada).

The Independent (1988) 18 November.

Informetrica Ltd (1988) *Economic Impacts of Enhanced Bilateral Trade: National and Provincial Results.*

Institute for Policy Analysis (1985) 'The Macroeconomic Impacts of Free Trade with the United States: Lessons from the Focus-Prism Models', *University of Toronto Working Paper*, November, pp. 85–6.

Lipsey, R.G. (1990) 'Canada and the US–Mexico Free Trade Dance', *Commentary*, 21 (September), C.D. Howe Institute.

Nimmo, G. (1990) 'Canada, USA, Mexico: A New FTA?', *Investing in Canada*, 4 (3), pp. 1–3.

Ohmae, K. (1985) *Triad Power* (New York: The Free Press).

Papadopoulos, N. (1986) *Canada and the European Community: An Uncomfortable Partnership?* (Montreal: The Institute For Public Policy).

Porter, M.E. (1990) *The Competitive Advantage of Nations* (London: Macmillan).

Porter M.E. (1991) *Canada at the Crossroads: The Reality of a New Competitive Environment*, Report Prepared for the Business Council on National Issues and the Government of Canada.

Reitsma, S. (1990) 'Canada–US–Mexico Trade Policy Options', *Canadian Business Review*, 17 (4), pp. 17–20.

Rugman, A.M. (1985) 'A Canadian Strategy for International Competitiveness', *Business Quarterly*, 50 (1), pp. 1–4.

Rugman, A.M. (1987) 'Living with Free Trade: How Multinationals will Adjust to Trade Liberalisation', *Business Quarterly*, 52 (2), pp. 85–90.

Rugman, A.M. and J.D'Cruz (1991) *Fast Forward: Improving Canada's International Competitiveness* (University of Toronto and Kodak Inc.).

Rugman, A.M. and J. McIlveen (1985) *Megafirms: Strategies for Canada's Multinationals* (London: Methuen).

Rugman, A.M. and A. Verbeke (1990) 'Canadian Business in a Global Trading Environment', in A.M. Rugman (ed.), *Research in Global Strategic Management*, vol. 1 (New York: JAI Press).

Rugman, A.M. and A. Verbeke (1991) 'Trade Barriers and Corporate Strategy in International Companies – the Canadian Experience', *Long Range Planning*, 24 (3), pp. 66–72.

Thompson, G. (1991) 'The Role of Economies of Scale in Justifying Free Trade: The Canada–USA Free Trade Agreement and Europe 1992 Compared', *International Review of Applied Economics*, 5 (1), pp. 47–76.

WEFA Group (1987) *Canada–US Free Trade: Opportunities, Risks and Prospects* (Wharton Econometrics).

Whalley, J. (1990) 'Now That the Deal is Over: Canadian Trade Policy Options in the 1990s', *Canadian Public Policy*, 16 (2), pp. 121–36.

Wonnacott, R.J. (1990a) 'Canada and the US–Mexico Free Trade Negotiations', *Commentary*, 21 (September), C.D. Howe Institute.

Wonnacott, R.J. (1990b) 'The Canada–US Experience in Auto Trade Since 1965', *Commentary*, 24 (December), C.D. Howe Institute.

11 The Single European Market Initiative: A Perspective from Canadian Companies*

with C.L. Pass and Kate Prescott

Historically, Europe and North America have forged strong trade and investment linkages. With the increasing 'regionalisation' of these areas, ensuing from the Single European Act 1986 (the so-called '1992' initiative) and the establishment of the North American Free Trade Agreement (1989), the future of these transatlantic flows has been called into question. The dominance of regional concerns and issues in both governmental and corporate decision-making has raised the spectre of 'inwardness', protectionism and the side-lining of GATT. This article looks at Canadian companies' views and responses to the Single European Market initiative. Unlike national governments, which tend to view trade and investment issues in a somewhat parochial manner, multinational companies (MNCs) formulate their foreign market-servicing strategies on a broader scale, using cross-border exporting, strategic alliances (joint ventures etc.) and1 overseas investment to reduce costs and enhance their marketing effectiveness. From their perspective, the formation of regional blocs may cause some temporary 'inconveniences' (the need to adjust to revised product specifications, technical standards, environmental protection measures and overt discrimination against 'outsiders' in the form, for example, of local content rules), but they also create greater opportunities for business expansion through their trade-creation effects. Moreover, the flexibility accorded to the multinational company through its ability to select a market-servicing mode most appropriate to the new circumstances can be used to minimise or remove strategic disadvantages (for example, in the face of discrimination against imports, MNCs may replace exporting by investing in a local manufacturing plant).

*Originally published in *British Journal of Canadian Studies*, vol. 10, no. 1, 1995, pp. 77–86.

A key objective of the European Union (EU) – formerly the European Community – is to secure the economic benefits of free trade through the creation of a 'common market' providing for the unrestricted cross-border movement of goods, services, capital and people. Initially, under the Treaty of Rome provisions (1958), attention was focused on the elimination of various governmental restrictions on interestate trade such as tariffs and quotas. Under the Single European Act 1986, the intention was to create a 'single market' (by '1992' if possible) through the elimination of obstacles to trade arising from historical differences in member countries' policies and practices; that is, to remove the present fragmentation of the EU into 'national' markets and to create a 'level playing-field' so that firms can produce and sell their products throughout the EU bloc without discrimination. To date, the European Commission has formulated some 400 'Directives' for eliminating disparities between members in respect of physical, technical and fiscal rules and regulations so as to create a unified EU-wide set of practices: for example, individuals and freight transport will be able to move across national frontiers without undergoing passport and customs checks; common technical specifications are to be introduced relating to product descriptions and design, labelling and packaging, health and safety standards, etc., while VAT and other sales taxes are to be applied on a uniform basis. These Directives are at various stages of implementation, being more comprehensively applied in some countries (including the UK) than others.

The harmonisation of EU practices and the creation of a barrier-free common market are expected to produce substantial economic gains, estimated by the authoritative Cecchini Report (1988) to be in the order of 4–6 per cent of each member's GDP. Concern, however, has been expressed by other countries that the EU will become more of a 'fortress', thereby limiting multinational trading opportunities (see Buckley, Pass and Prescott, 1992). This is not, however, the intent of the architects of the programme:

> The Internal Market will be beneficial both to EC and to non-EC firms since they will no longer have to deal with the national and technical barriers it is to abolish; in addition, the economic growth expected from completion of the Internal Market will have favourable consequences both for the EC and its trading partners...The Internal Market programme involves no weakening of the EC's commitment to respect its international obligations. (European Commission, 1988, p. 8).

Inevitably, some trade frictions with non-members will arise (such as reciprocity of market access – see Company 5, below – and local content complications; see Company 8, below), but such problems will be there with or without the internal market and may be more easily resolved if a non-EU country is dealing with a single authority rather than twelve national governments.

Generally speaking, the Canadian government sees the Single European Market programme as presenting an opportunity for Canadian companies to expand their European operations (see External Affairs and International Trade Canada, 1991). Europe has remained a somewhat neglected area despite the early promise of the 1976 'Framework Agreement' between Canada and the EU and other initiatives such as cooperation agreements between Canadian provincial governments and their counterparts in the EU:

> In the last decade, our exports to the EC have increased only slightly, despite a generally favourable Canadian exchange rate. In the meantime, our share of merchandise imports in the major EC markets has actually declined…the figures suggest that Canadians must be more aggressive …and must increase their rate of investment in the EC if they are to capitalise on the opportunities offered by the development of the Single Market. (External Affairs, 1991, pp. 18–19)

In sum,

> Penetration of this vast and sophisticated market will enhance any company's competitive position in the global market place. Success in the European market, however, demands an ability to respond rapidly to changing technological and business conditions. Few Canadian businesses will be able to prosper in the EC if all they do is to maintain an arm's-length trading relationship. (External Affairs, 1991)

This section presents details of the foreign market-servicing strategies of a sample of Canadian companies with business interests in the UK and EU. In-depth interviews were conducted with ten Canadian companies operating in the following areas: Company 1 – wood and wood products; Company 2 – lager drinks; Company 3 – transportation services; Company 4 – insurance; Company 5 – corporate banking and treasury services; Company 6 – reinsurance; Company 7 – telecommunications equipment and systems; Company 8 – computers; Company 9 – satellite/space equipment and systems; and Company 10 – food products. The sample was designed to reflect, in part, the importance of wood and wood products, food and drink, financial services and communication products and services in Canadian overseas trade and investment flows. The sampled firms vary greatly in size (and associated resources available for international expansion) and experience of international market, ranging from 'smaller' firms (overseas turnover under C$100 million), with only a limited international involvement, to 'larger' firms (overseas turnover C\$400 million plus), mainly established multinational concerns with extensive international operations. Table 11.1 summarises the sampled companies' current modes of servicing the European market and indicates some of their 'concerns' and possible changes in their servicing strategy in the light of the Single European Market initiative.

Table 11.1   Canadian firms: foreign market-servicing modes in the UK and EU

Com-pany	Current foreign market-servicing mode in the UK and EU	Likely impact of single European market on servicing strategy
1.	Established UK sales subsidiary (1967) (timber/wood/pulp). Acquisition of UK manufacturer of wood products. Strategic alliances (joint ventures) in the Netherlands and Germany (sourced by exports of timber and wood pulp from Canada).	Further joint ventures in mainland Europe. Deeper direct investment, including local sourcing to counter EU's 'protectionist' stance on imports of timber and wood pulp.
2.	Licensing deals with several UK brewers (Allied, Vaux) to gain access to 'tied' public-house chains. Local brewing of company's 'standard' draught lager brand, incorporating yeast product exported from Canada. Wider distribution of 'premium' packaged brand through licencees' public houses. Strategic alliance (joint venture) to build up public-house chain. Acquisition of two brewers in Italy.	Further European investments when opportunities present themselves. Wide diversity of demand across the market requires acquisition of, or strategic alliances with, local brewers with strong established brands. The company's own brands can be slotted into local product portfolios as appropriate.
3.	Established UK sales office (1986). European port calls to collect/deliver cargo, but no mainland offices.	Possibly sales offices in main European ports. Integration will benefit transportation companies in general, but the company is concerned that the EU might impose a 'flag' preference system giving EU-owned vessels priority over foreign fleets.

4. Long-established UK sales subsidiary (1893) which runs an extensive network of branch offices.

   Established sales office in the Republic of Ireland, but no other European business.

   The company has adopted a 'wait and see' posture for the present, unlike many UK insurers who have entered into strategic alliances with other European insurers and broad-based financial services groups.

5. Long-established treasury office in the UK (1870).

   Acquired UK broking business to give the company European legal status – important in obtaining 'freedom of access' under the 2nd Banking Directive. However, as yet, the company has no business outside the UK.

   May establish offices in other European financial centres (Paris, Brussels) if treasury business moves away from London. As with Company (4), the company has adopted a 'wait and see' stance. The issue of 'reciprocity' is being looked at by the EU and NAFTA authorities.

6. Established UK sales subsidiary (1987).

   Established sales/branch office in Brussels (1989) to develop European business contacts and 'monitor' new legislation.

   No immediate plans to set up further local offices.

7. Established UK sales subsidiary (1978) sourcing products from overseas plants. Established various manufacturing operations in England, Wales and Northern Ireland (1980s).

   Acquisition of major UK-based equipment manufacturer (1991) with European plants and sales network.

   Strategic alliances (joint ventures) to provide further expansion into Europe: Germany (1991), Poland (1992), Spain (1992) and France (1992).

   Further strategic alliances to widen and deepen access to 'big ticket' procurement contracts. Some concern at moves to harmonise technical standards around local firms' systems (under CEN/CENELEC) and 'local fiefdoms' in perpetuating procurement bias.

Table 11.1   (contd.)

Com-pany	Current foreign market-servicing mode in the UK and EU	Likely impact of single European market on servicing strategy
8.	Established UK sales office (1970) sourcing computers and peripherals from US-based parent and Canadian subsidiary. Exports to mainland Europe via distributors, sourcing from overseas plants and Ireland (see below). Established greenfield manufacturing plant in Republic of Ireland (1988) as an 'export' platform into the UK and mainland Europe.	Local-content issues are very much to the fore as the company's Irish plant sources some components from its overseas plants. The company is currently 'negotiating' with the European Commission to clarify local-content status, the likelihood being that more items will need to be sourced locally for its products to qualify as 'authentic' European products, thus avoiding import restrictions.
9.	Exports of 'know-how' and space/satellite equipment through UK and European strategic alliances (co-production and installation consortiums). Acquired US company (1989) producing related products which brought in a UK manufacturing subsidiary. Subsidiary used to 'coordinate' the company's participation in European strategic alliances.	Continuance of the strategic alliance format. Like Company (7), the company is concerned at the implications of CEN/CENELEC arrangements for 'foreign' companies – the issue of 'reciprocity' is being looked at by the EU and NAFTA authorities.
10.	Established UK manufacturing subsidiary (1968). Established and acquired manufacturing plants in Spain, the Netherlands, Belgium and France and sales offices/subsidiaries in EU markets. Cross-border exporting of some products to expand local product portfolios.	Will establish or acquire businesses to increase market penetration as appropriate. Development of 'pan-European' brands in certain product lines.

For some companies, the European Union bloc already contributes a sizeable proportion of their sales turnover, and the Single European Market initiative is seen as providing them with further opportunities for increasing their sales and profits. For example, European sales currently account for around

30 per cent of Company 1's turnover. In the past, the company relied mainly on exporting to supply the EU markets, selling wood pulp and timber directly to local sawmills and through local distributors. However, a number of changes in the industry have increased the importance of establishing a market presence through joint ventures and wholly-owned subsidiaries. The timber and paper industries in many countries have become more concentrated, reducing the number and increasing the power of indigenous competitors, and vertical integration has increased, while governments have imposed more exacting product specifications and environmental protection measures (for example, in the EU, a reduction in the chlorine content of wood pulp). In 1989, the company acquired the UK's third largest producer of wood panels and corrugated cases. The acquisition was viewed as providing an opportunity to expand in a rapidly growing market, benefiting from the UK company's existing sizeable market position and as a platform for introducing the company's 'innovatory' new panel-board product into the European market.

The company has established joint-venture operations in Germany and the Netherlands. The Dutch company (in which it has a 31 per cent equity stake) is a substantial supplier of coated and uncoated printing papers and paper packaging materials with an extensive EU network. Company 1 supplies wood pulp to the venture, and the Dutch company undertakes production and is responsible for marketing.

The European legislative environment is an important consideration for companies selling timber and paper products in this arena. 'Presence' has helped the company in its dealings with officialdom in negotiating standards and product-use applications. (It is to be noted that the Canadian Paper and Pulp Association has established an office in Brussels for the purpose of lobbying and ensuring a fair deal for Canadian firms.) Thus, overall, having an investment presence in Europe has helped the company to expand its business opportunities. The Single European Market initiatives are likely to provide further scope for increased market penetration through the harmonisation of product standards and the removal of procurement biases favouring indigenous suppliers. Company 1 is actively looking to forge further joint-venture alliances to enhance market access and, generally, compete against other suppliers (i.e. EU-based competitors, as well as exporters from Russia and increasingly from eastern European countries; Scandinavian suppliers continue to pose a particularly serious threat with the extension of the Single European Market directives to this area through the European Economic Association, and the increased emphasis on forward vertical integration). The 'protectionist' sentiments of the European Union bloc regarding imports of basic timber and wood pulp (involving price controls and quotas) have caused the company some concern in the past, but it feels that being an 'in-market' player has considerably strengthened its position for future expansion.

Company 2, Canada's second largest beer producer, is in the process of developing its business in the European Union, where it has a manufacturing and marketing investment in Italy and has concluded licensing agreements with a number of UK brewers covering manufacturing and distribution. In the UK, licensing local producers to manufacture their brands has been the main market-entry route chosen by overseas-based lager brewers because of the ownership of public houses by established indigenous brewers. This enables entrants to 'piggy-back' established distribution channels. Under the company's licensing agreements (or 'partnership agreements', as the company prefers to call them), the company exports the distinctive yeast component of the draught product to its UK licensees for incorporation into the local brewing operation, while the company's leading packaged premium lager is exported to licencees who undertake distribution and marketing. This strategy allows the company to retain some 'control' over its product while enabling the company to access a much wider distribution network than would have been possible by 'going it alone'. Licensing agreements have enabled the company to achieve a rapid rate of growth of sales and establish a sizeable market share (its leading brand is now among the top ten best- selling brands in the mainstream draught larger sector).

Company 2 believes that the Single European Market initiative will open up major opportunities. The beer market across the EU is fragmented, and the company takes the view that there is potential for new entrants to come into the market with a 'macro-brewery' aimed at servicing the main centres in member states (this may be, in the writers' opinion, 'optimistic' in view of the diversity in European beer tastes, requiring more of a 'customised' approach to one based on the 'global brand' theme). Apart from in the UK, the company is well represented in the Italian beer market, where it has three breweries and a national sales force and distribution network. The company is Italy's third largest brewer (a market which is dominated by overseas brewers), having acquired Birra Moretti and Prinz Brau in 1988. Further investments in Europe are high on the agenda, as the company intends to establish a strong European presence. The company's view is that current problems within GATT and the polarisation of economies into major trading blocs is raising barriers to business between the leading world markets and that a direct investment presence in key consuming markets is necessary to achieve profitable growth.

Company 10 specialises in the manufacture of frozen food products. Around 50 per cent of the company's turnover is generated in Europe. The

UK was identified in the 1960s as a promising growth market when it was expected to follow the US pattern of increasing demand for packaged convenience foods. The company established a greenfield manufacturing plant in 1968 to supply the UK market with frozen French-fry chips, and quickly established itself as market leader in this sector. The company's initial success in the UK provided the impetus for expansion into mainland Europe, where it now has manufacturing plants in the Netherlands (acquisitions), Spain (greenfield), France (greenfield) and Belgium (acquisitions). Adjacent markets are serviced by exports from these plants through sales subsidiaries. Some 'networking' is involved in these operations – the German market, for example, is serviced with product lines exported from the French and Dutch plants. The company is currently well placed in Europe, and to this extent the Single European Market initiative *per se* will make little difference to the company's strategic direction. Local consumer preferences will still dictate the need to develop products specifically for particular markets, but the company has already embarked upon the development of certain 'pan-European' brands which can be produced centrally and sold, with minor packaging and labelling adjustments, in all the main markets.

By contrast, a number of companies with a long-established presence in the UK, but no, or little, mainland European involvement, have treated the Single European Market initiative with reticence. For example, Company 4, established in the UK since 1893 and in the Republic of Ireland, has yet to formulate a broader-based European strategy. In the run-up to '1992', the company investigated the possibility of establishing sales offices in Belgium and Spain but decided not to proceed. Thus, at the present time, it has no European interests outside the UK and Ireland. The company's attitude on this remains 'cautious' to say the least, or even 'myopic'. The company is of the view that 'it is early days and the realities of the Single European Market remain filled with uncertainties'. It will 'wait and see', and monitor developments as they unfold. Interestingly, many UK financial groups, while equally sceptical of some of the more radical benefits which it is claimed will ensue from harmonisation of financial practices and freedoms to operate across borders, have nevertheless developed a stronger continental European presence, mainly using the strategic alliance mode (joint ventures and co-marketing agreements) which minimises entry costs by accessing partners' established distribution channels and avoiding head-to-head competition with incumbents.

The problem of market access to the European Union was mentioned by several of the companies in our sample. Restrictions on the importation of timber and wood pulp was of concern to Company 1, as noted above. The harmonisation of technical standards posed problems for Companies 7 and 9.

For example, in the telecommunications sector, Company 7 expressed concern at the way in which a number of leading indigenous suppliers were exerting 'pressure' on the European Commission to adopt formats which would exclude North American standards. Similarly, Company 9 (satellite equipment), while seeing the Single European Market initiative as providing opportunities for expansion, felt that the CEN/CENELEC arrangements as presently operated 'close out' foreign suppliers to a marked degree. Both companies felt that having a direct presence in the EU would help them develop a strong European 'persona'. Other areas of concern include reciprocity, procurement and local content, as discussed next.

Company 5 is a specialised treasury division of one of Canada's leading banks. It has been operating in the UK since the nineteenth century, reflecting the pivotal role played in Europe by London in foreign currency dealings, money-market and off-balance-sheet trading. The focus of the company's operations will remain UK-based, although if treasury business devolves away from London to other European centres such as Paris and Brussels the company is prepared to establish mainland offices to remain fully competitive. The company has been concerned at the 'reciprocity' sanctions incorporated in the second EU Banking Directive. Specifically, this requires foreign countries to allow open access to their financial markets in return for open access to the EU. Given that Canadian banking regulations currently limit foreign access to the Canadian market, some Canadian banks have sought to establish 'European status' by establishing or acquiring locally incorporated banks and securities firms in order to obtain unrestricted access to European financial markets. To this end, Company 5 acquired a UK broking business, which qualifies the company as a bona fide European financial institution with full rights of access.

Market access to some sectors of European business has been a problem because of procurement 'bias', particularly in the public sector. For example, overseas suppliers of telecommunications equipment have found it difficult to break into the European market, which hitherto has been tightly regulated by government and where in some countries public-sector monopolies have procured equipment from a 'select' group of established suppliers. Company 7 set up a UK sales subsidiary in 1978 but had little success in obtaining 'big ticket' orders from the then state-owned monopoly supplier of telecommunications services (British Telecom). Even after the privatisation of BT in 1984 and the liberalisation of the UK market, obtaining business continued to be difficult. In 1987, however, an opportunity for the company to advance its position in the UK market arose when a US concern sold its 27 per cent stake in a leading UK supplier to Company 7, and this was followed by full acquisition in 1991. This acquisition also provided the company with a strong entrée into mainland Europe, bringing with it manufacturing plants in France and

Ireland and a broad-based pan-European distribution network. The company has recently entered into strategic alliances with partners in Germany, Poland, France and Spain to obtain a stronger market presence. However, the company still has some concerns about 'Fortress Europe' and the perpetuation of procurement bias by 'local fiefdoms'.

Even a direct presence in the EU bloc may, in itself, be insufficient to secure full market access, as the Japanese have found in the car and photocopier markets. The issue of 'screwdriver' plants, sourcing components from outside the EU, remains in flux. One of our sample companies, Company 8 (computers), is currently 'negotiating' with the European Commission over local-content requirements. The company had established a manufacturing plant in the Republic of Ireland in 1988 to service the European market; previously it had exported computers to Europe from its Canadian and US plants. The Irish operation is a 'platform' for exports into Europe, with sales, marketing and after-sales facilities being undertaken by local sales offices and, in the case of mainland Europe, supported by a large distribution centre in Amsterdam. However, the potential of the European operation has been hampered by a local-content dispute. Certain components used in the manufacture of computers in Ireland are sourced from the USA and Japan. This has raised a question mark relating to the 'authenticity' of the final product as a bona fide European product and hence fully tradeable across EU markets without impediment. The likelihood is that the European Commission will require the company to increase the European content of its products in order to avoid trade impositions.

The general consensus of Canadian firms regarding the harmonisation programme is that it presents greater opportunity to offer products across the whole of the EU bloc. Thus, many companies are either contemplating establishing European operations or are in the process of expanding existing operations further. Economic integration in the EU is currently ongoing and in flux. The various 'single market' directives aimed at harmonising EU technical standards, product specifications, etc. are well advanced in many cases, but the move towards a fuller unification of members' economies, involving (as mooted in the Maastricht Treaty) a Single European currency, is less so. However, while it may be possible to harmonise 'supply-side' factors (for example, the introduction of common technical standards), this is often not possible to any great extent on the 'demand side' of the market where idiosyncratic and differentiated consumer preferences, reflecting deep-rooted national characteristics and cultural factors, are likely to continue to hold sway. Thus, the pan-European brand approach to servicing EU markets may well remain elusive, and careful attention to 'customisation' of products to meet local buyer tastes will be required.

For businesses domiciled outside the EU, market penetration and competitiveness can be enhanced by establishing an 'in-market' persona either through wholly-owned local investment or by joint-venture alliances with local partners. Apart from this, a local presence may be necessary in many instances in order to counteract various 'complications' relating to such matters as quota restrictions on 'sensitive' products (Company 1), 'reciprocity' giving equal freedoms of market access (Company 5), 'procurement' bias (Company 7), and 'local content' complications (Company 9).

The Canadian government and its agencies (Investment Canada, in particular) continue to exhort Canadian companies to 'think European' and not to become totally preoccupied with facing the opportunities and threats posed by the North American Free Trade Agreement. Similar considerations, of course, apply in reverse, with the NAFTA initiative providing considerable scope for British and EU firms to expand their involvement in North America. Thus, although the formation of regional blocs may have raised 'barriers to business' to some extent (cf. Company 2), the notion of regional blocs *per se* serving to 'polarise' the world trading system is clearly exaggerated.

References

Buckley, Peter J., C.L. Pass and K. Prescott (1992) *Servicing International Markets* (Oxford: Blackwell).

Cecchini, P. (1988) *The European Challenge 1992: The Benefits of a Single Market* (London: Wildwood House).

European Commission (1988) *Progress Report to the European Commission* (Brussels).

External Affairs and International Trade Canada (1991) *Moving Into Europe* (Ottawa).

12 Canadian–European Union Strategic Alliances*

with C.L. Pass and Kate Prescott

Strategic alliances with foreign partners are one means which a company can adopt to internationalise its business alongside exporting and wholly-owned foreign production and marketing subsidiaries.

This article reports the experiences of a number of Canadian companies which have sought to develop their business interests in Europe and enhance their worldwide capabilities by establishing alliances with European partners, mainly UK-based. The authors' interest in undertaking this work was prompted in part by our earlier study, *Canada–UK Bilateral Trade and Investment Relations* (1995), which highlighted various aspects of companies' foreign market-servicing strategies, including alliances. It also reflects the concern of the Canadian authorities to encourage Canadian companies to broaden their horizons beyond North America and to 'go global'. For companies unaccustomed to international business, and even those which have already gone down this road, strategic alliances with foreign partners can provide an opportunity to acquire new resources and competencies and to enter new markets or expand further in existing markets:

> Strategic alliances enable firms to position themselves in overseas markets without the high investments that were traditionally the only alternative to exporting. Strategic alliances not only save time and money, they also enable each partner to focus on what it does best, relying on the other to provide the skills, local savvy, resources or financing necessary to achieve success. (External Affairs and International Trade Canada, 1991, Executive Summary)

INTERNATIONALISATION STRATEGIES: AN OVERVIEW

Strategic alliances with foreign partners can enable firms to obtain access to worldwide technologies, know-how, capital and markets to augment their

---

* Originally published in *British Journal of Canadian Studies*, vol. 11, no. 2, 1996, pp. 254–64.

own resources and capabilities. Pooling resources and capabilities through alliances enables firms to achieve synergistic effects otherwise unobtainable on an individual basis. Partners can contribute established distribution and marketing networks, product and R&D facilities and local knowledge of the markets which they serve. International alliances, in particular, can ensure that products reach the marketplace more quickly and more effectively, especially where products need to be modified to meet local regulations covering product standards and packaging, and the preferences of local customers. Strategic alliances take two main forms. *Contractual agreements* in which partners, for example, agree to cooperate to make components or complete products (co-production), to distribute and market each other's products (co-marketing) and to develop new products (joint research and development), are called 'non-equity ventures'. *Joint ventures*, which involve the formation of a separate company which is owned by two or more 'parent' firms which each provide (in most cases) the equity for the business, are called 'equity ventures'.

While, as noted above, strategic alliances can yield positive benefits to partners, there are some potential drawbacks. Arm's-length cooperation agreements need careful planning and nurturing and involve 'agency' costs in negotiating, securing and monitoring contracts; they also require the establishment of mutual trust and commitment. Joint ventures go some way to implementing a stronger link between partners, but problems of joint control of operations again may limit the effectiveness of the alliance.

In practice, strategic alliances are used alongside exporting and wholly-owned foreign direct investment (FDI) in production and sales subsidiaries as a means of servicing international markets. Exporting from a centralised 'home' production plant is a relatively inexpensive and low-risk way of servicing a foreign market, enabling the firm to take full advantage of economies of scale. Unlike FDI, no overseas capital commitment (with its attendant risks) is required, and it is easy to withdraw from the market should the products fail to sell. However, the firm can be disadvantaged if imports are restricted by tariffs and quotas or by currency appreciation. Moreover, the use of independent agents and distributors to sell the firm's products may limit potential if it does not have control over the marketing of its products. This latter problem can be overcome by investment in a wholly-owned sales and marketing subsidiary. Wholly-owned FDI in the establishment of a local production plant may be attractive for a number of reasons. For example, it may enable the firm to lower its supply costs by taking advantage of low local wage rates and the elimination of long-haul transportation costs. Also, by its local presence in the market, the firm is in a better position to supply on a 'just-in-time' basis and to provide various back-up services such as repair and maintenance. However, FDI can be expensive and risky, especially in setting up a 'greenfield' plant. Alternatively, the firm could merge with, or take over, a local business, thus obtaining immediate access to local production facilities and established distribution networks.

How the firm chooses to service foreign markets will depend on an amalgam of considerations, including:

(1) firm-specific factors (the nature and 'uniqueness' of the firm's products and its resources and competencies, etc.). For example, small firms which have limited capital resources for expansion typically use the exporting mode to sell their products in foreign markets.

(2) industry-specific factors in target markets (level of seller concentration, availability of distribution networks, etc.). For example, if distribution networks are controlled by domestic suppliers, a strategic alliances with a local partner may be necessary to secure national coverage.

(3) country-specific factors (degree of economic maturity, government policies on trade and investments, etc.). For example, market access may be impeded by import controls, thus necessitating a local production presence; wholly-owned investments may be prohibited, forcing foreign firms to establish joint ventures with local partners.

Given the variety of these factors, there is no one general foreign market-servicing strategy which can be applied across the board. Rather, the firm must be pragmatic and be prepared to adapt its approach according to individual circumstances. Insofar as these factors are dynamic and changeable over time, the firm must also be prepared to be flexible and to change its strategies accordingly, switching, for example, from arm's-length exporting to an in-market investment.

EMPIRICAL STUDY OF STRATEGIC ALLIANCES BY CANADIAN COMPANIES WITH EUROPEAN PARTNERS

Interviews were conducted with the senior executives of eight Canadian companies and sixteen of their European alliance partners:

- Kenox's licensing agreement with Leigh Environmental (UK) relating to its innovatory wet-air oxidation waste-disposal system.
- Canadian Utilities' joint venture with BICC (UK) to build and operate a power station.

- MPR Teltech's agreement with Gooding Microwave (UK) and Precision Antennas (UK) relating to the development and manufacture of new satellite receiving equipment.
- BioChem Pharma's agreement with Glaxo (UK) relating to the development and co-marketing of an anti-AIDS drug.
- Allelix's agreements with Glaxo (UK), Hoechst-Roussel (Germany), Chiron (Netherlands) and Groupe Fournier (France) relating to the development and co-marketing of various antiviral and osteoporosis drugs.
- Nortel's joint ventures with Lagardère Group (France), Daimler-Benz Aerospace (Germany) and Olivetti (Italy) relating to the supply and distribution of telecommunications equipment.
- FastMAN's licensing agreement with Open Business Solutions (UK) relating to the installation of its computer software systems.
- Labatt's licensing agreements with Carlsberg-Tetley (UK) and Vaux (UK) and joint venture with Pubmaster (UK) to supply and distribute its lager beer.

The objective generally is to enhance competitive advantages and increase sales and profit-earning potential, and the sample of strategic alliances by Canadian companies reported here illustrates all the reasons cited above. Table 12.1 summarises the main features of a selected number of these alliances by type of alliance, objectives of the partners and partner responsibilities or tasks. (In the interests of brevity, only some of the strategic alliances by Allelix, Nortel and Labatt are recorded in Table 12.1).

With regard to resources, facilities and competencies, the two Canadian biopharmaceutical companies, for example, have relied extensively on the 'up-front' and 'milestone' payments worth millions of Canadian dollars provided by their alliance partners to fund ongoing R&D work. Likewise, CU Power Generation has reduced the capital cost of building a power-generation plant in the UK by a shared investment with its 50-50 joint-venture partner BICC. In some cases, the alliance format has been used to enable a firm to obtain the expertise of its partner to provide synergy: for example, the 'mixing and matching' of MPR Teltech's telecommunications know-how with that of Gooding's microwave expertise which has resulted in the development of new satellite receiving equipment; the installation and 'customisation' of FastMAN's MRP computer software package by Open Business Solutions in user companies; Nortel's access to GSM mobile phone technology through its 50-50 joint-venture company Matra Communication; and Allelix's alliance with Group Fournier, which cross-fertilises the former's biopharmaceutical specialism with the latter's expertise in the 'lipids' field.

Additionally, alliances enable firms to access local production facilities, as in the cases of MPR Teltech and Labatt, where the long-haul exporting of bulky products is too expensive and where an investment in an overseas production plant is uneconomic given the volumes involved. As also mentioned above, strategic alliances are often attractive as a means for a firm to enter a foreign market. Alliances are especially suited to accessing 'difficult' markets where entry is impeded by, for example, 'tied' distribution channels or local procurement bias, or where the authorities restrict imports and wholly-owned investments.

Table 12.1   Strategic alliances: summaries of alliance type, objectives and responsibilities

---

Kenox (Canada) – Leigh Environmental (UK), 1990

Type of alliance	Licensing agreement: waste-disposal technology.
Objectives	Kenox: First move into European market. Leigh: Exclusive UK rights to innovative technology.
Responsibilities	Kenox: 'Lead' designer and installer of its 'wet-air oxidation' technology, managing subcontractors to build plant and supply equipment. Leigh: Plant operator.

Canadian Utilities Power Generation (Canada) – BICC (UK), 1989

Type of alliance	50-50 equity joint venture, Thames Power: electricity generation.
Objectives	CU Power Generation: First move into European market. BICC: Power-plant builder – forward integration into electricity generation sector.
Responsibilities	CU Power Generation: Overall project management. Plant operator. BICC: Lead 'contractor'.

FastMAN (Canada) – Open Business Solutions (UK), 1994

Type of alliance	Installation and product development agreement: computer software applications.
Objectives	FastMAN: First move into European market. Will enable it to service the needs of global manufacturers in integrating their multi-site operations. Open Business Solutions: Access to innovative 'solutions' system, giving it competitive advantage.
Responsibilities	Joint: Development work on applications. Open Business Solutions: Marketing. Installation of FastMAN 3.4 software in client companies undertaking the necessary 'customisation' of the system to meet particular operational requirements.

Table 12.1   (contd.)

MPR Teltech (Canada) – Gooding Microwave and Precision Antennas (UK), 1994

Type of alliance	Product development and contract manufacturing/sales agreement: satellite receiving equipment.
Objectives	MPR Teltech: Further business expansion in Europe. Obtained contract from European Space Agency to develop and supply a new satellite receiving dish. ESA 'favours' collaborative contracts involving European partners. Access to Gooding's microwave know-how. Gooding: Further application of its microwave expertise. Precision: Extra business.
Responsibilities	Joint: MPR and Gooding to collaborate to produce a new satellite receiving dish. Gooding: Management of volume production of dishes (using subcontractors and antennas supplied by Precision) and pan-European marketing.

BioChem Pharma (Canada) – Glaxo (UK), 1990

Type of alliance	Product development and co-marketing agreement: pharmaceuticals. Glaxo has taken a 17 per cent equity stake in BioChem.
Objectives	BioChem: Access to funding for R&D. Access to Glaxo's worldwide marketing network. Glaxo: Access to new drugs to add to its product portfolio.
Responsibilities	BioChem: Basic research and sharing of know-how with partner. Canadian marketing rights to new products developed through the collaboration. Glaxo: Product development. Conduct of clinical trials and obtaining drug 'approval' from regulatory authorities. Production of new drugs. Marketing outside Canada.

Allelix (Canada): selected alliances

1. Glaxo (UK), 1989

Type of alliance	Initially, co-product development agreement: pharmaceuticals. Glaxo has taken a 9.7 per cent equity stake in Allelix. Joint venture established, 1993, co-development and co-marketing: pharmaceuticals.
Objectives	Allelix: Research synergies. Shared cost of development work. Access to Glaxo's worldwide marketing network. Glaxo: Access to new drugs to add to its product portfolio.
Responsibilities	Allelix: Development work and supply of 'active' ingredients. Co-marketing in Canada. Glaxo: Development work. Management of clinical trials and obtaining drug 'approval' from regulatory authorities. Production of new drugs. Marketing outside Canada.

The joint venture was terminated in 1995 as a result of Glaxo's decision to prioritise its R&D programme and concentrate its resources on fewer therapeutic categories; the equity stake was maintained.

2. Groupe Fournier (France), 1994

Type of alliance	Co-product development and co-marketing agreement: pharmaceuticals.
Objectives	Joint: Research synergies 'blending' Allelix's expertise in '3T' technology with Fournier's know-how and capabilities in 'lipids' field to develop new atherosclerosis drugs. Allelix: Access to funding for R&D. Access to Fournier's international marketing network. Fournier: Access to new drugs.
Responsibilities	Joint: R&D work. Allelix: Co-promotion rights in Canada. Fournier: Management of clinical trials and obtaining drug 'approval'. Production of new drugs. Marketing outside Canada.

Nortel (Canada): selected alliances

1. Lagardère Matra (France), 1992

Type of alliance	50-50 equity joint venture, Matra Communication: telecommunications equipment.
Objectives	Nortel: Market access – Matra's business links with monopoly operator, France Télécom, important in obtaining supply contracts. Access to Matra's European GSM mobile phone technology. Matra: Cash injection and achievement of 'critical mass' in competing against industry leaders. Access to Nortel's PBX equipment.
Responsibilities	Joint: Development of new telecom systems. Production and marketing of extended product line.

2. Daimler-Benz Aerospace (Germany), 1995

Type of alliance	50-50 equity joint venture company, Nortel Daimler: telecommunications equipment.
Objectives	Nortel: Market access – augmentation of its established presence in the build-up to market liberalisation in 1998. Daimler-Benz a 'high profile' company – useful in developing contacts. Daimler-Benz: Diversification into potentially lucrative growth market.
Responsibilities	Joint: The venture aims to produce and market telecom equipment for public and private networks.

John Labatt (Canada): selected alliances

1. Carlsberg-Tetley (UK), 1992

Type of alliance	Licensing, contract brewing and distribution agreement: lager beers.

Table 12.1   (contd.)

Objectives	Labatt: First move into European market. Local brewing cheaper than long-haul exporting. Key factor: access to 'tied' distribution network. Carlsberg-Tetley: Extension of product portfolio. Contract brewing adds to capacity utilisation and revenues.
Responsibilities	Labatt: Supplies yeast ingredients for its lagers and controls product specification. The UK subsidiary has overall responsibility for promotion (particularly national advertising) and 'free' trade sales. Carlsberg-Tetley: Brews and distributes through own national 'tied' public houses and supplies 'free' trade customers.

2. Pubmaster (UK), 1992

Type of alliance	50-50 joint venture, Maple Leaf Inns: beer retailing. All equity provided by Labatt.
Objectives	Labatt: Market access – vertical integration providing 'tied' outlets for its lagers. 'Reciprocal' trading enabling Labatt's lagers to access other brewers' estates. Retailing operation to be 'profit centre' in its own right. Pubmaster: Extension of its existing beer retailing operations.
Responsibilities	Labatt: Provision of finance for public-house acquisition programme. Pubmaster: Day-to-day management of retailing operations.

The joint venture was terminated in 1994 when Labatt decided to put its retailing operations on a more dedicated footing. It established its own retail subsidiary which took over the Maple Leaf estate and a number of public houses previously acquired by its sister company, Labatt Brewing Ltd.

In the case of four Canadian companies in the sample, their involvement in a strategic alliance marked their first entry into the European arena. For CU Power Generation, the company's electricity generation alliance, with BICC and through a subsidiary owned in partnership with three electricity distribution companies, has given it a viable customer base to justify a heavy up-front investment in power plant. For MPR Teltech, given that the European Space Agency 'favours' bids for contracts from consortia which include European partners, forging an alliance with two UK companies helped it to obtain a contract to design and supply satellite receiving equipment. In the case of Labatt, entry to the UK beer market through alliances with established brewers was seen as an imperative so as to obtain distribution through their 'tied' public-house networks. This approach was later augmented by, initially, a joint venture with an established public-house operator and then by the establishment of a wholly-owned beer retailing operation. Likewise, a joint venture with an established supplier, Matra Communication, in the French market has assisted Nortel to secure 'big ticket' equipment orders from France Télé-com, the country's monopoly provider of telecom services. Finally, in the case of the two Canadian pharmaceutical research specialists, BioChem Pharma and Allelix, one of the main advantages of their co-development alli-ances with a number of global pharmaceutical companies (Glaxo, Hoechst, Groupe Fournier) is the opportunity that they provide for any new drugs emerging from the collaboration to be marketed through the latter's distribu-tion networks both in Europe and worldwide.

The precise form that an alliance takes, whether contractual or equity-based, depends very much on the preferences of the companies concerned and the 'depth' and projected duration of the alliance. Generally, if there is a heavy investment requirement, the partner may decide to establish a separate equity-based joint-venture business unit, such as CU Power–BICC: Thames Power; Nortel–Lagardère: Matra Communication; Labatt–Pubmaster: Maple Leaf Inns. However, it is to be noted that contractual alliances can also be underpinned by equity investments, as was the case in Glaxo's alliances with BioChem and Allelix and in Hoechst's alliance with Allelix.

Irrespective of the form that an alliance takes, the responsibilities of each partner may be sharply delineated or combined and separated in a variety of ways. To take some examples, in the case of Kenox–Leigh, Kenox was re-sponsible for plant design and the installation of its 'wet-air oxidation' pro-cess while Leigh is the plant operator; in FastMAN–Open Business Solutions, FastMAN supplies the basic software package while Open Busi-ness Solutions is responsible for application and 'customisation' of the sys-tem to meet individual client company requirements; in CU Power–BICC, BICC's main function was to build the power plant, while CU Power will be responsible for the management of the plant. Other alliances, by contrast, are more multi-faceted. The BioChem–Glaxo alliance, for example, provides for joint development work on new drugs. Glaxo is responsible for the conduct of clinical trials, for obtaining regulatory approval and for worldwide pro-duction and marketing outside Canada. BioChem has the Canadian market-ing rights to any new drugs ensuing from the collaboration. In the case of Labatt and its alliances with Carlsberg-Tetley, Labatt supplies the distinctive yeast ingredient for its lagers and controls product specification. Carlsberg-Tetley undertakes contract brewing, distributes the brews through its own public houses and supplies free trade outlets. Labatt, however, retains overall responsibility for marketing, particularly national advertising campaigns.

The process of identifying and making contact with potential alliance part-ners is also of interest. Labatt's UK subsidiary 'sought out' regional brewers who were prepared to add its lagers to their real-ale portfolios; Nortel was aware from trade sources that Matra was 'in play', which prompted it to open negotiations with its parent, Lagardêre; CU Power and BICC were brought together by a London-based merchant bank which had assisted both companies on previous consortia projects, while MPR Teltech and FastMAN were put in touch with their UK partners by the Canadian High Commission in London. Kenox's involvement with Leigh came about as a result of an advertisement placed in a trade journal asking potential licenses to contact it, while Glaxo approached BioChem and Allelix after details of their research work were reported in the medical journal *Scrip*.

While in most cases strategic alliances yield the companies themselves 'net benefits', what impact do they have on Canada Inc.? There has been criticism in some quarters, most notably the labour movement, that overseas strategic alliances and FDI have served to weaken the Canadian economy. In particular, overseas joint-venture and wholly-owned investments, it is alleged, have resulted in the 'export' of Canadian capital, reducing domestic investment and displacing domestic jobs. In the case of Nortel, it was even hinted that they had largely lost their Canadian 'identity', that as a 'transnational' company their activities increasingly reflected their global ambitions and had produced little 'value added' for Canada. All of this, however, is very myopic, for three main reasons. First, trade and investment is a two-way process. In recent years, in particular, inward investment in Canada has greatly exceeded capital outflows, so that there has been a net addition to local capital formation (see Figure 12.1). Second, outward FDI is usually additional to a firm's domestic activities, representing a strategic response to an opportunity or threat in overseas markets (see Figure 12.2). Thus, FDI is normally to be seen as complementary to, rather than as a substitute for, domestic investment. Third, strategic alliances and wholly-owned FDI can bring local benefits through the acquisition of new skills and expertise and access to world markets. For example, in the cases of the two Canadian pharmaceutical companies in our sample (BioChem Pharma and Allelix), their domestic R&D efforts have been greatly enhanced by the financial assistance provided by their alliance partners, while their future export potential is underpinned by their ability to access their partners' international distribution networks. Similarly, MPR Teltech has enhanced its Canadian-based competencies in satellite technologies by its alliance with Gooding Microwave, while the incorporation of FastMAN's software in European-based multinationals such as Alcatel has had knock-on effects back into North America, as these companies are now using FastMAN to network their international operations.

A less convincing case for local benefit can be made in respect of CU Power Generation and John Labatt, since their alliances have more to do with obtaining access to hitherto restricted overseas markets. However, given limited opportunities for further expansion in their 'home' markets, overseas

Inward investment

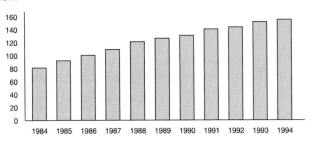

Outward investment

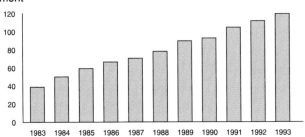

Figure 12.1   Canadian inward and outward foreign direct investment, 1984–94 (in C\$ billions)

Source: Statistics Canada.

expansion enlarges their profit-earning potential (with some of the extra profits likely to be repatriated) and generally underscores their corporate vigour.

CONCLUSION

Although many Canadian companies currently export to Europe and some have established a direct presence in European markets through wholly-owned investments and strategic alliances, the Canadian government would like to see more as a 'counterbalance' to Canada's present heavy reliance on the USA as a trade and investment partner. As reported in a previous study by the authors (Buckley, Pass and Prescott, 1995), there is an obvious danger that the formation of regional blocs such as the European Union and the North American Free Trade Agreement will favour intra-regional trade and investment to the detriment of global multilateral linkages. The Canadian government is alert to this possibility and has exhorted Canadian companies

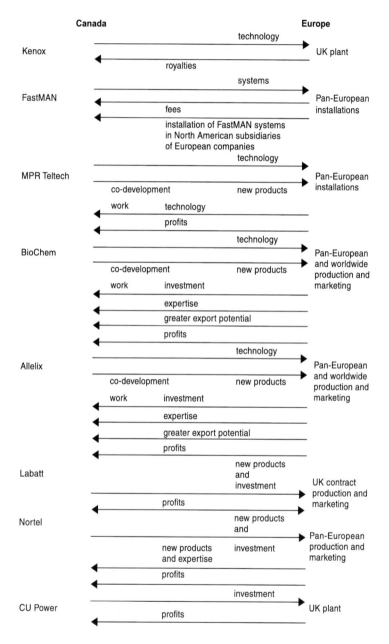

Figure 12.2   Summary of location of main operations and country-to-country benefits

to regard developments in the European Union as presenting an opportunity rather than as a threat:

> In the last decade, our exports to the EC have increased only slightly, despite a favourable Canadian exchange rate. In the meantime, our share of merchandise imports in the major EC markets has actually declined...the figures suggest that Canadians must be more aggressive...and must increase their rate of investment in the EC if they are to capitalise on the opportunities offered by the development of the Single Market. (External Affairs, 1991)

The present study clearly demonstrates the scope for using the strategic alliance mode to enter European markets. It appears, however, that Canadian companies in general have been somewhat tardy in taking up the government's clarion call for more strategic alliances. Despite an exhaustive search of company and 'official' databases, only a relatively small number of strategic alliances by Canadian companies with European partners were found in addition to the ones reported in this article.

References

Buckley, P.J., C.L. Pass and K. Prescott (1995) *Canada–UK Bilateral Trade and Investment Relations* (London: Macmillan).
External Affairs and International Trade Canada (1991) *Moving into Europe* (Ottawa).

13 An International Comparison of the Structure of National Foreign Market Servicing Strategies*

with Gordon E. Smith

INTRODUCTION

The purpose of this article is to compare the structure of foreign market servicing strategies of a number of the world's leading trading nations. The total foreign sales (TFS) of any nation are made up of its exports (X), sales arising from that country's foreign direct investments (I) plus licensed sales from exported know-how (L). Thus $TFS = X + I + L$.

The previous analyses of foreign market servicing have analysed the sales at individual firm level (Buckley and Pearce, 1979, 1981, 1984) or for one country (Buckley and Prescott, 1989). This article is the first to compare data across countries and therefore to shed light on national differences in foreign market servicing strategies as well as industry differences.

The following section briefly examines the theory of foreign market servicing, concentrating in particular on the sources of influence at the national level. The third section examines the research methods used in calculating the components of TFS and the data used. The fourth section presents the results for the countries analysed: the UK, USA, Germany, The Netherlands, Japan, France and Sweden. The final section draws out the implications of the analysis and points out crucial differences in the structure of TFS at national levels which have important implications for the structure of world trade.

---

* Originally published in *International Business Review*, vol. 3, no.1, 1994, pp. 71–94.

FOREIGN MARKET SERVICING STRATEGY

There is an extensive literature on the foreign market servicing strategies of companies which has been extensively reviewed by Buckley and Prescott (1989) and by Young *et al.* (1989). Much of the analysis takes place at the level of the firm using the twin concepts of internalisation and location to differentiate the three primary forms of foreign market servicing (exports, licensing and foreign direct investment, FDI) from each other. There is also a tradition of aggregating the 'world's largest firms' and analysing their collective foreign market servicing by reference to country of ownership, industry, size of firm and degree of multinationality (Buckley and Pearce, 1979, 1981, 1984). However, the analysis at the macro level, comparing national aggregates of exporting, licensing and investment sales is rare and exists in comprehensive form for only one country – the UK (Buckley and Prescott, 1989).

At its most simple, *X* can be differentiated from the other two methods by the location effect, as with exports the bulk of value-adding activity takes place in the home country, whilst the other two methods transfer much of value-adding activity to the host country. Similarly, *L* can be differentiated from *X* and *I* by the externalisation effect. *L* represents a market sale of intermediate goods or corporate assets by the firm. In licensing the firm sells rights and the use of assets to a licensee. In *X* and *I* such activities are internalised (Buckley and Casson, 1976, 1985). This has important implications. Broadly, then, the internalisation and location effects separate the three generic forms of market servicing as shown in Figure 13.1.

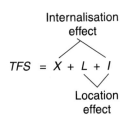

Figure 13.1   Internalisation and location effects in total foreign sales

These simple differentiations are, in practice, highly complex. First, comparative costs are not easily calculable or obvious. In multiproduct, process and functional firms the internal division of labour and the costs associated with each activity are difficult to assess accurately. Further, there are many complex interactions between the activities involved. Location abroad of some activities will have knock-on effects on home costs and on those of third countries within the firm's international network. Second, the costs and benefits of internalisation are nebulous and difficult to measure. Both sets of complication are entirely contingent on circumstances. The difficulties (and intellectual excitement) of these calculations is that the situation is dynamic and the determinants of choice of optimal market servicing strategies are continually shifting.

Cross-section analyses of market servicing are snapshot pictures at a moment in time of a continually changing process. This suggests that a dynamic analysis is essential. Assumptions in modelling which do not allow for changes in demand conditions – for instance, the existence of a 'presence effect' which results in an increased demand after the establishment of an investment presence (Buckley *et al.*, 1988) – are clearly inappropriate. Similarly, models which ignore the competitive process, in particular the role of 'defensive investment' established to protect a market share, are unlikely to capture the nuances of strategy. Models must be organic rather than static and capable of specifying the relationship between exports, licensing and FDI.

There are strong reasons for analysing the total foreign sales at national level and comparing the results. First, we can begin to highlight differences in the make-up of total foreign sales by firms of different nationalities. Countries with high export components in total foreign sales (e.g. Japan) will respond very differently over time to policy stimuli than will countries where investment sales are the preponderant element of TFS. This has profound importance in examining the impact of policy changes. Import restrictions by a particular country may have very different effects, if its major trading partners have heavily export dominated TFS, or are investment sales orientated. Second, differences between countries in the make-up of their foreign market servicing strategies are important elements in the structure of international competition. Third, changes in the composition of the TFS of a country are indicative of both changes in its internal economic structure and the way it approaches foreign markets, and so domestic policies should be informed by knowledge of the structure of TFS. Policies designed to encourage exports, for domestic payoffs, may fail if this conflicts with the desire of firms to invest in targeted foreign markets. Exchange rate targets will also shift the balance between different modes of servicing foreign markets. Thus it is important for any country to examine the structures of its trade. Exports of intermediate products may be a component of a strategy to finish those products in the final market via a direct investment in the finishing stages. Such 'mixed strategies' are sensitive to changes in location costs of all the activities involved and switching between modes of foreign market servicing can be triggered by minor changes in costs, demand patterns or external government policy. Fourth, international comparisons enable us to isolate industry effects, by identifying commonality of strategy within an industry across countries and thus to identify idiosyncrasies which arise from national origin. Finally trends in foreign market servicing strategies are important for policy not only at national level, but also at international level. Negotiations in the GATT 'Uruguay Round' show that services are a peculiarly sensitive issue. This is largely because of the peculiarities of the service industries arising from the fact that they must be performed *in situ* and cannot be conventionally exported. The extra issues arising from the investment related modes of foreign market servicing naturally complicate the negotiations. This raises the further point that services and the resource development sectors are very different from manufacturing in the possibilities of choice between exporting, licensing and FDI. This structure can be investigated in a preliminary fashion by our data, but there is much more work to do in this area (see in particular, Buckley *et al.*, 1992a).

RESEARCH METHODS

Introduction

For each home country studied, detailed export data were available from official sources (i.e. UN, IMP) whereas licensing and outward FDI data, available only from central bank sources, were generally more restricted (i.e. aggregated to broad industrial sector or listed according to important countries and regions). Hence, the tabulation of export data had to be made compatible with the data available for FDI and/or licensing for each home country, the availability and presentation of which tended to vary with the latter. Export and foreign investment industry classifications were reconciled for each home country. This was done by examining the FDI stock industry sector components (or royalty receipt data sources) given in government data, defining sector categories according to SITC codes and aggregating them as appropriate.

Raw export data were generally available in US$, whereas FDI and licensing data were often quoted in home country currency units. These were converted into a common currency (US$). Data sources are presented in the Appendix. The method of calculation of results is based upon that described by Buckley and Prescott (1989).

Exports

Introduction

For each home country, gross export values were used, since for most of the home countries studied, the contribution to exports of the subsidiaries of foreign companies based in the specified home country could not be deducted from gross export values, since the former data were not available.

Exports by Industry

Data for exports by industry were tabulated in formats compatible with the data available for FDI and licensing for the specified home country. These were expressed in terms of manufacturing sectors available, non-manufacturing and the all industry total for each year.

Exports by Country

Data for specified home country exports by destination were taken from *Direction of Trade Statistics Year Book* (1986, 1987, 1988), and tabulated in formats, compatible with the data available for FDI and licensing. Destination country/regional values were then adjusted in proportion to the ratio of manufacturing total to all industry total (i.e. manufacturing plus non-manufacturing totals) for each country of origin and for each year specified.

Licensing

Calculation of Sales Arising from Foreign Licensing

The raw data necessary for the calculation of licensed sales abroad by unaffiliated concerns (so as to eliminate double-counting) broken down by industry and country (or region) were available only for the UK, USA, and Germany. Data for Sweden were incomplete. For other countries (i.e. France, Japan, The Netherlands), only the total undistributed receipts, aggregated for both unrelated and related concerns, but generally excluding receipts on printed matter, sound recordings and performing rights, were available (for sources, see Appendix).

Licensed Sales Abroad by Industry

These are calculated from the raw data for each year as follows:

(1)   receipts for industry sectors were multiplied by 20, on the assumption that receipts averaged out at 5 per cent royalty on sales achieved;

(2) the sales figures were added up for manufacturing sectors to give the manufacturing total, and then added to the non-manufacturing contribution to give the overall total for licensing sales.

Licensed Sales Abroad by Country

The calculation of licensed sales for a particular home country varied according to the way in which the raw data were presented. However, where manufacturing sector receipts from unrelated concerns were not simultaneously available (i.e. payment country/region for each year), then for each survey year, the manufacturing receipts for each country making payment to the home country were multiplied by the ratio of unrelated concerns to total receipts (i.e. related plus unrelated concerns), and then by 20 (on the assumption that royalties averaged 5 per cent on sales achieved).

Foreign Direct Investment

The methodological problems associated with the collection and use of FDI data are well known and documented (Cantwell, 1992). However, despite these difficulties, it was felt that useful estimates of sales arising from FDI could be made in order to shed light on the key issues raised above.

Calculation of Sales from Outward Foreign Direct Investment

Depending upon the home country, outward FDI stock values were published every year, or every other year, over the period of investigation (1983 or 1984 to 1988). The exception was France, for which outward FDI data are available to 1987 only (at the time of writing this paper).

The contribution of manufacturing FDI, obtained directly from raw data or derived by calculation, was then multiplied by the appropriate sales: assets ratio for each year for manufacturing (or non-manufacturing where appropriate) and for country/region. These ratios were derived from data of US foreign affiliates, using surveys conducted for each year of interest and published in *Survey of Current Business* (Appendix 1).

Foreign Sales Arising from Home Country Foreign Direct Investment Industry

For each home country, the quoted stock value for each industry sector for each year was multiplied by the sales:assets ratio appropriate to that sector for that year, to give an estimate of sales derived from outward FDI.

Foreign Sales Arising from Home Country Foreign Direct Investment by Country/Region

The manufacturing FDI value for each country/region was derived directly from the raw data where available, or calculated by multiplying the quoted total value (manufacturing plus non-manufacturing total) by the ratio of manufacturing sector total to all industry total. These were then multiplied by the sales: assets ratio for the host country/region for the year in question. Sales for FDI in the USA were calculated by using the developed country average ratio for the year in question.

Final Calculations

Conceptual Framework

TFS is made up of exports (*X*) plus licensed sales (*L*) plus sales from foreign investment (*I*):

$$TFS = X + L + I$$

Home countries: UK, USA, Germany. The TFS for each industry or country was derived by adding up the appropriate values (each expressed in US$ million) for exports, licensed sales and sales from foreign investment, and the contribution of each mode of foreign market servicing (*X, L, I*) expressed as per cent TFS.

Home countries: The Netherlands, Japan, France, Sweden. The percentage contribution of licensed sales, distributed by industry sector or country, could not be calculated, as only aggregated totals for licence receipts were available. Hence, for these countries, only the distributed per cent contribution of exports and FDI sales could be derived, and tabulated.

If the values for licensed sales, derived from aggregated totals, are taken and added to the respective totals for exports and FDI sales, then the contribution of licensed sales to TFS for the four countries was found to be less than 10 per cent. However, it is unlikely that derived licensed sales related entirely to unrelated concerns. Hence, the real contribution of licensed sales, appropriate to unrelated concerns, for France, Japan and The Netherlands is probably a few per cent of TFS. Estimates for Sweden suggest that licensed sales amount to 3 per cent of TFS.

RESULTS: FOREIGN MARKET SERVICING AT NATIONAL LEVEL

This section presents the results for seven leading trading nations: the USA, Germany, Japan, the UK, The Netherlands, Sweden and France. Depending upon the source data, results were calculated, as far as possible, for the years 1984 to 1988 inclusive, but for reasons of brevity, results for two or three years only have been presented. Full tables of results are available on request from the authors. The breakdown of X, I and L by country and industry in percentage terms are presented in Tables 13.1–13.6. The geographical analysis is based on manufacturing sales only.

UK

Geographical Analysis

For the UK, the dominant form of foreign market servicing is exporting (Table 13.1). However, there are considerable differences between regions and individual countries. Export sales contributions higher than the global mean are seen for EC (76.78 per cent), EFTA (82.88 per cent), less developed countries (72 per cent) and the Middle East (99 per cent), whereas the FDI sales contribution is important for North America (58.64 per cent), Canada (59.82 per cent), USA (57.60 per cent), Africa (32.36 per cent), Asia (30.35 per cent) Latin America (43.45 per cent) and 'Other developed countries' (67.73 per cent). Intermediate FDI sales contributions are seen for Germany, Italy, The Netherlands, Portugal, Spain and Switzerland. Licensed sales are relatively unimportant (less than 10 per cent TFS) for all countries/regions, with the exception of Japan (26.32 per cent TFS).

Sector Analysis

Analysis by industry (Table 13.2) reveals that export orientated sectors are metals (81.86 per cent TFS), mechanical engineering (76.81 per cent), and transport equipment (81.83 per cent). Sectors strongly reliant on FDI sales are food, drink and tobacco (53.55 per cent), chemicals (46.51 per cent), electrical engineering (29.32 per cent) and paper (45.57 per cent). The difference between manufacturing industry and the non-manufacturing profile is significant, with non-manufacturing sales (73 per cent TFS) dominated by FDI sales. Licensed sales are a relatively unimportant component of TFS for all sectors, with the highest contributions (range 6–8 per cent TFS) seen in chemicals, transport equipment and paper.

Table 13.1 France, Sweden and UK: percentage of stated country manufacturing exports, FDI sales and licensed sales by country/region

	France 1987 (%)	Sweden 1986 (%)	Sweden 1988 (%)	UK 1984 (%)	UK 1987 (%)
Developed countries	X 82.8 I 17.8	X 71.9 I 28.1	X 63.4 I 36.6	X 54.6 I 42.1 L 3.3	X 59.8 I 36.7 L 3.5
EC	X 87.1 I 12.9	X 77.3 I 22.7	X 65.3 I 34.7	X 77.5 I 20.8 L 1.7	X 75.9 I 22.5 L 1.6
Belgium/Luxembourg	X 85.8 I 14.2	N/A	N/A	X 83.3 I 16.1 L 0.6	X 85.2 I 13.7 L 1.1
Denmark	X 98.0 I 2.0	X 77.5 I 22.5	X 63.6 I 36.4	X 88.9 I 10.0 L 1.1	X 92.8 I 6.4 L 0.8
France	– – –	X 76.8 I 23.2	X 67.8 I 32.2	X 81.7 I 16.6 L 1.7	X 81.3 I 16.7 L 2.0
Germany	X 92.6 I 7.4	X 83.3 I 16.7	X 78.9 I 21.1	X 74.2 I 24.4 L 1.4	X 76.7 I 21.2 L 2.1
Greece*	X 92.5 I 7.5	N/A	N/A	X 85.1 I 14.4	X 89.9 I 10.1
Ireland*	X 87.3 I 12.7	N/A	N/A	X 78.7 I 21.1	X 81.7 I 18.3
Italy	X 93.8 I 6.2	N/A	N/A	X 75.3 I 20.5 L 4.2	X 74.0 I 23.0 L 3.0
The Netherlands*	X 72.2 I 27.8	X 63.1 I 36.9	X 42.6 I 57.4	X 77.0 I 22.6	X 63.5 I 35.7
Portugal	X 89.4 I 10.4	N/A	N/A	X 73.6 I 24.0 L 2.3	X 62.0 I 36.2 L 1.8
Spain	X 97.2 I 2.8	X 65.8 I 34.2	X 66.4 I 33.6	X 61.9 I 28.5 L 9.6	X 69.5 I 28.4 L 2.2
UK	X 84.9 I 15.1	X 79.4 I 20.4	X 64.8 I 35.2	– – –	– – –
EFTA	X 76.4 I 23.6	X 84.3 I 15.7	X 68.0 I 32.0	X 81.8 I 16.4 L 1.8	X 87.5 I 10.0 L 2.5

Sweden	X 97.4	–	–	X 93.3	X 91.7
	I 2.6	–	–	I 6.0	I 6.6
				L 0.8	L 1.7
Switzerland	X 66.5	X 72.4	X 70.1	X 62.3	X 78.1
	I 33.5	I 27.6	I 29.1	I 34.2	I 18.7
				L 3.4	L 3.1
North America	X 60.7	N/A	N/A	X 31.6	X 37.5
	I 39.3			I 64.4	I 57.7
				L 4.0	L 4.8
Canada	X 68.2	N/A	N/A	X 17.0	X 38.2
	I 31.8			I 81.7	I 59.3
				L 1.3	L 2.5
USA	X 59.7	X 47.4	X 48.7	X 35.1	X 37.4
	I 40.3	I 52.6	I 51.3	I 60.3	I 57.4
				L 4.6	L 5.2
Japan	X 91.9	N/A	N/A	X 41.6	X 46.9
	I 8.1			I 26.6	I 27.0
				L 31.8	L 26.0
Other developed	X 81.8	X 63.0	X 64.4	X 24.6	X 31.0
countries	I 18.2	I 37.0	I 35.6	I 73.2	I 67.4
				L 2.2	L 1.6
Developing countries	X 91.7	X 80.8	X 73.1	X 71.9	X 72.3
	I 8.3	I 19.2	I 26.9	I 24.2	I 21.4
				L 3.9	L 6.3
Africa	X 90.6	N/A	N/A	X 60.8	X 63.3
	I 9.4			I 36.3	I 32.0
				L 2.9	L 4.6
Asia	X 95.8	N/A	N/A	X 62.7	X 63.2
	I 4.2			I 35.3	I 29.9
				L 2.0	L 6.9
Latin America	X 81.3	N/A	N/A	X 51.5	X 50.6
	I 18.7			I 45.4	I 42.9
				L 3.0	L 6.5
Brazil	X 58.2	X 33.6	X 19.4	N/A	N/A
	I 41.8	I 66.4	I 80.6		
Middle East*	X 98.8	N/A	N/A	X 98.9	X 99.2
	I 1.2			I 0.3	I 0.3
World total	X 84.3	X 73.2	X 64.8	X 57.7	X 62.0
	I 15.7	I 26.8	I 35.2	I 39.0	I 34.0
				L 3.4	L 4.0

Notes:
Acronyms: X, Exports; I, FDI sales; L, Licensed sales.
N/A, data not available. For countries/regions marked *, L is less than 1 per cent TFS.
For data sources on FDI, exports and licensed receipts, see Appendix.
Other developed countries, Australia, New Zealand and South Africa; for Sweden, Canada and Japan are included.

USA

Geographical Analysis

For the US, the dominant form of foreign market servicing globally is exporting (Table 13.3). Exports accounted for over 50 per cent of TFS for the whole of the period 1984 to 1988. FDI sales account for approximately 40 per cent of TFS of the USA and licensed sales for under 8 per cent. However, this global analysis conceals significant differences by region and individual country. For developed countries, the balance between exporting and sales from direct investment is much more equal (at approximately 45 per cent each) whilst licensed sales account for 8 per cent of the total. FDI sales are especially important in the EC, at over 57 per cent of TFS, rising rapidly (from 52 per cent in 1984).

Table 13.2   France, Sweden and UK: percentage of stated country exports, FDI sales and licensed sales by industry sector

	France 1987 (%)	Sweden 1986 (%)	Sweden 1988 (%)	UK 1984 (%)	UK 1987 (%)
Manufacturing total	X 83.7 I 16.3	X 73.3 I 26.7	X 64.8 I 35.2	X 58.3 I 37.9 L 3.8	X 61.8 I 33.6 L 4.6
Food, drink and tobacco	X 91.3 I 8.7	X 84.0 I 16.0	X 75.3 I 24.7	X 42.4 I 55.1 L 2.5	X 42.9 I 52.8 L 4.2
Chemicals	X 77.4 I 22.6	X 71.7 I 28.3	X 66.6 I 33.4	X 42.7 I 51.1 L 6.2	X 48.1 I 45.5 L 6.4
Metals	X 84.1 I 15.9	X 88.3 I 11.7	X 81.9 I 18.1	X 80.8 I 18.5 L 0.8	X 86.3 I 12.8 L 1.0
Mechanical engineering	X 92.9 I 7.1	X 67.5* 32.5*	X 58.3* I 41.7*	X 75.8 I 22.7 L 1.5	X 80.9 I 13.5 L 5.6
Electrical engineering	X78.0 I 22.0	X* I*	X* I*	X 66.0 I 32.3 L 1.7	X 70.3 I 28.7 L 1.0
Transport equipment	X 86.2 I 13.8	X* I*	X* I*	X 80.6 I 11.6 L 7.7	X 82.9 I 10.6 L 6.5
Paper	X 86.7 I 13.3	X 81.8 I 18.2	X 67.0 I 33.0	X 47.8 I 45.2 L 6.9	X 35.0 I 57.1 L 7.8

Other manufacturing	X 81.7	X 64.3	X 65.6	X 55.1	X 60.6
	I 18.4	I 35.7	I 34.4	I 41.4	I 35.3
				L 3.5	L 4.1
Total	X 29.6	X 32.9	X 35.3	X 25.2	X 21.2
non-manufacturing	I 70.4	I 67.1	I 64.7	I 73.1	I 72.5
				L 1.7	L 6.3
Overall total	X 76.0	X 69.0	X 62.1	X 43.1	X 47.2
(all industries)	I 24.0	I 31.0	I 37.9	I 54.1	I 47.6
				L 2.8	L 5.2

Notes:

Acronyms: X, Exports; I, FDI sales; L, Licensed sales.

For data sources on FDI, exports and licensed sales, see Appendix.

* Covers all engineering (for Sweden, engineering sectors have been aggregated). Additional results: textiles (France), X = 87.4%, I = 12.6%; textiles (Sweden), X = 96.6 (1986), X = 94.2 (1988), I = 3.4 (1986), I = 5.8 (1988); rubber (France), X = 52.7, I = 47.3; wood (Sweden), X = 81.8 (1986), X = 67.0 (1988), I = 18.2 (1986), I = 33.0 (1988).

FDI sales: (a) Data manipulation: FDI stock values (Fr, F., SEK, £) were converted to US$ (for rate of exchange, see *International Finance Statistics*, 1989, 1991), and then multiplied by the appropriate sales: assets ratio for manufacturing or non-manufacturing for the year in question (see Appendix).

Exports: (b) Sector categories: these have been collated so as to conform with the aggregated categories published by country FDI and royalty receipt sources (UK only). Food, drink and tobacco = Standard International Trade Classification, SITC (0 + 1 + 22 + 4); SITC 1, 22, 4 absent from Swedish data. Chemicals = SITC 5; Swedish sector also includes SITC 33 + 62. Metals = SITC (67 + 68 + 67). Engineering (Sweden) = SITC (7 + 87). Mechanical engineering = SITC (71 + 72 + 73 + 74). Electrical engineering = SITC (75 + 76 + 77). Transport equipment = SITC (78 + 79). Rubber = SITC 62. Textiles = SITC (65 + 84 + 26). Paper (including publishing) = SITC (64 + 892); paper and pulp (Sweden) = SITC (64 + 251). Wood = SITC (24 + 63). Total manufacturing = SITC (5 + 6 + 7 + 8) + food/drink contribution. Non-manufacturing total = all commodities total – total manufacturing.

Licensed Sales: UK – royalty receipt values (£) from 'unrelated' or unaffiliated sources were converted to US$ and then multiplied by 20.

France – royalty receipt data distributed by industry sector are not available. Only an aggregated total value (affiliated + non-affiliated) is available for 1987 (*Monthly Reports of Deutsche Bundesbank*, May 1988, vol. 40, no. 5, pp. 37–53; May 1990, vol. 42, no. 5, pp. 27–43). If this value is converted to US$, multiplied by 20, and expressed as % TFS, the estimated contribution of licensed sales (affiliated + non-affiliated) is less than 10%.

Sweden – using crude total royalty receipts (affiliated + non-affiliated) for 1988 (available from Deutsche Bundesbank sources), the overall contribution of licensed sales to TFS was calculated as 5.6%. However, using estimated 1986 unaffiliated royalty receipts (by averaging relevant data from the survey years 1985 and 1987) for manufacturing total to calculate total licensed sales for manufacturing, the contribution of 1986 licensed sales to TFS was 3%.

Especially high are the percentages for the Irish Republic, UK and Germany. In contrast FDI sales are lower in EFTA countries and especially low in Japan (at barely 20 per cent TFS). FDI sales are much lower in LDCs than in developed countries (23 per cent overall) except in Latin America (35–38 per cent TFS).

Table 13.3   USA and Japan: percentage of stated country manufacturing exports, FDI sales and licensed sales by country/region

	USA			Japan		
	1984 (%)	1987 (%)	1988 (%)	1984 (%)	1987 (%)	1988 (%)
Developed countries	X 47.7 I 44.3 L 8.0	X 44.7 I 46.6 L 8.7	X 46.2 I 45.4 L 8.4	X 87.2 I 12.8	X 85.1 I 14.9	X 78.7 I 21.3
EC	X 41.0 I 52.0 L 6.9	X 36.2 I 58.7 L 5.1	X 37.9 I 57.0 L 5.1	X 88.4 I 11.6	X 90.7 I 9.3	X 87.9 I 12.1
Belgium/Luxembourg	X 49.0 I 48.0 L 3.0	X 50.0 I 44.3 L 5.7	X 46.7 I 47.1 L 6.2	X 74.1 I 25.9	X 74.1 I 25.9	X 72.5 I 27.5
France	X 40.4 I 47.7 L 11.9	X 36.0 I 56.0 L 8.0	X 37.8 I 54.8 L 7.4	X 89.6 I 10.4	X 94.1 I 5.9	X 92.6 I 7.4
Germany	X 33.7 I 58.7 L 7.6	X 31.9 I 62.9 L 5.2	X 36.2 I 59.2 L 4.6	X 94.9 I 5.1	X 97.2 I 2.8	X 96.7 I 3.3
Ireland	X 25.4 I 74.6 L 0	X 23.2 I 76.8 L 0	X 22.3 I 77.7 L 0	X 82.0 I 18.0	X 84.5 I 15.5	X 85.9 I 14.1
Italy	X 41.1 I 45.6 L 13.3	X 32.9 I 58.8 L 8.2	X 33.6 I 57.4 L 8.9	X 95.8 I 4.2	X 97.6 I 2.4	X 97.1 I 2.9
The Netherlands	X 57.7 I 39.5 L 2.7	X 45.2 I 50.7 L 4.1	X 47.2 I 48.1 L 4.7	X 84.9 I 15.1	X 87.0 I 13.0	X 80.2 I 19.8
Spain	X 50.2 I 49.8 L 0	X 44.1 I 51.5 L 0	X 42.3 I 51.0 L 0	X 83.5 I 16.5	X 90.3 I 9.7	X 90.1 I 9.9
UK	X 36.7 I 56.4 L 6.9	X 32.7 I 64.0 L 3.4	X 34.7 I 62.2 L 3.1	X 84.9 I 15.1	X 86.8 I 13.2	X 81.7 I 18.3
EFTA	X 57.8 I 30.7 L 11.5	X 56.8 I 32.1 L 11.1	X 64.2 I 28.7 L 7.1	X N/A I N/A	X N/A I N/A	X N/A I N/A

Sweden	X 58.8	X 53.2	X 63.7	X N/A	X N/A	X N/A
	I 22.3	I 25.7	I 25.4	I N/A	I N/A	I N/A
	L 18.9	L 21.1	L 10.9			
Switzerland	X 54.9	X 49.2	X 56.3	X 85.8	X 92.3	X 92.7
	I 36.5	I 44.7	I 39.2	I 14.2	I 7.7	I 7.3
	L 8.6	L 6.1	L 4.5			
North America	X NA	X NA	X NA	X 86.3	X 82.5	X 73.5
	I NA	I NA	I NA	I 13.7	I 17.5	I 26.5
	L NA	L NA	L NA			
Canada	X 50.4	X 53.9	X 54.7	X 83.1	X 83.6	X 79.3
	I 48.1	I 44.2	I 44.1	I 16.9	I 16.4	I 20.7
	L 1.5	L 1.9	L 1.2			
USA	X –	X –	X –	X 86.6	X 82.5	X 73.1
	I –	I –	I –	I 13.5	I 17.5	I 26.9
	L –	L –	L –			
Japan	X 59.3	X 48.6	X 50.4	X –	X –	X –
	I 16.7	I 21.3	I 20.8	I –	I –	I –
	L 24.0	L 30.1	L 28.8			
Other developed countries	X 51.1	X 48.7	X 49.0	X 86.9	X 82.6	X 81.5
	I 41.9	I 41.7	I 43.7	I 13.1	I 17.4	I 18.5
	L 7.0	L 9.6	L 7.3			
Developing countries	X 73.7	X 71.2	X 71.9	X 82.8	X 82.6	X 81.2
	I 21.5	I 23.6	I 23.4	I 17.2	I 17.4	I 18.8
	L 4.8	L 5.2	L 4.8			
Africa	X 85.3	X 82.6	X 84.4	X 91.0	X 91.5	X 89.5
	I 10.8	I 12.3	I 13.8	I 9.0	I 8.5	I 10.5
	L 3.9	L 5.0	L 1.8			
Asia	X 77.5	X 76.9	X 77.9	X 82.4	X 84.7	X 83.6
	I 13.9	I 15.3	I 13.2	I 17.6	I 15.3	I 16.4
	L 8.6	L 7.9	L 8.9			
Latin America	X 61.5	X 60.6	X 60.7	X 64.2	X 59.3	X 56.3
	I 35.1	I 36.7	I 37.7	I 35.8	I 40.7	I 43.7
	L 3.4	L 2.7	L 1.7			
Middle East	X 98.9	X 90.8	X 95.1	X 97.6	X 95.1	X 94.0
	I 1.1	I 1.1	I 1.1	I 2.4	I 4.9	I 6.0
	L 1.1	L 8.1	L 3.2			
World total	X 54.8	X 51.3	X 53.0	X 86.1	X 84.4	X 79.9
	I 37.9	I 40.8	I 39.4	I 13.9	I 15.6	I 20.1
	L 7.2	L 7.9	L 7.6			

Notes:

Acronyms: X, Exports, I, FDI sales; L, Licensed sales (royalty receipt data on unaffiliated concerns for Japan are not available). NA, data not available.

For data sources on FDI, exports and royalty receipts, see Appendix.

The major host nations for US FDI in this region are Argentina, Brazil, Venezuela and Mexico (see data sources in Appendix). Although less than 8 per cent of US TFS overall, licensed sales represent nearly 29 per cent TFS to Japan, 8–13 per cent to Italy, 11–21 per cent to Sweden. Licensed sales to less developed countries are generally low.

Sector Analysis

Analysis by industry (Table 13.4) reveals that export-orientated industries are textiles and electrical and electronic components. Sectors strongly reliant on FDI sales are rubber, paper, chemicals and non-manufacturing. Licensed sales are most important in non-electrical machinery (14–16 per cent TFS).

Table 13.4 USA and Japan: percentage of stated country exports, FDI sales and licensed sales by industry sector

	USA			Japan		
	1984 (%)	*1987 (%)*	*1988 (%)*	*1984 (%)*	*1987 (%)*	*1988 (%)*
Manufacturing total	X 56.2 I 36.5 L 7.2	X 52.2 I 39.9 L 7.9	X 53.7 I 38.7 L 7.6	X 84.4 I 15.6	X 83.6 I 16.4	X 79.2 I 20.8
Food, drink and tobacco	X 68.1 I 26.1 L 5.9	X 53.7 I 38.6 L 7.7	X 57.7 I 35.0 L 7.4	X 48.0 I 52.0	X 43.1 I 56.9	X 36.2 I 63.8
Chemicals	X 42.4 I 50.1 L 7.5	X 39.7 I 51.9 L 8.3	X 38.9 I 53.3 L 7.8	X 58.1 I 41.9	X 64.3 I 35.7	X 60.4 I 39.6
Metals	X 46.2 I 47.6 L 6.1	X 43.4 I 48.5 L 8.1	X 44.7 I 48.4 L 6.8	X 74.1 I 25.9	X 70.1 I 29.9	X 67.6 I 32.4
Machinery	X 50.2 I 35.8 L 14.0	X 40.6 I 45.0 L 14.4	X 37.0 I 46.7 L 16.3	X 90.7 I 9.3	X 89.0 I 11.0	X 86.2 I 13.8
Electrical and electronic equipment	X 70.9 I 23.7 L 5.4	X 73.4 I 20.7 L 5.9	X 75.0 I 19.4 L 5.6	X 91.0 I 9.0	X 88.2 I 11.8	X 85.1 I 14.9
Transportation equipment	X 62.9 I 31.1 L 6.0	X 60.7 I 33.7 L 5.6	X 60.7 I 33.7 L 5.7	X 92.3 I 7.7	X 90.2 I 9.8	X 87.4 I 12.6
Motor vehicles	X 52.4 I 40.0 L 7.6	X 46.9 I 45.7 L 7.4	X 47.0 I 45.6 L 7.4	X NA I NA	X NA I NA	X NA I NA

Textiles	X 77.1	X 75.4	X 77.0	X 70.3	X 70.8	X 65.6
	I 20.1	I 21.0	I 19.6	I 29.7	I 29.2	I 34.4
	L 2.8	L 3.6	L 3.4			
Paper	X 34.7	X 35.3	X 35.5	X NA	X NA	X NA
	I 59.1	I 57.6	I 57.6	I NA	I NA	I NA
	L 6.2	L 7.0	L 6.9			
Rubber	X 25.5	X 27.2	X 29.4	X NA	X NA	X NA
	I 68.6	I 66.6	I 64.9	I NA	I NA	I NA
	L 5.8	L 6.3	L 5.7			
Total non-manufacturing	X 19.2	X 22.4	X 26.5	X 6.9	X 5.8	X 5.8
	I 75.9	I 71.7	I 67.6	I 93.1	I 94.2	I 94.2
	L 4.9	L 5.8	L 5.9			
Overall total (all industries)	X 43.2	X 42.4	X 45.3	X 67.1	X 64.8	X 60.5
	I 50.3	I 50.4	I 47.7	I 32.9	I 35.2	I 39.5
	L 6.4	L 7.2	L 7.0			

Notes:

Acronyms: X, Exports, I, FDI sales; L, Licensed Sales (royalty receipt data on unaffiliated concerns for Japan are not available). NA, data not available.

For data sources on FDI, exports and royalty receipts, see Appendix.

Details of data manipulation and sector categories are given in Table 13.2.

Germany

Geographical Analysis

The TFS of Germany are highly export-dominated (Table 13.5). About 80 per cent TFS (world total) are accounted for by the export mode, which is even higher at about 90 per cent TFS for LDCs. The most important locations for sales via FDI are Canada, USA, Latin America and non-European industrialised countries. Within Europe, only Switzerland, Spain and Belgium/Luxembourg approach 20 per cent of TFS via FDI. FDI sales are particularly low in Sweden. Licensed sales (at about 4 per cent TFS worldwide) reaches 30 per cent in Japan, 9 per cent in non-European industrialised countries and 8–10 per cent in Spain. Apart from Spain, licensed sales are very low in the EC.

Sector Analysis

The German sector analysis (Table 13.6) splits dramatically between manufacturing (at 80 per cent for export sales) versus non-manufacturing at (36–38 per cent for export sales). Within manufacturing, food, drink and tobacco, and metals are about 95 per cent export-dominated. Apart from non-manufacturing, FDI sales are significant in chemicals (26–31 per cent

TFS), electrical engineering (24–28 per cent) and road vehicle manufacturing (17–18 per cent). Licensed sales are of most importance in chemicals (9–10 per cent) and electrical engineering (6–8 per cent).

The Netherlands

Geographical Analysis

Worldwide sales from FDI account for about 40 per cent TFS ($X + I$), whereas the contribution of exports to TFS rise considerably in Ireland, Spain and Africa (Table 13.5). The proportion of TFS accounted for by exports to other

Table 13.5   Germany and The Netherlands: percentage of stated country manufacturing exports, FDI sales and licensed sales by country/region

	Germany			The Netherlands		
	1983 (%)	1985 (%)	1987 (%)	1984 (%)	1987 (%)	1988 (%)
Developed countries	X 77.5 I 18.6 L 3.9	X 78.8 I 17.0 L 4.2	X 78.9 I 17.3 L 3.9	X 56.0 I 44.0	X 62.5 I 37.5	X 59.9 I 40.1
EC	X 85.2 I 12.8 L 2.0	X 85.4 I 12.2 L 2.4	X 84.9 I 13.1 L 2.0	X 77.2 I 22.8	X 76.9 I 23.1	X 76.5 I 23.5
Belgium/Luxembourg	X 77.3 I 21.2 L 1.5	X 77.5 I 20.0 L 2.5	X 78.7 I 20.4 L 2.0	X 80.4 I 19.6	X 80.7 I 19.3	X 78.4 I 21.6
France	X 86.5 I 11.7 L 1.8	X 86.0 I 11.7 L 2.3	X 85.8 I 12.3 L 1.8	X 75.2 I 24.8	X 78.7 I 21.3	X 75.6 I 24.4
Germany	X – I – L –	X – I – L –	X – I – L –	X 85.6 I 14.4	X 86.1 I 13.9	X 84.1 I 15.9
Ireland	X NA I NA L NA	X NA I NA L NA	X NA I NA L NA	X 24.8 I 75.2	X 61.0 I 39.0	X 54.9 I 45.1
Italy	X 89.1 I 7.3 L 3.6	X 88.9 I 8.3 L 2.8	X 89.6 I 7.8 L 2.6	X 83.4 I 16.6	X 83.0 I 17.0	X 85.6 I 14.4
The Netherlands	X 87.4 I 12.0 L 0.6	X 87.4 I 12.0 L 0.6	X 85.0 I 14.1 L 0.9	X – I –	X – I –	X – I –
Spain	X 69.5 I 24.9 L 5.6	X 68.8 I 20.8 L 10.4	X 71.8 I 19.8 L 8.4	X 46.8 I 53.2	X 64.1 I 35.9	X 58.8 I 41.2

UK	X 88.5	X 88.7	X 87.5	X 62.2	X 56.0	X 62.3
	I 9.9	I 9.8	I 11.2	I 37.8	I 44.0	I 37.7
	L 1.7	L 1.5	L 1.3			
Sweden	X 89.3	X 90.1	X 90.7	X NA	X NA	X NA
	I 3.4	I 2.9	I 2.6	I NA	I NA	I NA
	L 7.3	L 7.0	L 6.7			
Switzerland	X 72.7	X 76.6	X 77.2	X 35.8	X 39.7	X 36.5
	I 24.9	I 20.5	I 19.3	I 64.2	I 60.3	I 63.5
	L 2.4	L 3.0	L 3.5			
Non-European industrialised countries	X 53.1	X 59.4	X 59.0	X NA	X NA	X NA
	I 37.4	I 31.6	I 32.3	I NA	I NA	I NA
	L 9.5	L 9.0	L 8.7			
Canada	X 36.7	X 47.2	X 49.7	X NA	X NA	X NA
	I 57.8	I 47.7	I 42.9	I NA	I NA	I NA
	L 5.5	L 5.1	L 7.4			
USA	X 51.8	X 57.9	X 57.0	X 12.1	X 15.9	X 14.2
	I 41.5	I 34.2	I 35.9	I 87.9	I 84.1	I 85.8
	L 6.5	L 8.0	L 7.1			
Japan	X 57.1	X 63.3	X 66.6	X 44.6	X 45.1	X 41.9
	I 12.9	I 12.5	I 14.4	I 55.4	I 54.9	I 58.1
	L 30.0	L 24.3	L 19.0			
Other developed countries	X 68.0	X 76.3	X 71.4	X 48.3	X 62.0	X 52.4
	I 21.8	I 17.0	I 20.9	I 51.7	I 38.0	I 47.6
	L 10.3	L 6.7	L 7.7			
Developing countries	X 89.7	X 88.2	X 86.7	X 47.2	X 53.2	X 46.3
	I 8.4	I 9.3	I 11.0	I 52.8	I 46.8	I 53.7
	L 1.9	L 2.5	L 2.3			
Africa	X 89.2	X 89.1	X 82.6	X 64.4	X 71.2	X 73.1
	I 10.3	I 9.3	I 16.4	I 35.6	I 28.8	I 26.9
	L 0.4	L 1.6	L 1.1			
Asia	X 87.0	X 89.0	X 89.8	X 48.0	X 53.4	X 51.7
	I 9.2	I 7.3	I 7.0	I 52.0	I 46.6	I 48.3
	L 3.7	L 3.7	L 3.2			
Latin America	X 58.8	X 55.9	X 57.3	X 28.0	X 33.6	X 21.2
	I 34.4	I 36.2	I 36.4	I 72.0	I 66.4	I 78.8
	L 6.8	L 8.0	L 6.3			
World total	X 79.9	X 80.3	X 79.8	X 57.1	X 62.9	X 59.8
	I 16.3	I 15.6	I 16.3	I 42.9	I 37.1	I 40.2
	L 3.7	L 4.1	L 3.9			

Notes:

Acronyms: X, Exports; I, FDI sales; L, Licensed sales (royalty receipt data on unaffili-ated concerns for Japan are not available). NA, data not available.

For data sources on FDI, exports and royalty receipts, see Appendix. For Germany, 'Other developed countries' = as for Table 13.1; for The Netherlands, 'Other de-veloped countries' also include Canada and EFTA less Switzerland.

countries ranges from 70–90 per cent. The USA market is largely serviced by FDI sales (83–88 per cent), as is the case with Japan (58 per cent in 1988). In less developed countries, Latin America (which also includes The Netherlands Antilles) is largely serviced by investment sales and the trend here is upwards.

Sector Analysis

The most FDI sales-intensive manufacturing sector is chemicals (which in the case of The Netherlands includes mining, quarrying and oil) at 59 per cent TFS in 1988 (Table 13.6). Non-manufacturing sales show the usual bias towards investment sales, but this form of foreign market servicing shows a dramatic decline from 81 per cent to 69 per cent TFS. Export-orientated sectors are food, drink and tobacco, and machines/engineering.

Japan

Geographical Analysis

Despite the rapid increase in Japan's FDI in recent years, Japan's TFS in manufacturing are still largely dominated by exports, although the world total has fallen from 86 per cent for exports to 79 per cent TFS (1988). The largest investment-sales percentages of TFS (Table 13.3) are in Latin America (44 per cent), North America (27 per cent), with the USA at 27 per cent, Belgium/Luxembourg (28 per cent), The Netherlands (20 per cent) and the UK (18 per cent). The geographical orientation of Japan is heavily towards the final markets of North America and selected countries within the EC, but Japan has a longstanding investment tradition in Latin America. The contribution of FDI related sales to TFS in Africa and the Middle East is low. The Asian contribution is intermediate at about 16 per cent (in 1988), the major recipients (according to data sources stated in Appendix 1) being Indonesia, Hong Kong, Singapore, Korea, People's Republic of China and Thailand.

Sector Analysis

Although the Japanese non-manufacturing sector is highly investment-sales dominated (94 per cent TFS, 1988), this is in sharp contrast to the 21 per cent of manufacturing sales accounted for by investment sales (Table 13.4). Within manufacturing, only in foodstuffs (at 64 per cent) are investment-backed sales dominant – chemicals at 40 per cent is the next highest. In electronics, transport equipment and other manufacturing, there is a strong upward trend in the investment sales percentage.

Table 13.6   Germany and The Netherlands: percentage of stated country exports, FDI sales and licensed sales by industry sector

	Germany			The Netherlands		
	1983 (%)	*1985 (%)*	*1987 (%)*	*1984 (%)*	*1987 (%)*	*1988 (%)*
Manufacturing total	X 80.0 I 16.2 L 3.8	X 80.4 I 15.6 L 4.1	X 79.8 I 16.4 L 3.9	X 58.3 I 41.7	X 63.0 I 37.0	X 60.0 I 40.0
Food, drink and tobacco	X 93.9 I 4.9 L 1.1	X 95.2 I 3.0 L 1.8	X 94.8 I 3.6 L 1.6	X 72.4 I 27.6	X 75.4 I 24.6	X 73.0 I 28.0
Chemicals	X 64.7 I 25.7 L 9.6	X 63.0 I 26.7 L 10.3	X 59.7 I 31.3 L 8.9	X 46.5 I 53.5	X 47.8 I 52.2	X 41.3 I 58.7
Metals	X 93.8 I 5.8 L 0.4	X 93.5 I 6.0 L 0.4	X 95.3 I 4.4 L 0.3	X 64.5 I 35.5	X 65.8 I 34.2	X 67.5 I 32.5
Mechanical engineering	X 85.3 I 11.5 L 3.2	X 86.2 I 11.1 L 2.7	X 87.9 I 9.5 L 2.6	X* I*	X* I*	X* I*
Electrical engineering	X 64.7 I 27.7 L 7.7	X 69.6 I 24.1 L 6.3	X 70.0 I 24.0 L 6.0	X* I*	X* I*	X* I*
Road vehicle manufacturing	X 81.0 I 17.8 L 1.1	X 80.1 I 16.9 L 3.0	X 80.3* I 16.5 L 3.2	X* I*	X* I*	X* I*
Other manufacturing	X 88.8 I 10.5 L 0.7	X 89.5 I 9.6 L 0.9	X 88.0 I 10.5 L 1.5	X 90.5 I 9.5	X 90.9 I 9.1	X 87.8 I 12.2
Total non-manufacturing	X 36.9 I 61.4 L 1.7	X 37.9 I 60.4 L 1.7	X 36.0 I 63.1 L 0.9	X 18.7 I 81.3	X 23.4 I 76.6	X 31.2 I 68.8
Overall total (all industries)	X 74.1 I 22.4 L 3.5	X 75.4 I 20.8 L 3.8	X 75.4 I 21.1 L 3.6	X 52.3 I 47.7	X 56.8 I 43.2	X 55.0 I 45.0

Notes:

Acronyms: X, Exports; I, FDI sales; L, Licensed Sales (royalty receipt data on unaffiliated concerns for Japan are not available). NA, data not available.

For data sources on FDI, exports and royalty receipts, see Appendix.

Details of data manipulation and sector categories are as given in Table 13.2. However, Dutch sources have aggregated 'chemicals' to include chemicals, mining/quarrying and oil; hence, 'chemicals' = SITC (5+3). 'Machines/engineering' (marked * in the above table) include metals, machines and electrical engineering; hence, 'machines/engineering' = SITC (67 + 68 + 69 + 7).

France

Geographical Analysis

Exports (Table 13.1) are the dominant form of market servicing in manufacturing within the EC (87 per cent TFS). The USA (40 per cent) and Switzerland (34 per cent) are the countries with the largest share of sales arising from FDI. Investment-related sales is 18 per cent TFS in developed countries, but only 8 per cent in developing countries, with Latin America and Brazil the exceptions at 19 and 42 per cent respectively.

Sector Analysis

Like most other countries, French manufacturing TFS (Table 13.2) are overwhelmingly export-dominated (84 per cent) whilst non-manufacturing TFS are dominated by FDI sales (70 per cent). Within manufacturing, rubber at 47 per cent, chemicals (22–23 per cent TFS) and electric/electronic equipment have the highest proportion of FDI sales.

Sweden

Geographical Analysis

Although Sweden's TFS in manufacturing are largely dominated by exports, the world total fell from 73 to 65 per cent between 1986 and 1988 (Table 13.1). The largest investment sales percentages of TFS are in the USA, Brazil and Switzerland, although most EC and EFTA countries and developing countries total show significant and rising percentages of sales attributable to FDI.

Sector Analysis

Swedish sector analysis (Table 13.2) reveals significant differences between manufacturing (at 65–73 per cent for exporting) and non-manufacturing (33.35 per cent TFS for exporting). Within manufacturing, export-dominated sectors are food, drink and tobacco (75.84 per cent), metals (82.88 per cent), textiles (94.97 per cent) and wood (81.86 per cent). Apart from non-manufacturing, FDI sales are most significant in chemicals (28.33 per cent), engineering (33.42 per cent) and paper and pulp (18.33 per cent).

A COMPARATIVE ANALYSIS OF GLOBAL MARKET SERVICING

Geographical Analysis

Several major issues in the world economy can be analysed using our data. These include: (i) cross flows within the 'Triad' of major trading nations (Japan, USA, EC), (ii) Intra EC-flows; (iii) differences between developed and developing nations as host countries; (iv) the individual orientations of the major source nations.

Cross Flows in the Triad

The picture of cross flows in the triad is complicated by the fact that the EC is made up of twelve nations. We can present data for only four of these: UK, Germany, France and The Netherlands. Information on licensed sales is only available for UK and Germany and this is unfortunate where Japan is the host country because licensed sales were 32 per cent TFS (1984) and 26 per cent (1987) for the UK, and 30 per cent (1983), 24 per cent (1985) and 19 per cent (1987) for Germany. Thus, licensing was a highly significant but declining element of TFS in European servicing of the Japanese market. France and The Netherlands (on partial data) represented contrasting pictures – only 8 per cent of TFS $(X + I)$ for French firms was represented by investment sales – the rest was export (1987). The Netherlands represented a 58 per cent/42 per cent split of investment to export sales in Japan in 1988. Thus, The Netherlands has followed a far more investment-led attack on the Japanese market than has France. Similarly, the UK had 27 per cent of sales in Japan arising from investment as against 14 per cent for Germany, which had a far more export-led strategy. The situation of EC investment in the USA is less complicated by licensed sales; these were 5 per cent of UK TFS and 7 per cent of German TFS in the US in 1987. Foreign licensed sales from EC to USA are therefore not insignificant. Sales arising from EC FDI in the USA are very important: 57 per cent for the UK and 36 per cent for Germany (of $X + L + I$) in 1987, 40 per cent for France, and 86 per cent for The Netherlands in the same year (of $X + I$). FDI in the US is rising for The Netherlands as a proportion of TFS, even from such a high base.

US TFS in Japan are becoming more investment orientated – from 17 per cent of TFS in 1984 they moved to 21 per cent in 1988, slightly down from 21 per cent in 1987. Licensed sales to Japan remain highly significant at 29 per cent in 1988. Export sales remain the largest proportion of US TFS to Japan at 50 per cent. The contrast with US TFS in the EC is stark. In 1988, 57 per cent of sales was direct investment related (slightly down from its peak in 1987 of

59 per cent). Licensing represented 5 per cent and exporting 38 per cent. In individual EC countries, the investment proportion varied from 78 per cent in Ireland and 62 per cent in UK to 31 per cent in Portugal and 22 per cent in Greece. The licensed sales proportion was highest in Italy (9 per cent).

Japanese foreign market servicing is still highly export orientated. Overall in 1988, exports were 80 per cent of manufacturing TFS $(X + I)$. This export proportion is actually higher for EC (at 88 per cent), than the world share. It is lower for the USA, where investment related sales account for 27 per cent of the total. For individual EC countries, Belgium/Luxembourg (27 per cent), The Netherlands (20 per cent), the UK at 18 per cent and Ireland 14 per cent (1988) are investment bases for Japan.

Overall, TFS flows among triad members are unbalanced. EC and USA bilateral flows are converging in the pattern of X, L and I but Japan is still very trade-orientated (X) in its outflows and, because of difficulties of penetrating the market in any other way, excessively L orientated in inflows – even in 1987/88.

Intra-EC Flows

Our data enable us to examine bilateral flows between UK, Germany, France and The Netherlands. Taking all the figures for 1987, the UK and The Netherlands contrast markedly with Germany and France. The UK has 23 per cent of TFS arising from foreign investment in the rest of the EC compared to 13 per cent for Germany (in both cases, licensed sales are small), The Netherlands has 23 per cent arising from foreign investment, in contrast to France's 13 per cent $(X + I)$. The highest share of I in TFS for the UK is The Netherlands (36 per cent) as it is for France (28 per cent). The lowest share of I for the UK is Greece (10 per cent); for France, it is Denmark (2 per cent) although Spain is remarkably small (3 per cent); for Germany, the lowest I share is Italy (8 per cent) and the highest is Belgium/Luxembourg (20 per cent). The lowest share of I in TFS for The Netherlands remarkably is Germany (14 per cent in 1987).

Overall strategies in intra-EC TFS obviously differ markedly. The UK and The Netherlands are investment-orientated, whereas France and Germany are trade-orientated. Different bilateral relations between pairs of countries obviously persist.

Developed versus Developing Countries

Taking the latest available year for each country, we find that the only source country with a greater share of investment sales in the developing world is The Netherlands. This is biased by investment in The Netherlands Antilles, but the proportion of $(X + I)$ represented by The Netherlands FDI sales is 54 per cent for developing countries and only 40 per cent for developed. In contrast, US FDI sales represent 45 per cent of TFS in developed countries and 23 per cent in developing countries, UK 37 per cent in developed and 21 per cent in developing (of $X + I + L$), France 18 per cent in developed and only 8 per cent in developing (of $X + I$). Japan now (1987) has a higher proportion of $(X + I)$ represented by investment in developed (21 per cent) than developing (19 per cent), but this has switched over the period under investigation in 1984 (the figures for I were 12 per cent for developed and 17 per cent for developing). The change over occurred in 1987, reflecting the buildup of large-scale FDI in the developed world, notably the UK and EC. Licensed sales are more significant in developing countries only for the UK (6 per cent versus 3 per cent); they are less significant for Germany and the USA.

Geographical Orientations of Individual Source Countries

Japan's basic preference for exporting over direct investment is never breached; Latin American I sales of 44 per cent are far ahead of any other host country or region, and the USA at 27 per cent and Belgium/Luxembourg's 28 per cent are the next most significant, although the switch away from exports towards investment is slowly evolving in other developed countries. Germany (80 per cent exports) and France (84 per cent exports) similarly maintain a high proportion of exporting. Germany has suffered expropriations after two world wars but has high investment proportions of TFS in Canada (43 per cent), USA (36 per cent) and non-European developed countries in general, with a significant investment share in Latin America (36 per cent). Similarly, France has high investment shares in TFS in USA (40 per cent), North America (39 per cent), with Brazil at 42 per cent and Canada (32 per cent).

The most investment-sales-orientated nations are The Netherlands (40 per cent of $(X + I)$) and USA (39 per cent of $(X + L + I)$). Dutch FDI hold a remarkably high share in the USA (86 per cent) and Latin America (79 per cent) and significant in Japan (58 per cent). US investment sales are proportionately greatest in the EC. UK investment sales reach their peak in Canada (59 per cent), USA (57 per cent), other developed countries (67 per cent), and in Latin America (43 per cent) in common with the other source countries. Sweden's highest I rate in TFS is in Brazil, a remarkable 81 per cent, with significant proportions in Switzerland (70 per cent), The Netherlands (57 per cent) and USA (51 per cent).

There are thus significant commonalities between the source countries. Latin America and Canada figure significantly as investment-dominated locations, as does the USA and (for investment in the EC), The Netherlands and UK. Political and linguistic links are important investment facilitators as UK investment in the Commonwealth illustrates (unpublished results).

Sector Analysis

The sector analysis enables us to make a comparison between manufacturing and non-manufacturing TFS shares. In all cases, the difference in shares of the components is very marked. In the case of Japan, this difference is truly spectacular. The proportions for manufacturing are X at 79 per cent, I at 21 per cent; for non-manufacturing, export sales account for only 6 per cent of TFS whilst investment sales represent 94 per cent of TFS. In descending order of the share of direct investment sales in TFS for non-manufacturing, we have UK 73 per cent, France 70 per cent, The Netherlands 69 per cent, Sweden 65 per cent and Germany 63 per cent. For the USA, there is also a wide difference between manufacturing FDI related sales (39 per cent) and non-manufacturing (68 per cent). These results are striking confirmations of the view that service industries will have a higher proportion of TFS represented by FDI, because many services are non-transportable and have to be performed *in situ* (Buckley *et al.*, 1992b). Licensing is not significantly higher in non-manufacturing than in manufacturing (it is approximately the same proportion for the USA's TFS, much less for Germany and somewhat greater for the UK), illustrating the importance of the control of operations in non-manufacturing.

Differences within sectors across source countries are illuminating. In food, drink and tobacco, Germany is much more export-orientated than the norm for its manufacturing industry (95 per cent versus 80 per cent); Sweden, France and The Netherlands are significantly more export-orientated and the US slightly more so. However, Japan is much more investment-sales-orientated than its manufacturing norm (64 per cent versus 21 per cent), and the UK is also more investment-orientated (53 per cent versus 34 per cent). Chemicals is generally a high export proportion sector, but in the case of Swedish and US FDI, the proportion of TFS in chemicals is lower than the country's norm. Investment sales are much higher than the norm for Germany (31 per cent for I), Japan (40 per cent for I) and The Netherlands (59 per cent for I).

In the large swathe of industries represented broadly by metals and engineering, some interesting contrasts emerge. In the Japanese case, metals emerge as an investment intensive sector (32 per cent for I in TFS against a norm of 21 per cent). In contrast, it is a low investment intensive sector for Germany – a tiny 4.4 per cent investment sales in TFS. Similarly, mechanical engineering is a low *I* intensive sector for Germany (10 per cent for *I*), whilst this is a high *I* sales sector for the USA (47 per cent with a very high *L* content also of 16 per cent). For the UK, all the broad engineering categories have low *I* content, whilst for Sweden engineering (at 42 per cent for *I*) is FDI intensive. The contrast in motor vehicles is also marked. The Japanese transportation sector still has a low *I* content (13 per cent), whilst the US *I* component is 34 per cent in transportation equipment and 46 per cent for *I* in motor vehicles. Clearly, Japanese internationalisation of investment in this sector has a long way to go.

Finally, we are able to make some comparisons in textiles, paper and rubber, although not across the complete sample of source countries where these industries are often included in 'other manufacturing'. In textiles, Japan has a high FDI sales component (34 per cent), well above its manufacturing norm. Sweden, by contrast, has a very low FDI content in textile TFS (6 per cent) and the US at 20 per cent is well below its manufacturing average. The UK and USA have high *I* proportions in paper – both over 57 per cent, whilst paper and pulp is low in *I* intensity in France (13 per cent) and about the norm for Sweden. Where rubber can be separately identified, it has a high *I* content (USA 65 per cent, France 47 per cent).

It is too fanciful to read across from these proportions of TFS by sector to success. It does seem that in similar sectors, different strategies are being followed by the source countries and that strategies are changing – often successful exporters become investors. However, with German engineering and much of Japanese industry, the strategy to date has been firmly fixed on global exporting from the national base.

CONCLUSION

It was suggested above that there were five major issues on which our analysis could shed light. First, our data have shown that there are profound differences in market servicing strategies between firms of different nationalities even when the same industry and the same target market are considered. Our analysis of foreign market servicing strategies *vis-à-vis* the Japanese market is a case in point. Second, even at the highly aggregated level at which we work, changes in foreign market servicing strategies are very evident. Our cross sectional, point-of-time picture does not disguise the dynamic nature of the process. The increasingly global nature of competition requires constant readjustment of strategies by firms. Third, government policies would be more effective if they paid more attention to the make-up of total foreign sales, both in the sense of what is feasible (it is pointless to encourage exporting if this is not the preferred way of firms in given sectors to pursue particular foreign markets) and what the competition is doing (it may be suicide to attempt to penetrate a market by exporting in the face of investment-led competition). The structure of sales is also worthy of attention; some stages of the value chain may be more effectively located abroad and this may help domestically located segments. Fourth, the structure of TFS responds to industry imperatives which are very different according to the nature of the particular products and supply conditions. There is no universally optimum solution to foreign market servicing strategies. Finally, at international level, it is crucial to recognise the differences in foreign market servicing strategies and the reasons for these differences, and to adopt a holistic attitude. Our data show that to liberalise one form of market servicing (e.g. exports) and not the others will merely produce distortions. This is particularly true in service sectors. These observations are of great importance for the current 'Uruguay Round' of GATT negotiations. The attention focused on TRIMS (trade related investment measures) and IRTMs (investment related trade resources) is belated recognition of this crucial issue.

References

Buckley, P.J. and M. Casson (1976) *The Future of the Multinational Enterprise* (London: Macmillan).

Buckley, P.J. and M. Casson (1985) *The Economic Theory of the Multinational Enterprise* (London: Macmillan).

Buckley, P.J., G.D. Newbould and J. Thurwell (1988) *Foreign Direct Investment by Smaller UK Firms* (London: Macmillan). First edition published as *Going International – The Experiences of UK Firms Overseas* (London: Associated Business Press).

Buckley, P.J., C.L. Pass and K. Prescott (1992a) *Servicing International Markets: Competitive Strategies of Firms* (Oxford: Basil Blackwell).

Buckley, P.J., C.L. Pass and K. Prescott (1992b) 'The Internationalisation of Service Firms, a Comparison with the Manufacturing Sector', *Scandinavian International Business Review*, 1 (1), pp. 39–56.

Buckley, P.J. and R.D. Pearce (1979) 'Overseas Production and Exporting by the World's Largest Enterprises – A Study in Sourcing Policy', *Journal of International Business Studies*, 10 (1) (Spring) pp. 9–20.

Buckley, P.J. and R.D. Pearce (1981) 'Market Servicing by Multinational Manufacturing Firms: Exporting versus Foreign Production', *Managerial and Decision Economics*, 2 (4) (December) pp. 229–46.

Buckley, P.J. and R.D. Pearce (1984) 'Exports in the Strategy of Multinational Firms', *Journal of Business Research*, 12 (2) (June) pp. 209–26.

Buckley, P.J. and K. Prescott (1989) 'The Structure of British Industry's Sales in Foreign Markets', *Managerial and Decision Economics*, 10 (3) (September) pp. 189–205.

Cantwell, J.A. (1992) 'The Methodological Problems Raised by the Collection of Foreign Investment Data', *Scandinavian International Business Review*, 1 (1), pp. 86–102.

United Nations Centre on Transnational Corporation (UNCTC) (1992) *World Investment Report 1992: Transnational Corporations as Engines of Growth* (New York: UNCTC).

Young, S., J. Hamill, C. Wheeler and J.R. Davies (1989) *International Market Entry and Development* (Hemel Hempstead: Harvester Wheatsheaf).

Appendix: Data Sources

Exports

International Trade Statistics Yearbook (1986, 1987, 1988), vol. 1; Trade by Country, UN.
Direction of Trade Statistics Yearbook (1986, 1987, 1988). IMF.
UK: *Business Monitor*, MQ10, various issues.

Royalty Receipts

Aggregated totals for France, Japan, The Netherlands, Sweden:
Monthly Reports of Deutsche Bundesbank, May (1988), vol. 40, no. 5, pp. 37–53; May (1990), vol. 42, no. 5, pp. 27–43.
Japan (additional source): *Balance of Payments Monthly*, April (1990), no. 285, pp. 41–6, International Department, The Bank of Japan.
Germany: *Monthly Reports of the Deutsche Bundesbank* (1984), vol. 36, no. 7, pp. 23–38; May (1986), vol. 38, no. 5, pp. 27–42; May (1988), vol. 40, no. 5, pp. 37–53.
Sweden: *SCB Statistics Sweden*, based on photocopies of relevant tables from *Statistical Reports*, series U14/SM (1985, 1987).
UK: *British Business* (August 15, 1986), pp. 48–9; (September 4, 1987), pp. 24–5; (August 12, 1988), pp. 28–9; (September 15, 1989), pp. 26–7.
USA: *Survey of Current Business* (June, 1986), vol. 66, no. 6, pp. 36–73; (September, 1986), vol. 66, no. 9, pp. 40–63; (September, 1990), vol. 70, no. 9, pp. 37–72.

Foreign Direct Investment

France: *Note d'Information*, no. 86, 'Encours des investissements direct français a l'etranger au 31 Decembre 1987' (Avril, 1989), pp. 1–20.
Germany: 'Statistische Beihefte zu den Monatsberichten der Deutschen Bundesbank', Reihe 3, Zahlungsbilanz Statististik (Marz, 1985), no. 3, pp. 1–32.
Monthly Report of Deutsche Bundesbank (March, 1985), vol. 37, no. 3, pp. 28–34; (March, 1987), vol. 39, no. 3, pp. 20–32; (April, 1989), vol. 41, no. 4, pp. 23–32.
Japan: *EXIM Review* (1985), vol. 6, no. 2, pp. 21–55; (1988), vol. 8, no. 2, pp. 76–103; (1989), vol. 9, no. 2, pp. 70–111.

'Trends in Japan's Direct Investment Abroad in FY 1989'. Provisional English Translation of article in *Research Institute of Overseas Investment Bulletin* (July, 1990). The Export-Import Bank of Japan.

Netherlands: personal communication, De Nederlandsche Bank, Balance of Payments Department, Amsterdam.

Sweden: B. Swedenborg, G. Johansson-Grahn and M. Kinnwall (1988) 'Den Svenska Industries Utlands investeringar, 1960–86', tables B.1, B.2 (pp. 178, 179), Industriens Utrednings Institut, Stockholm. F. Rockert (1990:2) *Quarterly Review*, Sveriges Riksbank 'Reinvested Earnings and Direct Investment Assets', pp. 14–19.

UK: *Business Monitor* (1986, 1988), MA4, Overseas Transactions: (1984, 1987), MO4 (1984, 1987), Census of Overseas Assets.

USA: *Survey of Current Business* (August, 1987), vol. 67, no. 8, pp. 58–84; (August, 1988), vol. 68, no. 8, pp. 42–68; (August, 1989), vol. 69, no. 8, pp. 62–88; (August, 1990), vol. 70, no. 8, pp. 56–98.

Sales: Assets Ratios

The tables used for calculation of sales:assets ratios were those that referred to 'Selected Data for Nonbank Foreign Affiliates, Major Industry and Area of Affiliate' for the specified year. The non-manufacturing ratio for each year was derived from the average for petroleum, wholesale trade, finance, services and 'others'.

Survey of Current Business (September, 1986), vol. 66, no. 9, pp. 27–39; (June, 1987), vol. 67, no. 6, pp. 26–37; (June, 1988), vol. 68, no. 6, pp. 85–96; (June, 1990), vol. 70, no. 6, pp. 31–44.

Exchange Rates

The values used were taken from *International Financial Statistics* (1989, 1991).

14 Japanese Transfer Pricing Policy: A Note*

with Jane Frecknall-Hughes

INTRODUCTION

In the past three years, the financial press has devoted a good deal of coverage to the alleged use of transfer pricing policies by multinationals to gain a tax advantage. Such a tax advantage accrues because different countries may constitute tax havens or because the overall tax may be lower for a variety of reasons, thus resulting in higher profits (and taxes) in the home country of the parent/holding company or a third country, which thereby benefit from the use of another country's resources.

In November and December 1995 Glaxo Wellcome was the particular focus of press attention when it contended that the Inland Revenue did not have the right to go back over the transfer pricing transactions in tax years which had been left open. It failed in its contention. Such issues only come to public notice when they reach the courts or when the companies involved themselves reveal details. Although data are scarce, transfer pricing investigations do seem numerous. A recent study by Ernst and Young, which investigated 210 multinationals, found that 49 per cent were being investigated in respect of transfer pricing issues, while 83 per cent had at some stage been involved in a transfer pricing dispute (*Financial Times*, 23 November 1995, p. 11). Although this press report does not specify where the multinationals investigated are based, these percentages do at least give some indication of the scope of the issue. The *Financial Times* article quoted above refers to an adjustment which resulted in additional tax from one company alone of £1,638 million in 1994–5. The payer's name remains unknown. Although it may be inferred from the tone and context of the article that this was a transfer pricing adjustment, the actual wording of the Inland Revenue report quoted in the newspaper itself only refers to 'adjustments' resulting in additional tax. Such adjustments need not be transfer pricing related: that they may be so is press speculation. As anyone involved in corporate tax knows, adjustments to profits arise for many different reasons.

---

* Originally published in *Applied Economics Letters*, vol. 4, 1997, pp. 13–17.

The activities of Japanese multinationals appear to have stimulated the interest of Revenue authorities in the USA and the UK in respect of transfer pricing. The *Sunday Times* 'Insight' column on 22 March 1992 (p. 1) refers to Sony's alleged activities in this area and points to the low levels of tax paid by other Japanese firms operating in the UK, specifically mentioning Toshiba UK, Mitsubishi Electric and Hitachi Consumer Products. Matsushita is quoted as an instance of Revenue investigation in the USA, together with its arrangement with the Internal Revenue Service (IRS) to agree ahead of time fair prices for intercompany transactions.

THE PROBLEM

The issues of pricing in a decentralised uni-national company are well known and are analysed by Hirshleifer (1986). The problem occurs when a company taxable under one jurisdiction (company 1) allegedly sells products at an inflated price to another company under common control (company 2), this latter company being taxable under a different jurisdiction. Company 2 thus pays a higher price than it would if it had purchased the same products from an external unconnected third party, and consequently makes lower profits, and company 1's profits are therefore higher (see Figure 14.1). The concern of the Revenue authorities is that the payment of any inflated purchase price siphons profits back to an overseas jurisdiction.

In the UK, the relevant tax legislation is Section 770 of the Income and Corporation Taxes Act 1988 (ICTA 1988), under which the Board of the Inland Revenue may direct that 'the like consequences shall ensue as would have ensued if the property had been sold for the arm's length price' – that is, the price for which the products could have been purchased from an unconnected party. Hence an adjustment to taxable profits can be made. Determining an arm's length price in practice is extremely difficult, particularly in the case of a multinational which may have a particular strength in certain products, such that no real competitors or comparatives exist outside the entity in question. Indeed in the case of the Japanese multinationals quoted above, all are electronics giants and even if they are considered as competitors, they all stand accused in the press of the same sort of practices, so it becomes even harder to sort out an independent price.

THE CONTINUUM

A number of studies has been done on the problem of transfer pricing which have examined the issue from a variety of perspectives (Emmanuel and

Mehafdi, 1994, chapter 3 includes a comprehensive survey). It would seem that such surveys inherently assume that transfer pricing issues occur for the same reasons in all cases – a deliberate exploitation of intra-group trade to the tax disadvantage of host countries, and this is very much the tone that colours all press reports, as the above quotes instance. While multinationals in many instances may be guilty of this deliberate exploitation, no one seems to have queried whether this blanket assumption holds true in all cases. It is the contention of this note that it does not, particularly in regard to Japanese companies which have been singled out for attention by Revenue authorities, especially in the USA. Examination of existing academic analysis of Japanese pricing policies in global context will cast serious doubt on the validity of the press allegations. However, the fact of such intense press interest does raise the question whether there is something unique about Japanese company practices or culture that give rise to this degree of attention.

The Japanese point of view seems to be that the companies are doing nothing unusual or illegal: 'Sony said that if such price manipulation occurred, it was against its policies and in defiance of company rules' (*Sunday Times*, 22 March 1992, p. 1). Deliberate price manipulation may not, however, be the issue here, but rather one should ask what is the norm for the 'Japanese firm', and consider that what *it* would consider as price manipulation is not the same sort of practice that would so be regarded in, say, certain Western business cultures, which regard Japanese practices in a more hostile manner, as a result of the differing perspective from which they are viewed.

The difference in approach to pricing between Japan and the UK/USA is fundamental and it is the argument put forward in this note that the current transfer pricing issues should be viewed in this light. Comparative studies of European and Japanese firms show how this different perception works (Sparkes *et al.*, 1987). The traditional European approach is based on cost plus a mark-up or contribution. If the consequent price was too 'high' then any downward price movement starts with a reduction in the mark-up or contribution. The Japanese approach works differently: the price is set according to what the market will bear, and then an examination of the costs is done, and if these absorb too much of the required contribution margin, pressure is exerted on suppliers/subcontractors to produce and supply at lower costs. The contribution margin is thus protected by this approach (often referred to as target costing in management accounting textbooks). Sparkes *et al.* show the Japanese margin split into net contribution, a contingency element and administrative expenses (see Figure 14.2).

The example used by Sparkes *et al.* assumes that the whole of the 75 per cent cost of the Japanese company derives from suppliers/subcontractors, which is deemed reasonable '*because the supplier may well be the workshop*

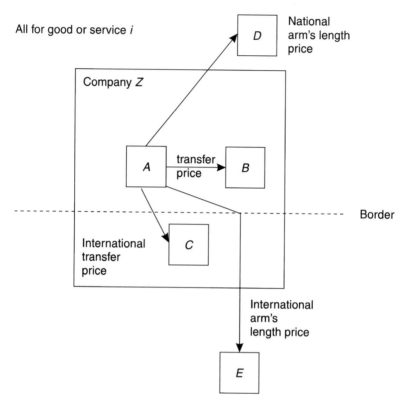

All for good or service *i*

National arm's length price

Company *Z*

D

transfer price

A

B

- Border

International transfer price

C

International arm's length price

E

If *C* > *E* or *C* < *E* manipulated prices?
Other comparators *C* = *D*
                   C = *B* (both internal)

Figure 14.1   Intercompany transfer prices

division of the same company selling to sales division' (italics are the authors'). The workshop division's pricing structure will therefore be done on the assumption that the 75 per cent cost to the purchasing division is all the income that it *can* receive, and so will control its own costs similarly, either internally or by pressuring its own suppliers. The aim is to protect the margin above costs in all cases. However, these margins may be reduced when the firm finds itself facing competition in the outside market, and the Japanese firm will forgo administrative expenses, contribution and contingency, if absolutely necessary (thus effectively selling at marginal cost), so the pricing is therefore very flexible. This seems particularly true of exports from Japan, either sold on to world markets through subsidiaries or exported directly. Sales at marginal cost (plus a minimal contribution) to the home-based company will be profitable if all other overheads are recovered from the home market, and if this is protected against foreign investment by the Japanese government (as seems likely – see below), then such sales will be profitable from a group's perspective. The operation of costing such as this also is a useful defence against price manipulation – the Japanese company is selling at costs which do not try to recover fixed overheads, so therefore *cannot* be artificially high. In some cases there have been allegations of 'dumping' goods cheaply in foreign markets in breach of EC regulations, and it is hard to see how a company could be hit by allegations of dumping and transfer pricing manipulation without appreciating the pricing structures from this perspective. Generally, however, the firm will seek to maintain its contribution by exerting pressure on the supplier. If the supplier is a company under its control with all its output guaranteed sold to this purchaser, the supplier will not need a contingency in its own cost structures, as it is not selling to the outside world and will not face the pressures of an external market. There is empirical evidence to suggest that such relationships exist even between companies which are not associated with a particular group (Yoshikawa *et al.*, 1989).

The implication is that all Japanese firms operate pricing structures in a similar way, and the larger the firm or group, the more powerful its market position for doing so. The idea seems to be that it is the group as one entity which will make a profit centrally. The generation of profit for the home-based company is therefore the element which drives the pricing structure, and transcends any ideas of individual company and national boundaries: the profit will not be divided among companies whose efforts help earn those profits. (See Figure 14.3, which reveals the same pricing structure as Figure 14.2, but from the perspective of an international group *as a single entity*. It shows where individual company or national boundaries may possibly occur, but also how irrelevant they would be in this interpretation of the pricing structure.) This seems to be an idea which is central to Japanese concepts of management, in so far as individual contributions are valuable only so far as they help achieve a wider objective. Buckley and Mirza comment on the diacritical features of Japanese style management in comparison with Western/European style. Of particular relevance to the argument here is the view of the firm as a collective body (the individual is totally devoted to the firm) with stress on cooperative teamwork, collective decision-making and information transmitted by implicit understanding, collective participation and planning, group responsibility, collusive relationship of government, business and labour, and concurrence of the firms' goals and the life goals of individuals. While these features are listed as part of an

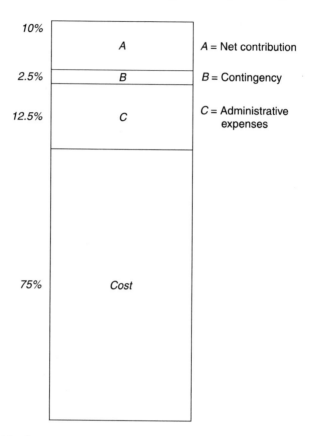

Figure 14.2   Japanese pricing

ideal typology, it is nevertheless acknowledged that a very real structural difference remains.

If such features are so predominant in Japanese corporate life, it is to be expected that they will colour every expression of it, not least the relationship of subsidiary companies to the Japanese parent and the pricing policies in respect of goods sold to the outside world.

THE RELEVANCE TO TRANSFER PRICING

In a situation where a Japanese firm sells products to an associated company overseas, the Japanese firm does not perceive itself to be a supplier, whereas

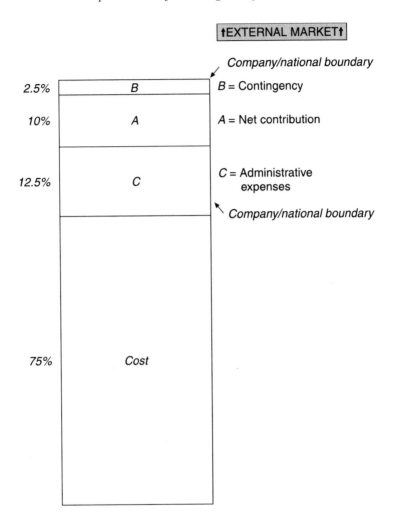

↑EXTERNAL MARKET↑

Figure 14.3   Product costing from group perspective

tax authorities are obliged to apply a statutory hypothesis and perceive it precisely *as* an independent supplier (and so selling at an 'inflated' price). The Japanese view seems to be that it is extending its own arm or employing an agent to deal with its overseas sales (although the legal set-up may not be an agency under UK law). The overseas company 'serves' the group: it does not see itself as a separate entity expecting to make a profit independently. Much credence is given to this by the presence on local boards of directors of Japanese nationals who are closely connected with the parent company, even if they have no official status there. Hence if the same sort of pricing philosophy is followed, then the price the ultimate market will bear will be the deciding factor. In the case of a company based in Japan selling items to a subsidiary in the UK, the price at which they will be sold will be similar to that at which the subsidiary will sell on to the UK market. The Japanese company will therefore structure its costs accordingly so that the group receives the majority of the profit. Thus the cost to the Japanese UK subsidiary will therefore be virtually the same as the price for which it will sell the goods. To allow for local costs and conditions, in this case the home company will probably be prepared to forgo its contingency margin, and thus the UK subsidiary will make a little profit – perhaps a margin of 2 per cent or so after deduction of UK costs. In this context, the comments of a former sales and marketing manager at Sony make sense: 'I was a professional salesman, yet I was set a goal of zero profits' (*Sunday Times*, 23 March 1992, p. 1). The parent company thus can 'squeeze' contribution margins as well as costs. The Japanese overseas subsidiary is thus not regarded as a profit centre in its own right, therefore there is no incentive to increase subsidiary profits. From the Japanese point of view, profit in a subsidiary company is dysfunctional.

In cases where a Japanese controlled subsidiary operating in the UK manufactures goods which are sold on to Europe or America, the price it receives, if it sells to another associated company, will again be close to the price the ultimate market will bear, thus giving rise to the allegation that sales are made at artificially low prices and profits again artificially depressed. If this is looked at from the perspective outlined above, then the element of artificiality is mitigated, and it can also be understood easily why goods can be sold to different countries at different prices – because the market in those countries is in a different condition or is of a different sort and will bear a different price. It is not driven by product costs, and represents a commercial price.

CONCLUSION

If the on-going transfer pricing problems facing Revenue authorities are examined from this perspective, then it can be seen that they derive from a different way of pricing and costing, rather than from a deliberate manipulation of pricing to transfer profits back to the home country, and the denials by the Japanese multinationals of anything unusual begin to make more sense. However, this is not to suggest that they are not capable of realising the effect that their strategy has on countries where they have local bases of operation. The above explanation does not make the problems faced by Revenue authorities disappear but it does change the context in which they are set. The idea of trying to find a 'fair price' (USA) or an 'arm's length price' (UK) thus does not always fully accord with pricing principles obtaining, as such principles are endemic to entirely different business cultures.

This note examines only Japanese companies because it is widely known that they operate target costing: indeed it is assumed to be a particular Japanese phenomenon. It is not known to what extent other, non-Japanese multinationals operate target costing, and hence similar transfer pricing policies. In the light of the ever-current interest of the financial press in the tax affairs of such groups, this is an issue which needs further academic investigation.

References

Financial Times, 23 November 1995, p. 11.

Sunday Times, 'Insight', 22 March 1992, pp. 1 and 16.

Buckley, P.J. and H. Mirza (1985) 'The Wit and Wisdom of Japanese Management: An Iconoclastic Analysis', *Management International Review*, 25, 16–32.

Emmanuel, C. and M. Mehafdi (1994) *Transfer Pricing* (London: Academic Press).

Hirshleifer, J. (1986) 'Internal Pricing and Decentralised Decisions', in C.P. Bonini, R.K. Jaedicke and H.M. Wagner (eds), *Management Controls: New Directions in Basic Research* (New York and London: Garland Publishing) pp. 27–37.

Sparkes, J.R., P.J. Buckley and H. Mirza (1987) 'A Note on Japanese Pricing Policy', *Applied Economics*, 19 (6), 729–32.

Yoshikawa, T., J. Innes and F. Mitchell (1989) 'Japanese Management Accounting: A Comparative Survey', *Management Accounting*, November, 20–23.

Index